d.

Fin

GREAT IRISH STORIES OF CHILDHOOD

GREAT IRISH
STORIES
OF CHILDHOOD

Edited by
Peter Haining

SOUVENIR PRESS

First published 1997 by
Souvenir Press Ltd,
43 Great Russell Street, London WC1B 3PA
and simultaneously in Canada

ISBN 0 285 63359 7

Photoset by Rowland Phototypesetting Ltd,
Bury St Edmunds, Suffolk
Printed in Great Britain by
Creative Print & Design Group (Wales), Ebbw Vale

For
my son, Sean
who has enriched the childhoods
of so many others

CONTENTS

INTRODUCTION

When the celebrated Irish poet Seamus Heaney delivered his Nobel lecture in Stockholm in December 1995, after being awarded the prestigious prize for his contribution to literature, he began his speech by describing his secluded childhood on a farm in Derry. It was, he said, a place into which the outside world normally only intruded in the form of voices on the radio. He recalled perching on the arm of a sofa, his ear glued to the set in order to hear through the family racket that was going on all around him. 'I was avid not just for the BBC news,' he told his audience of academics and dignitaries from all over the world, 'but also for the adventures of Dick Barton and Biggles.'

William Trevor, one of Ireland's foremost short-story writers, has vividly recalled being sent away to a boarding school in the hills beyond Dublin. Here one of the great pleasures of the group of schoolfriends to which he belonged was cycling down into the city in the early evening to eat vast fry-ups at the Green Rooster café. 'From there we'd go to the Shelbourne Hotel to try to persuade the hall porter to give us a drink,' says Trevor. 'But he never would. There was a boy called Popeye Jameson— one of the whiskey people—who'd say, "I think my father is staying here at the moment," and they'd reply, "I don't think he is, sir." That would be the end of that and we'd have to cycle back.'

Maeve Binchy, the international best-selling novelist who was born in County Dublin, first began to experience the pangs of love which she writes about so movingly in her books, as an adolescent on visits to Dublin. 'A cousin took me to Bewley's for coffee when I was 15—and the most boring teenager in the world—and she listened to my views on the future,' Maeve recalled in a recent article. 'I fell in love there, too, and that was wonderful. On the other hand, a friend told me there that her boyfriend was unfaithful and we cried for a whole morning.'

Three famous Irish writers recalling memories of their youth— one from childhood, one from schooldays and the other from adolescence. Together they form a mixture of nostalgia, adventure and emotion: exactly the same kind of experiences we have all known and gone through during those days between infancy and adulthood when the world is still new, older people are still (mostly) admirable, and life has not yet had a chance to shape irrevocably one's personality for good or evil. In their maturity, many writers and poets have turned for inspiration to that time of growing up; few, it seems, have done so with more honest emotion and objectivity than the Irish.

What makes the memories of an Irish childhood so fascinating is not just the diversity of backgrounds from which they spring— villages deep in the heart of the countryside on the one hand and crowded city streets on the other—but also the religious, social and moral issues which have always pulled at all those growing up in Ireland, be they boys or girls. All these elements have provided a wealth of inspiration for native writers, enabling them to create stories that are warmly nostalgic, illuminated by the discovery of knowledge, fraught with emotional conflict, and even, at times, with experiences of fear and the unknown.

For some, these formative moments have happened when they were very young; to others while they were at school; and to the rest during those painful teenage years of adolescence. Because these three categories divide childhood probably as neatly as it is possible to do, the stories in this collection have likewise been arranged chronologically, thereby providing the reader with a journey from the days of innocence to the growth of knowledge through experiences that are entertaining, instructive and pecu- liarly Irish. This said, there is much in the pages that follow which will strike a chord in the memory of any reader—for the search for self-expression and freedom which drives on the young of Ireland is the motivation of many others, too.

The vitality of youngsters can often be an inspiration to the older generation, even in unlikely circumstances—a theme developed by several of the contributors to this book. Seamus Heaney's remarks about Dick Barton and Biggles—an enthusiasm for whom I shared during the late Forties and early Fifties— remind me of a story about another young literary 'hero', the mischievous Just William, in the books by Richmal Crompton. In one of the tales about him, 'The Cure', William is dispatched to Ireland where his great-aunt is dying. The intention of the boy's harassed parents is that he should see the old lady one last time before she dies. Instead, the irrepressible William not only brings a smile to his great-aunt's drawn Irish countenance, but even gives her a new lease of life!

In this book, the full range of childhood emotions is to be found, from laughter to tears, in stories by some of the leading Irish writers of this century. Most of their tales, it would seem, are based on personal experience, and what *is* invented is surely only to protect the innocent. Few love children and a story more than the Irish; put together they are, I believe, irresistible.

Peter Haining
September 1996

1

THE AGE OF INNOCENCE

Memories of Growing Up

MANKEEPERS AND
MOSSCHEEPERS

Seamus Heaney

Memories of the earliest days of childhood are usually isolated and curiously random, as Seamus Heaney (1939–), winner of the 1995 Nobel Prize for Literature, has demonstrated in a number of his best-selling volumes of poetry. Born the eldest of nine children in a three-roomed, thatched farmstead named Mossbawn, at Castledawson in County Derry, he has returned again and again to his formative years, writing about his family and the human and physical landscape around their farm. As a Catholic in Northern Ireland, he remembers his family as quiet, watchful, oblique and shy, all of the children urged by their mother, 'Whatever you say, say nothing.' Speaking about his childhood in Derry when accepting the Nobel prize, Heaney described the tensions he had faced as 'ethical, anaesthetical, moral, political, metrical, sceptical, cultural, topical, typical, post-colonial and, taken all together, simply impossible.'

Despite this, he was undoubtedly a bright child. At the age of eleven he won a scholarship to St Columba's College, a Catholic boarding school in Londonderry, and from there went to Queen's University, Belfast, where he graduated in 1961 with a First in English. He then became a teacher at St Thomas's Secondary School in West Belfast where he came under the influence of the headmaster, Michael McLaverty, the novelist and short-story writer (also a contributor to this collection), who encouraged him to continue writing the poetry he had begun while at university and published in a few local magazines and papers. Soon he was breaking into prestigious journals like the New Statesman, *and in 1966 published his first collection,* Death of a Naturalist. *By the end of the Sixties, with his reputation as a major poet growing rapidly and the Troubles having broken out in Belfast, he moved south to Glanmore in County Wicklow where he has remained.*

The world of Seamus Heaney's childhood can be found in any number of his poems like 'Alphabets' and 'Mid-Term Break', but 'Mankeepers and Mosscheepers' is something rather different. It is one of his infrequent pieces of prose in which he vividly recalls his early days in the fields and groves of Mossbawn, where his imagination was first excited by the sights and sounds which were later to appear in his verse. One of the most evocative pieces about the early days of childhood I know, it shows how wise he was to disregard his mother's well-intentioned advice . . .

*   *   *

I do not know what age I was when I got lost in the pea-drills in a field behind the house, but it is a half-dream to me, and I've heard about it so often that I may even be imagining it. Yet, by now, I have imagined it so long and so often that I know what it was like: a green web, a caul of veined light, a tangle of rods and pods, stalks and tendrils, full of assuaging earth and leaf smell, a sunlit lair. I'm sitting as if just wakened from a winter sleep and gradually become aware of voices, coming closer, calling my name, and for no reason at all I have begun to weep.

All children want to crouch in their secret nests. I loved the fork of a beech tree at the head of our lane, the close thicket of a boxwood hedge in the front of the house, the soft, collapsing pile of hay in a back corner of the byre; but especially I spent time in the throat of an old willow tree at the end of the farmyard. It was a hollow tree, with gnarled, spreading roots, a soft, perishing bark and a pithy inside. Its mouth was like the fat and solid opening in a horse's collar, and, once you squeezed in through it, you were at the heart of a different life, looking out on the familiar yard as if it were suddenly behind a pane of strangeness. Above your head, the living tree flourished and breathed, you shouldered the slightly vibrant bole, and if you put your forehead to the rough pith you felt the whole lithe and whispering crown of willow moving in the sky above you. In that tight cleft, you sensed the embrace of light and branches, you were a little Atlas shouldering it all, a little Cernunnos pivoting a world of antlers.

The world grew. Mossbawn, the first place, widened. There was what we called the Sandy Loaning, a sanded pathway between old hedges leading in off the road, first among fields and then through a small bog, to a remote farmhouse. It was a silky, fragrant world there, and for the first few hundred yards you were safe enough. The sides of the lane were banks of earth topped with broom and ferns, quilted with moss and primroses. Behind the broom, in the rich grass, cattle munched reassuringly. Rabbits occasionally broke cover and ran ahead of you in a flurry of dry sand. There were wrens and goldfinches. But, gradually, those lush and definite fields gave way to scraggy marshland. Birch trees stood up to their pale shins in swamps. The ferns thickened above you. Scuffles in old leaves made you nervous and you dared yourself always to pass the badger's sett, a wound of fresh mould in an overgrown ditch where the old brock had gone to earth. Around that badger's hole, there hung a field of dangerous force. This was the realm of bogeys. We'd heard about a mystery man who haunted the fringes of the bog here, we talked about mankeepers and mosscheepers, creatures uncatalogued by any naturalist, but none the less real for that. What was a moss-cheeper, anyway, if not the soft, malicious sound the word itself made, a siren of collapsing sibilants coaxing you out towards bog pools lidded with innocent grass, quicksands and quagmires? They were all there and spreading out over a low, birch-screened apron of land towards the shores of Lough Beg.

That was the moss, forbidden ground. Two families lived at the heart of it, and a recluse, called Tom Tipping, whom we never saw, but in the morning on the road to school we watched his smoke rising from a clump of trees, and spoke his name between us until it was synonymous with mystery man, with unexpected scuttlings in the hedge, with footsteps slushing through long grass.

THE DEATH OF PEGGY MEEHAN

William Trevor

William Trevor (1928–) has also drawn extensively in his work on what he remembers as 'an itinerant childhood in the small towns of Ireland' where his father, a manager in the Bank of Ireland, was constantly being moved to new positions. Born in Mitchelstown, County Cork, he and the family occupied a series of homes in Youghal, Skibbereen, Tipperary Town, Enniscorthy and Maryborough (now called Port Laoighise). Although the removals considerably curtailed young William's education—on several occasions he missed as much as six months' schooling— and this prevented him from making many friends, he now believes those early years provided him with the sense of curiosity about the human condition which is a hallmark of his writing. He remembers, too, that the marriage of his parents was not a happy one—his father was a man who loved talking to people and telling stories, while his mother was very capricious, fickle and eccentric, and there was a constant sense of an argument brewing between them. Their only common interest was a love of the cinema, although they both enjoyed quite different types of film. William Trevor's own visits to the pictures remain deeply etched in his memory 'like escapes to paradise'. Later, in his teens, he was to be sent to a boarding school in Dublin and afterwards made up for lost time by taking a degree at Trinity.

Today, William Trevor is highly regarded as novelist, script-writer for radio and television, and a master of the short story. He has won numerous literary awards, including the Whitbread Prize which he is the only writer to have collected twice. 'The Death of Peggy Meehan' combines two of the major influences of William Trevor's childhood, loneliness and the cinema, in a haunting tale of a seven-year-old and his desperate longing for friendship.

*   *   *

Like all children, I led a double life. There was the ordinariness of dressing in the morning, putting on shoes and combing hair, stirring a spoon through porridge I didn't want, and going at ten to nine to the nuns' elementary school. And there was a world in which only the events I wished for happened, where boredom was not permitted and of which I was both God and King.

In my ordinary life I was the only child of parents who years before my birth had given up hope of ever having me. I remember them best as being different from other parents: they were elderly, it seemed to me, two greyly fussing people with grey hair and faces, in grey clothes, with spectacles. 'Oh, no, no,' they murmured regularly, rejecting on my behalf an invitation to tea or to play with some other child. They feared on my behalf the rain and the sea, and walls that might be walked along, and grass because grass was always damp. They rarely missed a service at the Church of the Holy Redeemer.

In the town where we lived, a seaside town thirty miles from Cork, my father was employed as a senior clerk in the offices of Cosgriff and McLoughlin, Solicitors and Commissioners for Oaths. With him on one side of me and my mother on the other, we walked up and down the brief promenade in winter, while the seagulls shrieked and my father worried in case it was going to rain. We never went for walks through fields or through the heathery wastelands that sloped gently upwards behind the town, or by the river where people said Sir Walter Ralegh had fished. In summer, when the visitors from Cork came, my mother didn't like to let me near the sands because the sands, she said, were full of fleas. In summer we didn't walk on the promenade but out along the main Cork road instead, past a house that appeared to me to move. It disappeared for several minutes as we approached it, a trick of nature, I afterwards discovered, caused by the undulations of the landscape. Every July, for a fortnight, we went to stay in Montenotte, high up above Cork city, in a boarding-house run by my mother's sister, my Aunt Isabella. She, too, had a grey look about her and was religious.

It was here, in my Aunt Isabella's Montenotte boarding-house, that this story begins: in the summer of 1936, when I was seven. It was a much larger house than the one we lived in ourselves, which was small and narrow and in a terrace. My Aunt Isabella's was rather grand in its way, a dark place with little unexpected half-landings, and badly lit corridors. It smelt of floor polish and of a mustiness that I have since associated with the religious life, a smell of old cassocks. Everywhere there were statues of the Virgin, and votive lights and black-framed pictures of the Holy Child. The residents were all priests, old and middle-aged and young, eleven of them usually, which was all the house would hold. A few were always away on their holidays when we stayed there in the summer.

In the summer of 1936 we left our own house in the usual way, my father fastening all the windows and the front and back doors and then examining the house from the outside to make sure he'd done the fastening and the locking properly. We walked to the railway station, each of us carrying something, my mother a brown cardboard suitcase and my father a larger one of the same kind. I carried the sandwiches we were to have on the train, and a flask of carefully made tea and three apples, all packed into a sixpenny fish basket.

In the house in Montenotte my Aunt Isabella told us that Canon McGrath and Father Quinn were on holiday, one in Tralee, the other in Galway. She led us to their rooms, Canon McGrath's for my father and Father Quinn's for my mother and myself. The familiar trestle-bed was erected at the foot of the bed in my mother's room. During the course of the year a curate called Father Lalor had repaired it, my aunt said, after it had been used by Canon McGrath's brother from America, who'd proved too much for the canvas.

'Ah, aren't you looking well, Mr Mahon!' the red-faced and

jolly Father Smith said to my father in the dining-room that evening. 'And isn't our friend here getting big for himself?' He laughed loudly, gripping a portion of the back of my neck between a finger and a thumb. Did I know my catechism? he asked me. Was I being good with the nuns in the elementary school? 'Are you in health yourself, Mrs Mahon?' he inquired of my mother.

My mother said she was, and the red-faced priest went to join the other priests at the main dining-table. He left behind him a smell that was different from the smell of the house, and I noticed that he had difficulty in pulling the chair out from the table when he was about to sit down. He had to be assisted in this by a new young curate, a Father Parsloe. Father Smith had been drinking stout again, I said to myself.

Sometimes in my aunt's house there was nothing to do except to watch and to listen. Father Smith used to drink too much stout; Father Magennis, who was so thin you could hardly bear to look at him and whose flesh was the colour of whitewash, was not long for this world; Father Riordon would be a bishop if only he could have tidied himself up a bit; Canon McGrath had once refused to baptise a child; young Father Lalor was going places. For hours on end my Aunt Isabella would murmur to my parents about the priests, telling about the fate of one who had left the boarding-house during the year or supplying background information about a new one. My parents, so faultlessly regular in their church attendance and interested in all religious matters, were naturally pleased to listen. God and the organisation of His Church were far more important than my father's duties in Cosgriff and McLoughlin, or my mother's housework, or my own desire to go walking through the heathery wastelands that sloped gently upwards behind our town. God and the priests in my Aunt Isabella's house, and the nuns of the convent elementary school and the priests of the Church of the Holy Redeemer, were at the centre of everything. 'Maybe it'll appeal to our friend,' Father Smith had once said in the dining-room, and I knew that he meant that maybe one day I might be attracted towards the priesthood. My parents had not said anything in reply, but as we ate our tea of sausages and potato-cakes I could feel them thinking that nothing would please them better.

Every year when we stayed with my aunt there was an afternoon when I was left in charge of whichever priests happened to be in, while my parents and my aunt made the journey across the city to visit my father's brother, who was a priest himself. There was some difficulty about bringing me: I had apparently gone to my uncle's house as a baby, when my presence had upset him. Years later I overheard my mother whispering to Father Riordon about this, suggesting—or so it seemed—that my father had once been intent on the priestly life but had at the last moment withdrawn. That he should afterwards have fathered a child was apparently an offence to his brother's feeling of propriety. I had the impression that my uncle was a severe man, who looked severely on my father and my mother and my Aunt Isabella on these visits, and was respected by them for being as he was. All three came back subdued, and that night my mother always prayed for much longer by the side of her bed.

'Father Parsloe's going to take you for a walk,' my Aunt Isabella said on the morning of the 1936 visit. 'He wants to get to know you.'

You walked all the way down from Montenotte, past the docks, over the river and into the city. The first few times it could have been interesting, but after that it was worse than walking on the concrete promenade at home. I'd have far preferred to have played by myself in my aunt's overgrown back garden, pretending to be grown up, talking to myself in a secret way, having wicked thoughts. At home and in my aunt's garden I became a man my father had read about in a newspaper and whom, he'd said, we must all pray for, a thief who broke the windows of jewellers' shops and lifted out watches and rings. I became Father Smith, drinking too much stout and missing the steps of the stairs. I became Father Magennis and would lie on the weeds at the bottom of the garden or under a table, confessing to gruesome crimes at the moment of death. In my mind I mocked the holiness of my parents and imitated their voices; I mocked the holiness of my Aunt Isabella; I talked back to my parents in a way I never would; I laughed and said disgraceful things about God and the religious life. Blasphemy was exciting.

'Are you ready so?' Father Parsloe asked when my parents and my aunt had left for the visit to my uncle. 'Will we take a bus?'

'A bus?'

'Down to the town.'

I'd never in my life done that before. The buses were for going longer distances in. It seemed extraordinary not to walk, the whole point of a walk was to walk.

'I haven't any money for the bus,' I said, and Father Parsloe laughed. On the upper deck he lit a cigarette. He was a slight young man, by far the youngest of the priests in my aunt's house, with reddish hair and a face that seemed to be on a slant. 'Will we have tea in Thompson's?' he said. 'Would that be a good thing to do?'

We had tea in Thompson's café, with buns and cakes and huge meringues such as I'd never tasted before. Father Parsloe smoked fourteen cigarettes and drank all the tea himself. I had three bottles of fizzy orangeade. 'Will we go to the pictures?' Father Parsloe said when he'd paid the bill at the cash desk. 'Will we chance the Pavilion?'

I had never, of course, been to the pictures before. My mother said that the Star Picture House, which was the only one in our town, was full of fleas.

'One and a half,' Father Parsloe said at the cash desk in the Pavilion and we were led away into the darkness. THE END it announced on the screen, and when I saw it I thought we were too late. 'Ah, aren't we in lovely time?' Father Parsloe said.

I didn't understand the film. It was about grown-ups kissing one another, and about an earthquake, and then a motor-car accident in which a woman who'd been kissed a lot was killed. The man who'd kissed her was married to another woman, and when the film ended he was sitting in a room with his wife, looking at her. She kept saying it was all right.

'God, wasn't that great?' Father Parsloe said as we stood in the lavatory of the Pavilion, the kind of lavatory where you stand up, like I'd never been in before. 'Wasn't it a good story?'

All the way back to Montenotte I kept remembering it. I kept seeing the face of the woman who'd been killed, and all the bodies lying on the streets after the earthquake, and the man at the end, sitting in a room with his wife. The swaying of the bus made me feel queasy because of the meringues and the orangeade, but I didn't care.

'Did you enjoy the afternoon?' Father Parsloe asked, and I told him I'd never enjoyed anything better. I asked him if the pictures were always as good. He assured me they were.

My parents, however, didn't seem pleased. My father got hold of a *Cork Examiner* and looked up the film that was on at the Pavilion and reported that it wasn't suitable for a child. My mother gave me a bath and examined my clothes for fleas. When Father Parsloe winked at me in the dining-room my parents pretended not to notice him.

That night my mother prayed for her extra long period, after the visit to my uncle. I lay in the dimly lit room, aware that she was kneeling there, but thinking of the film and the way the people had kissed, not like my parents ever kissed. At the convent elementary school there were girls in the higher classes who were pretty, far prettier than my mother. There was one called Claire, with fair hair and a softly freckled face, and another called Peggy Meehan, who was younger and black-haired. I had picked them out because they had spoken to me, asking me my name. I thought them very nice.

I opened my eyes and saw that my mother was rising from her knees. She stood for a moment at the edge of her bed, not smiling, her lips still moving, continuing her prayer. Then she got into bed and put out the light.

I listened to her breathing and heard it become the breathing which people have when they're asleep, but I couldn't sleep myself. I lay there, still remembering the film and remembering being in Thompson's and seeing Father Parsloe lighting one cigarette after another. For some reason, I began to imagine that I was in Thompson's with Father Parsloe and the two girls from the convent, and that we all went off to the Pavilion together,

swinging along the street. 'Ah, isn't this the life for us?' Father
Parsloe said as he led us into the darkness, and I told the girls
I'd been to the Pavilion before and they said they never had.

I heard eleven o'clock chiming from a nearby church. I heard
a stumbling on the stairs and then the laughter of Father Smith,
and Father Riordon telling him to be quiet. I heard twelve chiming
and half past twelve, and a quarter to one, and one.

After that I didn't want to sleep. I was standing in a classroom
of the convent and Claire was smiling at me. It was nice being
with her. I felt warm all over, and happy.

And then I was walking on the sands with Peggy Meehan. We
ran, playing a game she'd made up, and then we walked again.
She asked if I'd like to go on a picnic with her, next week
perhaps.

I didn't know what to do. I wanted one of the girls to be my
friend. I wanted to love one of them, like the people had loved
in the film. I wanted to kiss one and be with one, just the two
of us. In the darkness of the bedroom they both seemed close
and real, closer than my mother, even though I could hear my
mother breathing. 'Come on,' Peggy Meehan whispered, and then
Claire whispered also, saying we'd always be best friends, saying
we might run away. It was all wrong that there were two of them,
yet both vividly remained. 'Tuesday,' Peggy Meehan said. 'We'll
have the picnic on Tuesday.'

Her father drove us in his car, away from the town, out beyond
the heathery wastelands, towards a hillside that was even nicer.
But a door of the car, the back door against which Peggy Meehan
was leaning, suddenly gave way. On the dust of the road she was
as dead as the woman in the film.

'Poor Peggy,' Claire said at some later time, even though she
hadn't known Peggy Meehan very well. 'Poor little Peggy.' And
then she smiled and took my hand and we walked together
through the heathery wastelands, in love with one another.

A few days later we left my Aunt Isabella's house in Montenotte
and returned on the train to our seaside town. And a week after
that a new term began at the convent elementary school. Peggy

Meehan was dead, the Reverend Mother told us, all of us assembled together. She added that there was diphtheria in the town.

I didn't think about it at first; and I didn't connect the reality of the death with a fantasy that had been caused by my first visit to a cinema. Some part of my mind may passingly have paused over the coincidence, but that was all. There was the visit to the Pavilion itself to talk about in the convent, and the description of the film, and Father Parsloe's conversation and the way he'd smoked fourteen cigarettes in Thompson's. Diphtheria was a terrible disease, my mother said when I told her, and naturally we must all pray for the soul of poor Peggy Meehan.

But as weeks and months went by, I found myself increasingly remembering the story I had told myself on the night of the film, and remembering particularly how Peggy Meehan had fallen from the car, and how she'd looked when she was dead. I said to myself that that had been my wickedest thought, worse than my blasphemies and yet somehow part of them. At night I lay in bed, unable to sleep, trying hopelessly to pray for forgiveness. But no forgiveness came, for there was no respite to the images that recurred, her face in life and then in death, like the face of the woman in the film.

A year later, while lying awake in the same room in my aunt's boarding-house, I saw her. In the darkness there was a sudden patch of light and in the centre of it she was wearing a sailor-suit that I remembered. Her black plaits hung down her back. She smiled at me and went away. I knew instinctively then, as I watched her and after she'd gone, that the fantasy and the reality were part and parcel: I had caused this death to occur.

Looking back on it now, I can see, of course, that that feeling was a childish one. It was a childish fear, a superstition that occurring to an adult would cause only a shiver of horror. But, as a child, with no one to consult about the matter, I lived with the thought that my will was more potent than I knew. In stories I had learnt of witches and spells and evil spirits, and power

locked up in people. In my games I had wickedly denied the
religious life, and goodness, and holiness. In my games I had
mocked Father Smith, I had pretended that the dying Father
Magennis was a criminal. I had pretended to be a criminal myself,
a man who broke jewellers' windows. I had imitated my parents
when it said you should honour your father and your mother. I
had mocked the holiness of my Aunt Isabella. I had murdered
Peggy Meehan because there wasn't room for her in the story I
was telling myself. I was possessed and evil: the nuns had told
us about people being like that.

I thought at first I might seek advice from Father Parsloe. I
thought of asking him if he remembered the day we'd gone on
our outing, and then telling him how, in a story I was telling
myself, I'd caused Peggy Meehan to be killed in a car accident
like the woman in the film, and how she'd died in reality, of
diphtheria. But Father Parsloe had an impatient kind of look
about him this year, as if he had worries of his own. So I didn't
tell him and I didn't tell anyone. I hoped that when we returned
to our own house at the end of the stay in Montenotte I wouldn't
see her again, but the very first day we were back I saw her at
four o'clock in the afternoon, in the kitchen.

After that she came irregularly, sometimes not for a month
and once not for a year. She continued to appear in the same
sudden way but in different clothes, and growing up as I was
growing up. Once, after I'd left the convent and gone on to the
Christian Brothers', she appeared in the classroom, smiling near
the blackboard.

She never spoke. Whether she appeared on the promenade or
at school or in my aunt's house or our house, close to me or at
a distance, she communicated only with her smile and with her
eyes: I was possessed of the Devil, she came herself from God.
In her eyes and her smile there was that simple message, a
message which said also that my thoughts were always wicked,
that I had never believed properly in God or the Virgin or Jesus
who died for us.

I tried to pray. Like my mother, kneeling beside my bed. Like
my aunt and her houseful of priests. Like the nuns and Christian

Brothers, and other boys and girls of the town. But prayer would not come to me, and I realised that it never had. I had always pretended, going down on my knees at Mass, laughing and blaspheming in my mind. I hated the very thought of prayer. I hated my parents in an unnatural manner, and my Aunt Isabella and the priests in her house. But the dead Peggy Meehan, fresh from God's heaven, was all forgiveness in her patch of light, smiling to rid me of my evil spirit.

She was there at my mother's funeral, and later at my father's. Claire, whom I had destroyed her for, married a man employed in the courthouse and became a Mrs Madden, prematurely fat. I naturally didn't marry anyone myself.

I am forty-six years old now and I live alone in the same seaside town. No one in the town knows why I am solitary. No one could guess that I have lived with a child's passionate companionship for half a lifetime. Being no longer a child, I naturally no longer believe that I was responsible for the death. In my passing, careless fantasy I wished for it and she, already dead, picked up my living thoughts. I should not have wished for it because in middle age she is a beautiful creature now, more beautiful by far than fat Mrs Madden.

And that is all there is. At forty-six I walk alone on the brief promenade, or by the edge of the sea or on the road to Cork, where the moving house is. I work, as my father worked, in the offices of Cosgriff and McLoughlin. I cook my own food. I sleep alone in a bed that has an iron bedstead. On Sundays I go hypocritically to Mass in the Church of the Holy Redeemer; I go to Confession and do not properly confess; I go to Men's Confraternity, and to Communion. And all the time she is there, appearing in her patch of light to remind me that she never leaves me. And all the time, on my knees at Mass, or receiving the Body and the Blood, or in my iron bed, I desire her. In the offices of Cosgriff and McLoughlin I dream of her nakedness. When we are old I shall desire her, too, with my shrunken, evil body.

In the town I am a solitary, peculiar man. I have been rendered so, people probably say, by my cloistered upbringing, and probably add that such an upbringing would naturally cultivate a morbid imagination. That may be so, and it doesn't really matter how things have come about. All I know is that she is more real for me than anything else is in this seaside town or beyond it. I live for her, living hopelessly, for I know I can never possess her as I wish to. I have a carnal desire for a shadow, which in turn is His mockery of me: His fitting punishment for my wickedest thought of all.

THE FIRST OF MY SINS

Brian Friel

A schoolmaster's son, Brian Friel (1929–) has utilised his experiences of a childhood growing up in Ireland in several of the plays which have earned him recognition as one of today's leading playwrights—notably Philadelphia, Here I Come *(1964),* Aristocrats *(1981) and* Translations *(1983). Born in Omagh, County Tyrone, Friel was an observant youngster always aware of a certain distance between himself and other children because of his father's profession. His insight into the minds of children was further enlarged when he followed in his father's profession, and for ten years, between 1950 and 1960, worked as a primary and intermediary schoolteacher in Derry. Writing in his spare time, he was finally able to become a full-time author in the Sixties. His early short stories, which often focused on the rigid social and religious codes in villages and small towns of Donegal and Derry, won him recognition in the* New Yorker *and* Saturday Evening Post, *but it was the success of* Philadelphia, Here I Come *on Broadway and then as a film which made Friel's reputation, and since then he has devoted much of his energy to writing plays.*

A number of stories about childhood are to be found in his collections, A Saucer of Larks *(1962) and* The Gold in the Sea *(1966), including 'Everything Neat and Tidy' in which a disaster forces young Johnny to abandon his private world of role-playing and enter the world of adult conduct, and 'The Illusionist' featuring the annual visit of a magician to a rural primary school and its impact on the children, which is clearly based on personal experience. 'The First of My Sins', written in 1965, is the story of an eight-year-old boy approaching his first confession and wrestling with what he must tell the priest. Few other pieces of fiction have so knowingly caught this landmark moment in any child's life.*

*   *   *

I can recall the precise moment in my childhood when I had the first intimation of the real meaning of sin. It occurred on a Friday evening in the June of my eighth year, the day before I made my first confession. Mother and I had had a row—it ended with mother shouting, 'You are nothing but an animal—a dirty little animal!' and slapping my face—and I had run, bawling, out of the house and down to the bank of the stream that flowed past the foot of our garden. I remembered I was wearing my new shoes to break them in for the next day, and in my blind rush through the garden I had stepped into a cake of cow-dung. That finished me altogether. A slap on the face merely pricks one's pride but cow-dung on new shoes shatters one's dignity. I flung myself on the ground and was screaming my head off when I felt a hand on my shoulder and heard Uncle George's voice behind my neck. I was aware that he was trying to console me in his awkward way but I kept up my screaming for a time to establish my wretchedness. He got down on his knees beside me and asked what had happened. I told him. He raised me into a sitting position on the bank—I was then at the sniffling stage—and pulled handfuls of grass, and began wiping the manure off my new shoes, and all the time he talked and talked, no doubt to distract me, about the great city of London where he lived and about the Royal Majestic Hotel where he worked. I did not understand half of what he was saying, but his voice was soft and comforting, and I was content just to listen. And it was then, when he was telling me about his job as night porter, that I had the sudden, momentary intuition of what sin really is. I will not pretend that I knew fully—for that matter, I am still far from certain—but there, on the bank of that yellow stream listening to Uncle George rambling on as if he were talking to himself, I got a flicker of real understanding, and that lightning intelligence was so different to what I had been taught by Sister Benignus, my teacher, or by Father Clancy, who examined our catechism lessons, or by mother, who had me gurgling prayers before I could walk, so different but so illuminating, that I felt suddenly very wise and very crafty and very old.

Uncle George had appeared out of the blue a fortnight before, and as soon as I saw him I was disappointed. I imagine he was about fifty then, tall and loose and ungainly, and when he walked his shoulders and arms worked in unison with his feet so that, with every step he took, one side of his body swivelled forward. His face was pale and disturbed every so often by a muscular twitch in his right cheek which drew his features into a quick, unhappy smile. His eyes were shy and constantly on the move in case, if they rested for any length on one place, they might see anything. I knew from mother, his sister, that he had run away to sea as a boy and that he had travelled the world, and night after night I had dreamed of him and his great exploits. And I might have forgiven him his appearance if he had told me tales of high adventure and mutiny and pirates. But this great loping giant, who arrived unannounced one morning and who spent his days tramping around the Tyrone countryside, seldom spoke, and I never saw him except at meal times when he ate voraciously and smiled his bleak involuntary smile at father's persistent banter. I told any of my friends who asked me about our visitor that he was suffering from shell-shock.

Everybody assured me that my first confession would be the happiest day of my life, a day I would always remember; and as that Saturday drew near life certainly became more and more blissful. Father bought me a new bicycle. Mother got me a new suit and new shoes. Auntie Mary sent me £1 and Auntie Kathleen 30/- (it was her privilege, as my godmother, to outdo Auntie Mary). Sister Benignus gave me a pair of rosary beads and Father Clancy presented me with a white prayer book, inscribed 'To a great little man' (I considered the description accurate and could not understand why it brought tears to mother's eyes). Indeed I was beginning to wonder what further ecstasy confession itself would bring when on the eve of the big event mother and I had the row and I was plunged into despair—and dung.

We had got the half-day off school that Friday afternoon, and when I went home I found mother ironing my new suit to smooth out the shop creases. I jumped up on a stool on the other side of the ironing board and watched. The next day was suddenly very close to us.

'You go to church at ten?' mother said.

I nodded my head.

'Will Sister Benignus be there?'

I said she would.

'I suppose you know what you're going to tell the priest, David?'

'Of course!' I said.

'Of course,' she said.

'Bless-me-Father-for-I-have-sinned. Please-Father-this-is-my-first-confession. Please-Father-I . . .'

'No, no, no, David. Don't tell me. That is something for the priest alone. I don't want to hear your sins.'

'I don't care,' I said indifferently. 'I told Sister Benignus.'

'Did you?'

'We all did. You know—a sort of practice.'

'Yes?'

'She just laughed at me.'

'Laugh? Why did she laugh?'

'How would I know?' I said.

She hung the jacket on a coat hanger and spread the trousers on the board. 'You must have said something that made her laugh.'

'I told her what I'm going to tell the priest: Please-Father-this-is-my-first-confession. Please-Father-I-killed-a-cat-once. That-is-all-Father.'

Mother smiled across at me. I thought for a second she was going to kiss me. But she went on ironing. 'Yes, that was a naughty thing to do, killing that cat. And you're sorry, aren't you?'

'In a way. But it ate Roger.' Roger had been my pet rabbit.

'Still, you're sorry you killed it?'

'I suppose so,' I said. I put my cheek on the warm surface of the ironing board and remembered Roger.

'David, don't you think you should mention to the priest what happened last Tuesday week?'

'Mm?'

'I can't talk to you lying down like that. Sit up.'

I sat up.

'I said should you not tell the priest what happened last Tuesday week?'

'When was that?'

'The day we went to see Auntie Mary.'

'Did I do something wrong?'

'Don't you remember?' she said. 'She and I were having a cup of coffee and you crawled under the table. Remember?' She was using the tone of voice she used when we had visitors.

'What did I do?' I was genuinely interested.

'Well,' she said, 'you crawled under the table—she and I were sitting, chatting—and you crawled under the table—and—and—and you pulled up her skirt.'

'Oh, that!' I said, disappointed.

'You did, you know, David.'

'I only wanted to see the colour of her knickers. I told you that.'

'I know. I know. But still . . .' Her face was flushed with the heat of the iron. 'And I merely mention it now, David, in case you think you might like to tell the priest about it. It was—it was a naughty thing to do.'

'That was no sin!'

'It was naughty.'

'Sister Benignus told me it was no sin. So there!'

Mother looked quickly at me. 'Told you? Did you ask her?'

'Course I did. Because I knew I was right and you were wrong.'

'What did you say to her?'

'I told her,' I said patiently, 'that I pulled up Auntie Mary's skirt to see what colour her knickers were, and that she squealed, and that you wouldn't speak to me all the way home in the bus. And I asked her was it a sin.'

'And what did she say?'

'She said, "Run away and have a bit of sense. She's easy made squeal." That's what she said. So there!'

'No need to make a face at me, David,' mother said. 'I'm only trying to help you.'

But I knew she was annoyed with me. Her mouth had gone tight. 'And there's another thing,' she said.

'Another what?'

'That fight you had with Tony Brennan last Monday. Don't you think you should tell that to the priest tomorrow?'

'Tell what?'

'That you hit Tony with your fist.'

'That was no sin!'

'Did I say it was, David?'

'You said I should tell the priest. Why should I tell him if it wasn't a sin?'

'I'm merely suggesting things you might have overlooked, things I myself might consider telling if I were you.'

'It was his fault. He hit me first.'

'Two wrongs don't make a right. And, anyhow, you must have made him angry.'

'He wouldn't kiss me,' I explained. She thought I said 'kick'.

'And why should he kick you, for heaven's sake?'

'I didn't say kick—I said kiss! We were all kissing each other, Billy Kerrigan and Eamonn Shine and Paul Shiels and Sean O'Donnell, and Tony wouldn't join in. And when I tried to make him he hit me and I hit him back.' I knew by her face that she did not understand.

'I told you before!' I said. 'You must have forgotten!'

'No,' she said softly. 'You never told me why he hit you in the first place.'

'Anyhow, we're pals now again,' I said.

'When—when did this happen, David?' she asked, smoothing very slowly.

'What?'

'This—this kissing.'

'In the toilets. At lunchtime.'

'Yes?'

'Well, that's all. It was just a game. And Tony got angry.'

'A kissing game?'

'Not the way you kiss,' I said, because I could see that she still did not understand. 'This was fun kissing—you know?— just touching tongues. And when I went to Tony with my tongue out he wouldn't put out his tongue because he said my tongue was dirty. And then he hit me because I was going to make him kiss me.' She did not speak. 'So I hit him back,' I concluded.

'I think you should mention that to the priest, David.'

'What?'

'What you have just told me, the whole thing exactly as you have told me.'

'That was no sin!'

'David, it is the priest's job to advise you on what is right and what is wrong. He might think that this—this game is not a nice game for young boys.'

'The kissing game?'

'Whatever you call it,' she said.

'I'm not going to tell him about the games we play!' I said stoutly.

'I think you should, David. He will be able to tell you if it is wrong.' She paused. 'Yes. Tell him exactly as you told me and then ask his advice. Father, you'll say, is this—this game we play sinful or not.' She began working briskly again. 'Now, we have a real confession to make, haven't we? First, we killed the cat. Second, we looked up Auntie Mary's skirt. And third, we played this—this kissing game—with other boys. Don't you agree? Are you listening to me, David? I said don't you agree?'

I should have said yes just to satisfy her and then gone ahead with the confession I had rehearsed. But some stubbornness, some vague sense of independence, took possession of me.

'No,' I said sullenly.

'No—what?'

'The cat is the only thing I'm going to tell.'

'David—'

'I told you why I pulled up her skirt: I just wanted to see the colour of her knickers!' I was shouting in self defence. 'And the kissing game was only a game, and I hit Tony because he hit me! That was no sin either! And I'm not going to tell things like that to the priest!'

'David, if your mother tells you to—'

'Father Clancy said it in school. The priest wants to hear nothing but your sins, he said; he doesn't want to hear what you had for your breakfast or how far you can spit. That's what he said.'

'I'm telling you, David, that there are certain things—'

'I don't care what you say. I know! Father Clancy told us!'

'How dare you speak to me like that!'

Now the two of us were shouting. 'I'll tell about the cat but I'll tell nothing else! I won't! I won't!'

'David!'

'I won't! I won't! I won't.'

We both got the smell of burning at the same time.

'Oh, God!' said mother, snatching up the iron. But the damage was done. A brown triangle, the shape of the iron, was imprinted on the seat of my new trousers.

'Oh, God!' mother groaned. 'Your suit's ruined! Ruined!' Suddenly her anger overflowed. 'And it's all your fault, you little brat, you!' It was then she slapped my face with her open hand. 'D'you know what you are?' she shouted. 'You're nothing but an animal—a dirty little animal!'

And that was why I had run, bawling, out of the house and down to the bank of the stream where Uncle George found me, and wiped the manure off my feet, and comforted me with his soft voice, and distracted me with his rambling conversation.

There are times when I imagine I remember every detail of that scattered soliloquy, when I think I can recall everything that Uncle George said to me. But I know I cannot. What I do remember, vividly, is the drowsy heat of the evening sun, and the noise of the stream, and the smell of grass and dung, and the bleak flitting smile on his face, and his glancing looks at mine. And I remember, too, parts of what he said.

He had held dozens of jobs, he told me, all over the world—docker, insurance man, sailor, mechanic, prospector, labourer, soldier; and always he had left them because—and I have no doubt about the expression he used—'because people were always bribing you, smiling and bribing you at the same time.' I asked him about his job as night porter in the Royal Majestic Hotel and he told me that he had left it, too, because people kept slipping him money and winking at him and squeezing his elbow. 'Do you see?' he kept saying. 'Do you see? Do you see? Do you see?' repeating the staccato words again and again so that I tried, tried desperately, to understand him. I cannot have understood. But, young as I was, I got an inkling of what he was trying to tell me: that evil abounded, all over the world; and that evil-doers were people who smiled, and somehow, with their smiles and their sly intimacy, involved others in their corruption; and that one had to keep going from place to place and from job to job to avoid being corrupted by them.

'There,' he said, jumping to his feet. 'Those shoes are cleaner now, aren't they?'

I looked at them. 'Mother warned me to stay off the grass,' I said. I was on the verge of tears again.

'Tell you what,' he said. 'Go back to the house; and go up to my room; and in the case under the bed you'll find a pair of brushes and a tin of polish. Give the shoes a good rub and they'll look as good as new.'

'You come with me,' I said.

The muscle twitched and the eyes slid all over the place. 'I think I'll go for a walk,' he said. 'You go ahead. Under the bed. In the case. Okay?' And off he strode as if he were being followed.

Because I was nervous of meeting mother I slipped in the back door and went cautiously up to Uncle George's room. I found the cardboard case and the brushes in it and cleaned my shoes. They looked as good as new. Then, when I was putting the brushes back, I noticed a small bundle, covered with newspaper, in the corner of the case. I felt it. It was hard. I tore a corner off the paper and stuck a finger into the hole. The finger found a smooth, cold surface. My curiosity was too strong: I opened the parcel. It contained six knives and six forks and six spoons, each with the letters RMH on the handle. My Uncle George had stolen them! My Uncle George was a thief!

Mother ignored me when I went down to the kitchen. She moved from the cooker to the table and back to the cooker, and brushed past me as if I were not there.

I asked when tea would be ready.

'You owe me an apology, David,' she answered.

'Sorry,' I said dutifully.

'I hope you are,' she said. 'Any boy about to make his first confession and shouting at his mother like that! Shame on you!' Usually when we had a row, she kissed me when we made it up. But that day she told me to stop hanging around and make myself useful.

I did all the little jobs that always merited a hug: I set the table for her; I carried in the extra chair from the sitting-room; I brought in coal for the night. But still she froze me. I could endure it no longer. I had to have her affection.

'Do you want to hear a secret?'

'If you wish to tell me,' she said.

'It's a big secret,' I said temptingly.

She did not speak.

'It's the biggest secret I ever had,' I said.

'If you're going to tell me, then tell me. If you're not, run upstairs and leave out fresh underclothes. You're having a bath after tea.'

I sidled over to the cooker and stood beside her. 'I'll tell you,' I said.

'What is it? What is it?' She did not even look at me.

I hesitated for a moment, long enough to weigh the revelation I was about to make against her warm love which I hoped to win in exchange. I made the choice.

'Whisper,' I said. She stooped down to me.

'Uncle George is a thief,' I said into her ear. 'His case is full of knives and forks and spoons that belong to the London hotel!'

Through the wall that separated my bedroom from the living-room I heard the row that night. Father spoke occasionally, placatingly, and Uncle George did not speak at all; it was mother who made all the noise. She shouted and sobbed and moaned, and the words 'disgrace' and 'thief' pierced into me again and again. It kept on for a long time and then there was silence. But still I did not sleep. Then I heard Uncle George moving about in his room upstairs and then the front door was opened and shut and then there was no more sound.

Mother woke me with a kiss and said gently, 'David, darling, do you know what day this is?' It was a glorious June morning. I had a special breakfast in the dining-room (I usually ate at the kitchen table) and mother attended to me as if she were a waitress.

Then we walked hand-in-hand to the church and on the way we met Billy Kerrigan and his mother, and Paul Shiels and his mother, and Sean O'Donnell and his mother, each couple hand-in-hand just like mother and myself. All the mothers chatted away and we smirked at one another in embarrassment.

We stopped at the door of the church. Mother fixed my hair and pulled down my jacket so that the burn on the trousers was concealed. 'Ready?' she said.

'Is Uncle George gone away?' I asked.

'He is,' she said. 'Let's not talk about him.' She adjusted my collar. 'Remember our little chat yesterday?'

'Yes.'

'And the three things to tell the priest?'

'Yes.'

'And you're sorry for them?'

'Yes.'

'Good,' she said. 'Good boy. Now, in you go. I'll be waiting for you when you're finished.'

I took my place in the queue. When my turn came I went into the little box. I told the priest what I had done to Uncle George; and when he said, 'Is that all, son?' I told him again because he obviously did not understand the enormity of my sin. But he nodded his head and said, 'I know. I know. Is there nothing else?'

'No, Father,' I said. He gave me absolution and asked me to pray for him.

I came out into the golden church and walked towards the row of eager, smiling mothers kneeling at the back.

RED JAM ROLL, THE DANCER

Brendan Behan

Former Borstal boy and would-be terrorist, Brendan Behan (1923–1964) is another of Ireland's most acclaimed playwrights of the twentieth century, whose anti-heroic works The Quare Fellow *(1956), a study of life in a prison on the night of a hanging, and* The Hostage *(1958), about a Cockney soldier imprisoned in a Dublin brothel, were huge box-office successes with audiences throughout Europe. Born in Dublin, one of three sons of a house-painter, Brendan was a quick-witted, mischievous child, forever on the verge of trouble with the law as he grew up in one of the city's most deprived areas. However, his youthful pranks became something more sinister when, at the age of 16, he crossed to Liverpool and was arrested by the police. In a statement to CID officers in Lime Street Police Station, Behan claimed he had 'come over to fight for the Irish Workers' and Small Farmers' Republic, for a full and free life for his countrymen, North and South, and for the removal of British Imperialism from Irish affairs'. Too young to be imprisoned, he was sentenced to three years' Borstal training, but on his release was soon in trouble again and for the next ten years spent most of his time behind bars. In 1958 he published his autobiography,* Borstal Boy, *and although the book was banned in the Republic (and, curiously, in Australia) it marked the arrival of a unique and irreverent literary talent.*

In later newspaper essays and short stories, Behan earned the reputation of being a writer who 'sends language out on a swaggering spree, ribald, flushed and spoiling for a fight.' Tales of his childhood such as 'Up and Down Spion Kop', 'We Took

Over a Castle' and 'What Are They At With the Rotunda' are colourful pictures of growing up in a rapidly changing Dublin. One thing that never changed was Behan's love of a fight— whether a battle with words or actual fisticuffs—and 'Red Jam Roll, the Dancer' shows that this fighting spirit was in him even as a nine-year-old.

*   *   *

I am reminded of boxing matters by an encounter I had this day with a former opponent of mine, pugilistically speaking. I do not mean that our encounter this day was a pugilistic one, but it was pugilistically speaking we last spoke. And that, at the lane running alongside the railway end of Croker Park.

Our street was a tough street, and the last outpost of toughness you'd meet as you left North Dublin for the red brick respectability of Jones's Road, Fitzroy Avenue, Clonliffe Road, and Drumcondra generally.

Kids from those parts we despised, hated and resented. For the following sins: they lived in houses one to a family, which we thought greedy, unnatural and unsocial; they wore suits all the one colour, both jacket and pants, where we wore a jersey and shorts; they carried leather schoolbags where we either had a strap round our books or else a cheap check cloth bag.

Furthermore, it was suspected that some of them took piano lessons and dancing lessons, while we of the North Circular Road took anything we could lay our hands on which was not nailed down.

We brought one of them to our corner and bade him continue his performance, and thereafter any time we caught him, he was brought in bondage to the corner of Russell Street and invited to give a performance of the dance: hornpipe, jig, reel, or slip jig.

This young gent, in addition to being caught red-footed, was by colouring of hair red-headed, and I've often heard since that they are an exceedingly bad-tempered class of person which, signs on it, he was no exception. For having escaped from his exercises by reason of an approaching Civic Guard, by name

'Dirty Lug', he ran down to the canal bridge which was the border of our territory, and used language the like of which was shocking to anyone from Russell Street and guaranteed to turn thousands grey if they hailed from some other part.

However, our vengeance for the insults heaped upon us by this red-headed hornpiper, that thought so bad of giving the people an old step on the corner of the street, was not an empty one.

One day, not alone did we catch him, but he'd a jam roll under his oxter—steaming hot, crisp and sweet from the bakery—and the shortest way from Summerhill to where he lived was through our street. He was tired, no doubt, with wearing suits and living in a house with only his own family and carrying that heavy leather schoolbag, not to mind the dancing lessons; no doubt he thought he had a right to be tired, and he took the shortest way home with the cake for his ma.

He could see none of our gang, but the fact that he didn't see us didn't mean we were not there. We were, as a matter of fact, playing 'the make in' on Brennan's Hill down by the Mountjoy Brewery when his approach was signalled by a scout, and in short order 'the make in' was postponed while we held up the red fellow and investigated his parcel.

We grabbed the booty, and were so intent on devouring the jam roll that we let the prisoner go over the bridge and home to plot his vengeance.

He was a hidden villain all right. Long weeks after, myself and Scoil (or Skull, have it any way you fancy) Kane were moseying round Croker, not minding anything in particular. Kerry was playing Cavan in hurling or Derry was playing Tyrone in anything, but it wasn't a match of any great import to any save relations and friends, and a dilatory class of a Sunday afternoon was being had by all, when the Scoil (Skull) and myself were surrounded by a gang, if you please, from Jones's Road, and who but the red-headed dancing master at the head of them.

But we didn't take them seriously.

'Sound man, Jam Roll,' said I, not knowing what else to call him.

'I'll give you jam roll in a minute,' said Jam Roll.

'You're a dacent boy,' said I, 'and will you wet the tea as you're at it?'

'Will you stand out?' says Jam Roll.

'I will,' said I.

'In the cod or in the real?'

'The real,' said I; 'd'you take me for a hornpiper?'

He said no more but gave me a belt so that I thought the Hogan Stand had fallen on me. One off the ground. The real Bowery Belt.

'Now,' says he, when I came to, 'you won't call me Jam Roll again.'

'You were wrong there, Jam Roll.'

THE TROUT

Sean O'Faolain

Unlike Brendan Behan, the novelist and biographer Sean O'Faolain (1900–1991) grew up in a genteel home in Cork with his father, a dedicated member of the Royal Irish Constabulary, and his devoutly Catholic mother. According to his autobiography, Vive Moi! *published two years after his death, his childish imagination was 'fed by the shows and rituals of the local theatre, the Catholic Church and the British Empire', and for even the slightest misdemeanours he earned a beating with the cane. While still in his teens, however, he rebelled against his background and, following the Easter Rising in 1916, joined the IRA as a bomb-maker, 'an essentially inglorious job which girls could have done as well or better,' he later wrote. Returning to graduate from University College, Cork, he studied for an MA at Harvard and then worked as a teacher in America, England and Ireland before publishing his first collection of short stories,* Midsummer Night Madness, *in 1932, prior to becoming a full-time writer. He married his childhood sweetheart, Eileen, whom he had first met at school, introducing himself by dipping her long ponytail in an inkwell and then 'politely handing it to her'. She, too, became a writer and published the widely praised volume* Irish Sagas and Folk Tales *(1954).*

For much of his life, Sean O'Faolain was a leading figure in the Irish cultural world, although some of his more outspoken and sexually explicit stories did land him in trouble with the Censorship Board. Among his many varied short stories are several which hark back to his youth, such as 'The Judas Touch', about a little boy desperately imploring his mother to let him go

*to the forbidden pleasure of the cinema (as he himself had done),
and 'The Man Who Invented Sin', about some young students
getting innocent fun from studying the Irish language. 'The Trout'
is a particularly evocative story of sunny childhood days on
holiday and is especially interesting because it features a young
girl named Julia. Sean O'Faolain had a daughter named Julia
who, like her parents, has become a writer and appears later in
this collection with her own special memory of childhood.*

*   *   *

One of the first places Julia always ran to when they arrived in
G—— was The Dark Walk. It is a laurel walk, very old, almost
gone wild, a lofty midnight tunnel of smooth, sinewy branches.
Underfoot the tough brown leaves are never dry enough to
crackle: there is always a suggestion of damp and cool trickle.

She raced right into it. For the first few yards she always had
the memory of the sun behind her, then she felt the dusk closing
swiftly down on her so that she screamed with pleasure and raced
on to reach the light at the far end; and it was always just a little
too long in coming so that she emerged gasping, clasping her
hands, laughing, drinking in the sun. When she was filled with
the heat and glare she would turn and consider the ordeal again.

This year she had the extra joy of showing it to her small
brother, and of terrifying him as well as herself. And for him the
fear lasted longer because his legs were so short and she had
gone out at the far end while he was still screaming and racing.

When they had done this many times they came back to the
house to tell everybody that they had done it. He boasted. She
mocked. They squabbled.

'Cry babby!'

'You were afraid yourself, so there!'

'I won't take you any more.'

'You're a big pig.'

'I hate you.'

Tears were threatening so somebody said, 'Did you see the
well?' She opened her eyes at that and held up her long lovely

neck suspiciously and decided to be incredulous. She was twelve and at that age little girls are beginning to suspect most stories: they have already found out too many, from Santa Claus to the Stork. How could there be a well! In The Dark Walk? That she had visited year after year? Haughtily she said, 'Nonsense.'

But she went back, pretending to be going somewhere else, and she found a hole scooped in the rock at the side of the walk, choked with damp leaves, so shrouded by ferns that she only uncovered it after much searching. At the back of this little cavern there was about a quart of water. In the water she suddenly perceived a panting trout. She rushed for Stephen and dragged him to see, and they were both so excited that they were no longer afraid of the darkness as they hunched down and peered in at the fish panting in his tiny prison, his silver stomach going up and down like an engine.

Nobody knew how the trout got there. Even old Martin in the kitchen-garden laughed and refused to believe that it was there, or pretended not to believe, until she forced him to come down and see. Kneeling and pushing back his tattered old cap he peered in.

'Be cripes, you're right. How the divil in hell did that fella get there?'

She stared at him suspiciously.

'You knew?' she accused; but he said, 'The divil a know'; and reached down to lift it out. Convinced she hauled him back. If she had found it then it was her trout.

Her mother suggested that a bird had carried the spawn. Her father thought that in the winter a small streamlet might have carried it down there as a baby, and it had been safe until the summer came and the water began to dry up. She said, 'I see,' and went back to look again and consider the matter in private. Her brother remained behind, wanting to hear the whole story of the trout, not really interested in the actual trout but much interested in the story which his mummy began to make up for him on the lines of, 'So one day Daddy Trout and Mammy Trout . . .' When he retailed it to her she said, 'Pooh.'

It troubled her that the trout was always in the same position;

he had no room to turn; all the time the silver belly went up and down; otherwise he was motionless. She wondered what he ate and in between visits to Joey Pony, and the boat and a bathe to get cool, she thought of his hunger. She brought him down bits of dough; once she brought a worm. He ignored the food. He just went on panting. Hunched over him she thought how, all the winter, while she was at school he had been in there. All winter, in The Dark Walk, all day, all night, floating around alone. She drew the leaf of her hat down around her ears and chin and stared. She was still thinking of it as she lay in bed.

It was late June, the longest days of the year. The sun had sat still for a week, burning up the world. Although it was after ten o'clock it was still bright and still hot. She lay on her back under a single sheet, with her long legs spread, trying to keep cool. She could see the D of the moon through the fir-tree—they slept on the ground floor. Before they went to bed her mummy had told Stephen the story of the trout again, and she, in her bed, had resolutely presented her back to them and read her book. But she had kept one ear cocked.

'And so, in the end, this naughty fish who would not stay at home got bigger and bigger and bigger, and the water got smaller and smaller . . .'

Passionately she had whirled and cried, 'Mummy, don't make it a horrible old moral story!' Her mummy had brought in a Fairy Godmother, then, who sent lots of rain, and filled the well, and a stream poured out and the trout floated away down to the river below. Staring at the moon she knew that there are no such things as Fairy Godmothers and that the trout, down in The Dark Walk, was panting like an engine. She heard somebody unwind a fishing-reel. Would the *beasts* fish him out!

She sat up. Stephen was a hot lump of sleep, lazy thing. The Dark Walk would be full of little scraps of moon. She leaped up and looked out the window, and somehow it was not so lightsome now that she saw the dim mountains far away and the black firs against the breathing land and heard a dog say, bark-bark. Quietly she lifted the ewer of water, and climbed out the window and scuttled along the cool but cruel gravel down to the maw of the tunnel. Her pyjamas were very short so that when she splashed water it wet her ankles. She peered into the tunnel. Something alive rustled inside there. She raced in, and up and down she raced, and flurried, and cried aloud, 'Oh, Gosh, I can't find it,' and then at last she did. Kneeling down in the damp she put her hand into the slimy hole. When the body lashed they were both mad with fright. But she gripped him and shoved him into the ewer and raced, with her teeth ground, out to the other end of the tunnel and down the steep paths to the river's edge.

All the time she could feel him lashing his tail against the side of the ewer. She was afraid he would jump right out. The gravel cut into her soles until she came to the cool ooze of the river's bank where the moon-mice on the water crept into her feet. She poured out watching until he plopped. For a second he was visible in the water. She hoped he was not dizzy. Then all she saw was the glimmer of the moon in the silent-flowing river, the dark firs, the dim mountains, and the radiant pointed face laughing down at her out of the empty sky.

She scuttled up the hill, in the window, plonked down the ewer and flew through the air like a bird into bed. The dog said bark-bark. She heard the fishing-reel whirring. She hugged herself and giggled. Like a river of joy her holiday spread before her.

In the morning Stephen rushed to her, shouting that 'he' was gone, and asking 'where' and 'how'. Lifting her nose in the air she said superciliously, 'Fairy Godmother, I suppose?' and strolled away patting the palms of her hands.

THE RING

Bryan MacMahon

*Bryan MacMahon (1909–) was born in the market town of
Listowel in County Kerry and during his childhood developed
an enduring delight in the rivers, lakes and mountains of the
local countryside, bounded on the west by the rolling breakers
of the Atlantic and on the north by the Shannon estuary. According to his own account, 'much of my casual education was gathered in the work-shops of local saddlers, smiths and shoemakers,
where I listened, fascinated, to the thrust and parry of magic
words.' The rich tradition of local folklore also captured his
imagination and found its way, initially, into his school essays
and, later, into short stories, plays and poetry. MacMahon's life
has been spent almost entirely in Listowel as a teacher and later
headmaster of the local school. His skill as a natural storyteller
was signalled when his early work was published in Sean
O'Faolain's magazine,* The Bell, *and he reached an even wider
audience with his collections* The Lion-Tamer *(1948) and* The
Red Petticoat *(1955). He enjoyed still greater acclaim for his
novels* Children of the Rainbow *(1952) and* The Honey Spike
(1967), as well as a number of plays, notably The Song of the
Anvil *(1960). MacMahon has continued to write since his retirement from teaching, and his autobiography,* The Master *(1990),
was a best-seller in Ireland.*

*Bryan MacMahon has written several tales about his child-
hood, most of which are set in Listowel and have made him, in
the words of fellow Irish writer Benedict Kiely, 'as essential to
his own locality as the ancient stone monuments of the Dingle
peninsula'. The selection here, 'The Ring', observes the idiosyn-*

*crasies of the older generation through a child's eyes—and in
particular the stubbornness of one old lady.*

*   *   *

I should like you to have known my grandmother. She was my
mother's mother, and as I remember her she was a widow with
a warm farm in the Kickham country in Tipperary. Her land was
on the southern slope of a hill, and there it drank in the sun
which, to me, seemed always to be balanced on the teeth of the
Galtees. Each year I spent the greater part of my summer holidays
at my grandmother's place. It was a great change for me to leave
our home in a bitter sea-coast village in Kerry and visit my
grandmother's. Why, man, the grass gone to waste on a hundred
yards of the roadside in Tipperary was as much as you'd find in
a dozen of our sea-poisoned fields. I always thought it a pity to
see all that fine grass go to waste by the verge of the road. I
think so still.

Although my Uncle Con was married, my grandmother held the
whip hand in the farm. At the particular time I am trying to recall,
the first child was in the cradle. (Ah, how time has galloped away!
That child is now a nun in a convent on the Seychelles Islands.)
My Uncle Con's wife, my Aunt Annie, was a gentle, delicate girl
who was only charmed in herself to have somebody to assume the
responsibility of the place. Which was just as well indeed, consider-
ing the nature of woman my grandmother was. Since that time when
her husband's horse had walked into the farmyard unguided, with
my grandfather, Martin Dermody, dead in the body of the car, her
heart had turned to stone in her breast. Small wonder to that turning,
since she was left with six young children—five girls and one boy,
my Uncle Con. But she faced the world bravely and did well by
them all. Ah! but she was hard, main hard.

Once at a race-meeting I picked up a jockey's crop. When I
balanced it on my palm it reminded me of my grandmother.
Once I had a twenty-two-pound salmon laced to sixteen feet of
Castleconnell greenheart; the rod reminded me of my grandmother. True, like crop and rod, she had an element of flexibility,

but like them there was no trace of fragility. Now after all these years I cannot recall her person clearly; to me she is but something tall and dark and austere. But lately I see her character with a greater clarity. Now I understand things that puzzled me when I was a boy. Towards me she displayed a certain black affection. Oh, but I made her laugh warmly once. That was when I told her of the man who had stopped me on the road beyond the limekiln and asked me if I were a grandson of Martin Dermody. Inflating with a shy pride, I had told him that I was. He then gave me a shilling and said, 'Maybe you're called Martin after your grandfather?' 'No,' I said, 'I'm called Con after my Uncle Con.' It was then my grandmother had laughed a little warmly. But my Uncle Con caught me under the armpits, tousled my hair and said I was a clever Kerry rascal.

The solitary occasion on which I remember her to have shown emotion was remarkable. Maybe remarkable isn't the proper word; obscene would be closer to the mark. Obscene I would have thought of it then, had I known the meaning of the word. Today I think it merely pathetic.

How was it that it all started? Yes, there was I with my bare legs trailing from the heel of a loaded hay-float. I was watching the broad silver parallels we were leaving in the clean after-grass. My Uncle Con was standing in the front of the float guiding the mare. Drawing in the hay to the hayshed we were. Already we had a pillar and a half of the hayshed filled. My grandmother was up on the hay, forking the lighter trusses. The servant-boy was handling the heavier forkfuls. A neighbour was throwing it up to them.

When the float stopped at the hayshed I noticed that something was amiss. For one thing the man on the hay was idle, as indeed was the man on the ground. My grandmother was on the ground, looking at the hay with cold calculating eyes. She turned to my Uncle Con.

'Draw in no more hay, Con,' she said. 'I've lost my wedding ring.'

'Where? In the hay?' he queried.

'Yes, in the hay.'

'But I thought you had a keeper?'

'I've lost the keeper, too. My hands are getting thin.'

'The story could be worse,' he commented.

My grandmother did not reply for a little while. She was eyeing the stack with enmity.

' 'Tis in that half-pillar,' she said at last. 'I must look for it.'

'You've a job before you, mother,' said Uncle Con.

She spoke to the servant-boy and the neighbour. 'Go down and shake out those couple of pikes at the end of the Bog Meadow,' she ordered. 'They're heating in the centre.'

'Can't we be drawing in to the idle pillar, mother?' my Uncle Con asked gently.

'No, Con,' she answered. 'I'll be putting the hay from the middle pillar there.'

The drawing-in was over for the day. That was about four o'clock in the afternoon. Before she tackled the half-pillar my grandmother went down on her hands and knees and started to search the loose hay in the idle pillar. She searched wisp by wisp, even sop by sop. My Uncle Con beckoned to me to come away. Anyway, we knew she'd stop at six o'clock. 'Six to six' was her motto for working hours. She never broke that rule.

That was a Monday evening. On Tuesday we offered to help— my Uncle Con and I. She was down on her knees when we asked her. 'No, no,' she said abruptly. Then, by way of explanation, when she saw that we were crestfallen: 'You see, if we didn't find it I'd be worried that ye didn't search as carefully as ye should, and I'd have no peace of mind until I had searched it all over again.' So she worked hard all day, breaking off only for her meals and stopping sharp at six o'clock.

By Wednesday evening she had made a fair gap in the hay but had found no ring. Now and again during the day we used to go down to see if she had had any success. She was very wan in the face when she stopped in the evening.

On Thursday morning her face was still more strained and drawn. She seemed reluctant to leave the rick even to take her meals. What little she ate seemed like so much dust in her mouth. We took down tea to her several times during the day.

By Friday the house was on edge. My Uncle Con spoke guard-edly to her at dinner-time. 'This will set us back a graydle, mother,' he said. 'I know, son; I know, son; I know,' was all she said in reply.

Saturday came and the strain was unendurable. About three o'clock in the afternoon she found the keeper. We had been watching her in turns from the kitchen window. I remember my uncle's face lighting up and his saying, 'Glory, she's found it!' But he drew a long breath when again she started burrowing feverishly in the hay. Then we knew it was only the keeper. We didn't run out at all. We waited till she came in at six o'clock. There were times between three and six when our three heads were together at the small window watching her. I was thinking she was like a mouse nibbling at a giant's loaf.

At six she came in and said, 'I found the keeper.' After her tea she couldn't stay still. She fidgeted around the kitchen for an hour or so. Then, 'Laws were made to be broken,' said my grandmother with a brittle bravery, and she stalked out to the hayshed. Again we watched her.

Coming on for dusk she returned and lighted a stable lantern and went back to resume her search. Nobody crossed her. We didn't say yes, aye or no to her. After a time my Uncle Con took her heavy coat off the rack and went down and threw it across her shoulders. I was with him. 'There's a touch of frost there tonight, mother,' said my Uncle Con.

We loitered for a while in the darkness outside the ring of her lantern's light. But she resented our pitying eyes so we went in. We sat around the big fire waiting—Uncle Con, Aunt Annie and I. That was the lonely waiting—without speaking—just as if we were waiting for an old person to die or for a child to come into the world. Near twelve we heard her step on the cobbles. 'Twas typical of my grandmother that she placed the lantern on the ledge of the dresser and quenched the candle in it before she spoke to us.

'I found it,' she said. The words dropped out of her drawn face.

'Get hot milk for my mother, Annie,' said Uncle Con briskly.

My grandmother sat by the fire, a little to one side. Her face was as cold as death. I kept watching her like a hawk but her eyes didn't even flicker. The wedding ring was inside its keeper, and my grandmother kept twirling it round and round with the fingers of her right hand.

Suddenly, as if ashamed of her fingers' betrayal, she hid her hands under her check apron. Then, unpredictably, the fists under the apron came up to meet her face, and her face bent down to meet the fists in the apron. 'Oh, Martin, Martin,' she sobbed, and then she cried like the rain.

NOT LIKING TO PASS THE ROAD AGAIN

Patrick O'Brian

Although Patrick O'Brian (1914–) suffered from a debilitating illness in his childhood, which meant he was unable to attend school regularly, his poor health was to prove a mixed blessing for his later career as a best-selling novelist of Napoleonic seafaring yarns. Following the death of his mother just after the First World War, O'Brian was sent to live with relatives in County Clare and here he was recommended by a doctor to get as much sea air and sailing as possible to help his condition. He quickly learned the intricacies of sailing—including how to hand, reef and steer a yacht—and later took part in a number of races in ocean-going craft. From these invigorating days of his youth came the first seeds of inspiration for what would later become his famous series of novels about a captain in Nelson's navy, Jack Aubrey RN of the HMS Surprise, *and his friend, Dr Stephen Maturin, an Irish physician. Described as 'among the best novels to have been written in English over the last 25 years', they have won many well-known admirers, including the round-the-world yachtsman, Sir Francis Chichester, the American film star Charlton Heston and the English politician William Waldegrave. Although O'Brian has fought shy of personal publicity, his books have become a cult and in America* The Patrick O'Brian Newsletter *is issued regularly to keep readers informed of new adventures and provide a glossary of the arcane language which the author frequently uses.*

Prior to the publication, in 1970, of the first book in the Jack

Aubrey series, Master and Commander, *O'Brian had written two novels for children,* The Road to Samarkand *(1954) and* The Golden Ocean *(1956), as well as a number of short stories, many drawn from life, and several focusing on his childhood in Ireland. 'Not Liking to Pass the Road Again' is perhaps the most evocative—a tale of childhood audacity and terror which conjures up emotions that anyone who, as a small child, has ever been drawn to a place of mystery will understand.*

*   *   *

The road led uphill all the way from the village; a long way, in waves, some waves steeper than others but all uphill even where it looked flat between the crests.

There was a tall thick wood on the right hand for the first half: for a long time it had been the place of the Scotch brothers. They were maniacs, carpenters by trade, Baptists; and one had done something horrible to his brother.

I have forgotten now why I thought that only one brother still lived in the wood: perhaps I had been told. I used to throw things into the wood.

At first they were small things, bits of twig or pebbles from the middle of the road, the loose stuff between the wheel tracks; I threw them furtively, surreptitiously, not looking, just into the nut bushes at the edge. Then I took to larger ones, and on some bold days I would stand in an open wide part of the road flinging heavy stones into the wood: they lashed and tore the leaves far within the wood itself. It was a place where there had been a traction engine and where they had left great piles of things for the road.

Quite early in the summer (there were a great many leaves, but they were still fresh and the bark was soft and bright) I was there and I had two old chisels without handles; they were brown and their cutting edges were hacked and as blunt as screw drivers, but their squared angles were still sharp. I had gashed a young tree with one, throwing it; it had taken the green bark clean from the white wood.

I had them purposely this bold day prepared, to throw them in with desperate malice—I was almost afraid of them then. I did not throw them far, but flat and hard and oh God the great bursting crashing in the wood and he came, brutal grunting with speed.

Before my heart had beat I was running. Running, running, running, and running up that dreadful hill that pulled me back so that I was hardly more than walking and my thin legs going weaker and soft inside.

I could not run, and here under my feet was the worst hill beginning. At the gap by the three ashes I jigged to the left, off the road to the meadow: downhill, and I sped (the flying strides) downhill to the old bridge and the stream full-tilt and downhill on the grass.

Into the stream, not over the bridge, into the water where it ran fast over the brown stones: through the tunnel of green up to the falls I knew the dark way. I knew it without thinking, and I did not put a foot on dry ground nor make a noise above the noise of the water until I came to the falls and then I stepped on a dry rock only three times all the way up the wide mouth. It is easier to climb with your hands and feet than to run on a bare road. And I came out into the open for an instant below the culvert on the road, a place where I could look back, back and far down to the smooth green at the foot of the old bridge.

It was still there, casting to and fro like a hound, but with inconceivable rapidity. Halfway up the meadow sometimes to hit back on the line, so eager, then a silent rush to the water's edge and a check as if it had run into a stone wall: then over and over again, the eager ceaseless tracing back and fro. Vague (except in movement), uncoloured, low on the ground.

There was a cart on the road now, well above the ruined cottage, and I went home. I changed my boots without being seen—they had kept the water out for a long time, although I had been up to my knees at once; in the end the water had come in down from my ankles, quite slowly.

That night and afterwards, when I told the thing over to myself I added a piece to make the passing of the road again more bearable. In the added piece my mother came in and said that we were all to be careful when we went out because there was a mad dog. 'Hugh was found on the old bridge,' she said (Hugh was one of the farm boys), 'at the foot of the old bridge, with his face bitten. They have taken him to hospital, but he will not speak yet.'

LADY-IN-WAITING

Anne McCaffrey

*Although born in America, Anne McCaffrey (1926–) has lived
in County Wicklow for many years, on a farm called Dragonhold-
Underhill in acknowledgement to her series of a dozen fantasy
novels about the Dragonriders of Pern. Beginning with*
Dragonflight *in 1968, they have since sold more than 20 million
copies and been translated into 18 languages. The place is something of a mecca for her predominantly younger readers, and
Anne, a silver-haired, jolly lady, is a legend among local people.
She became fascinated with Celtic lore as a child and wrote
her first story in 1943, while at boarding school, following a
precognitive experience when she sensed her father was in danger
and later learned he had been in a torpedo attack while serving
off the coast of Algeria. McCaffrey was for some years involved
in the stage and opera, before turning to writing full-time and
winning several prestigious awards for her best-selling books.
When she is not writing, she runs a livery stable in County
Wicklow training three-day-event horses—a number of which
have been successful in international competitions—and she also
lectures in secondary schools and universities.*

*Anne McCaffrey's long association with Ireland and its people
has given her a special affection for the country, as well as a
deep understanding of its problems. 'Lady-in-Waiting' is one of
several stories which draw on this personal knowledge to explore
the emotions within a family where the father has been killed by
a bomb explosion in a pub. She once remarked that her stories
are 'messages of hope for forlorn children' and this is certainly
true of the following tale, in which a commonplace game like*

dressing up becomes a strange and emotional experience for both the young children and their mother.

*   *   *

'Mummie, Sally wants to play dress-up,' said Frances, her pointed little face contorted with the obligation to accommodate her first guest in the new house.

'I do, too,' said six-year-old Marjorie, pouting her plump cheeks in anticipation of refusal.

Sally Merrion just stood in the loose semicircle about Amy Landon's kitchen table, her dubious but polite expression challenging her hostess.

'Dressing up seems a very good idea for such a drizzling day,' Amy replied calmly. To give herself a moment to think what she could possibly find for them to play in, she finished pouring the steaming bramble jelly into the jar.

Fran caught her breath as a gobbet on the lip of the saucepan splashed and instantly dissolved, colouring pink the hot water in which the jars were steeped.

'What had you planned to dress up as?'

'Ladies-in-waiting,' said Sally, recovering from the initial surprise of agreement but still determined to put her hostesses to the blush.

There was such an appeal in Fran's soft eyes that Amy was rather certain that the notion of this particular costume was all Sally's.

'Wadies-in-waiting,' Marjorie said, frowning and pouting as if to force her mother to accept.

'We'd be very careful,' Fran said in her solemn way.

'I know you would, pet,' Amy replied, smiling gentle reassurance.

Not for the first time, Amy wondered how long it would take the sensitive Frances to recover from the shock of her father's death: his brutal murder, Amy amended in the deepest part of her mind. Peter had been a victim of a bomb thrown without warning into a London pub.

She disciplined her thoughts sternly back to the tasks at hand:

pouring the bramble jelly and figuring out how to comply with her daughters' needs.

'Werry careful,' Marjorie said, bobbing her head up and down while Sally Merrion waited to be surprised.

'Of course you would, love,' Amy assured the child, knowing that Fran could be depended upon to make certain that her younger sister was careful.

'Frances is a real dote,' Amy's mother often said with pride, since the child resembled her in feature and colouring, 'and more help than the twins, I'm sure, despite their being older. The poor wee fatherless lambkins,' she'd recently taken to adding in a tone that stiffened Amy's resolve to make the move that had indirectly caused Peter's death.

During the first days of her bereavement, the hideous irony of his dying had given her a passionate dislike for Tower Cottage. The only reason Peter had been in that pub at that critical moment was to phone her the good news that he'd signed the mortgage contract for a house that would take them away from the increasingly dangerous city streets: a house in the grey-stoned hills of Dorset, with its own orchard and gardens, and a paddock for a pony; the kind of rural, self-sufficient life that Amy and he had known as children.

Her parents, and his, had urged her to repudiate the contract, to stay close to them so they could give her the comfort, protection and aid that a young widow with four growing children would undeniably need.

Stubbornly and contrary to her prejudice towards Tower Cottage, Amy Landon had honoured that agreement, citing to her parents that the life-insurance policy required by the mortgage company now gave her the house free and clear.

'You could say that Peter died to secure Tower Cottage,' Amy had told the parental conclave. 'It *is* far away from London and I want to *get* far away from London. I want to abide by the plans my Peter and I made. I'm well able for the life. It isn't as if I weren't country-bred . . . Just because *you* wanted to retire to the city . . .'

'But, all alone . . . so far from a village . . . and neighbours,' her father and Peter's had argued.

'I'm hardly alone with four children. Young Peter's as tall as I and much stronger. We're scarcely *far* from a village when there're shops, a post office, *and* a pub a half mile down the lane. As for neighbours . . . I'll have too much to do to worry about neighbours.'

And the fewer the better, she'd amended to herself. She abhorred the pity, even the compassion, accorded her for her loss. She was weary of publicity, of people staring blur-eyed at herself and her children. They'd all be spoiled if this social sympathy continued much longer: spoiled into thinking that the world owed them something because politics . . . or was it madness? . . . had deprived them of their father.

'My mother keeps a special box,' Sally Merrion was saying to draw Amy's thought back to the present, to the low-beam kitchen redolent of bubbling bramble berries, sealing wax, and the casserole baking in the old Aga cooker. 'It's got clothes my grandma and great-gran wore.'

Amy wondered if she'd ever use those maxiskirts again. 'I've some things in the blanket chest . . .' She hesitated. She couldn't leave the jelly half-poured and she resisted the notion, once again, that there was something about the box room that made her loath to enter it.

'Don't worry, Mother. I wouldn't touch anything *good*,' Fran said, patently relieved that her mother had risen to the need. 'And you daren't leave the jelly.'

'Wadies-in-waiting?' asked Marjorie in a quavering voice.

'Yes, yes, love. Go along then, girls. I really must finish the jelly. Fran, you can use those long skirts of mine. And there're old sheets in the blanket chest . . .' Why on earth be afraid of a blanket-chest? But a frisson caught her between her shoulders. 'They'd make lovely flowing robes . . .'

From the scornful expression on Sally's face, Amy wondered what on earth the child was permitted to use in her own home. Cheeky girl.

Amy concentrated on the jelly, finishing the first pan of jars and getting the next ready before her maternal instinct flared. Back in the kitchen, separated from the main section of the cottage

by the pantry, and thick walls, she could hear nothing. She'd
better check. She pushed open the pantry door and the high happy
voices of the girls, affecting adult accents, carried quite audibly
down the stairwell. They were obviously playing there on the
landing in front of the box room. Satisfied, Amy returned to her
jelly.

She found unexpected satisfaction, she mused, in these homely
preparations against the winter. Atavistic, Peter would have called
her. The summer had not been kind to the land and its bounty
was reduced, or so the villagers had said, but Amy Landon had
no fault to find. The apple and pear trees of Tower Cottage were
well laden when you considered that there'd been no one to
prune, spray or fertilise them: and how there came to be beetroot,
potatoes, cabbage, carrots and swedes in the kitchen garden, Amy
didn't know. The villagers had rolled their eyes and each suggested someone else as the Good Samaritan. Her circumstances
were known in the village, so she concluded that some kindhearted soul did not wish her to feel under obligation. Nonetheless, the abundance of the garden meant that she could manage
better on the spartan budget she allowed herself. (She would
make no unnecessary inroads on savings that were earmarked to
see young Peter through secondary school and college. And she
refused to think in terms of compensation money.) With the cost
of all commodities rising, she must grow or raise as much as
possible on her property.

Mr Suttle, who ran the tiny shop at the crossroads, had told
her that old Mrs Mallett had kept chickens: she had owned Tower
Cottage before the Alderdyces bought it. (The Alderdyces, now,
they hadn't lived there very long: come into money sudden like,
and bought a grand house nearer London only they didn't get to
live in their new house because they died of a motor accident
before ever they reached it.) While Mr Suttle hadn't heard of
chickens living wild like that for two years or more, then returning
to their own run, there was no other explanation for the flock
that now pecked contentedly around the barn behind Tower Cottage, and obediently laid their eggs for Patricia to find.

To her father's amusement, and young Peter's delight, Amy

had purchased a Guernsey cow, for what was the sense of having a four-acre meadow and a barn unexpectedly full of hay if one didn't use them. Mr Suttle had knowledgeably inspected the same stable and hay, pronounced the one fit to house cattle and the other well enough saved to be eaten by the cow, and applauded little Mrs Landon's sense.

Old Mrs Mallett, who'd been spry to the day of her peaceful death, had kept chickens, cow, and pig (Mr Suttle thought he might be able to find Mrs Landon a piglet to fatten for Christmas) and lived quite well off her land, and kept warm and comfortable in Tower Cottage.

Amy assured Mr Suttle that this was also her intention, and she thanked him for his advice, but she rather felt the piglet could wait until she was accustomed to managing cow, chickens and children.

Actually, it was young Peter who managed the cow, after instructions from the farmer who'd sold them the beast. And Patricia, Peter's twin, cared for the chickens. The two vied with each other to prove their charges in that curiously intense competition reserved to twins.

Amy sealed the bramble jelly and began to stick on the labels that Fran had laboriously printed for her. All of them had picked the berries the day before, a warm, sunny Sunday, and made a game of the work, arriving home in the early September dusk, berry-full and berry-stained, with buckets of the rich dark fruit. The only deterrent to complete happiness for Amy had been the absence of her husband: this was what he had wanted for his family and he wasn't alive to share it. In poignant moments like this, her longing for him became a physical illness.

She must continue to force such negative thoughts from her mind: the children had had enough gloom, enough insecurity. She must find contentment in the fact that they were indeed living as Peter had so earnestly desired.

Young Peter came in with the milk pail, the contents frothy and warm. Patricia was just behind him with eggs from her hens.

'I think Molly likes me,' Peter announced as he usually did when the Guernsey had let down her milk for him with no fuss.

'Another dozen eggs, Mummie,' said Patricia, taking her basket into the larder and carefully arranging the freshest in the front of the moulded cardboard.

Peter heaved the bucket up to the counter and got out the big kettle, whereupon he began to measure the milk before heating it. He was keeping a record of Molly's output as against her intake, so that they would have accurate figures on how much their milk and butter were costing them. He was all for trying to make soft cheese, too, since there were herbs along the garden path for seasoning.

High on the wall by the pantry door, the old bell tinkled in its desultory fashion, announcing a caller at the front door.

Wondering who that could be since the few people with whom she was acquainted would know that she'd be in the kitchen this time of day, Amy half ran to the front hall, wiping her hands as she went and pulling fussily at her jumper, aware that it was jelly-sticky. She gave the door the hefty yank it required and discovered Sally's mother about to use the huge clumsy knocker.

'Good heavens, Mrs Landon . . .'

'I'm terribly sorry to keep you standing on the doorstep, Mrs Merrion . . .'

'I can't thank you enough for minding Sally . . .'

'No bother. Such a nasty day, the girls have been playing dress-up.'

In mutual accord, the two women crossed the square front hall to the stairs. Above them some charade was in progress: they could hear Sally announcing dire news in a loud and affected voice.

'Sally dear, it's Mummie come to collect you.'

'Oh, Mummie, did you have to come just now?'

Amy and Mrs Merrion exchanged amused glances at the distressed wail of protest. As they looked up, Sally was leaning over the upper balustrade, her face framed by a gauzy blue, the folds of heavy blue sleeves falling to cover her hands on the railing.

'I'm just denouncing the traitor in our midst who was de . . . dee . . . what did you say he was doing to us, Fran?' Sally turned her head and nearly lost the heavy headdress.

'Sally love'—Mrs Merrion's voice was patient and level—
'I've got to pick up the meat for tea and your father from the
station. There's only just time to get to Mr Suttle's before . . .'

'Oh, Mummie . . .' Sally's tone was piteous, and undoubtedly
tears were being repressed.

Amy heard Fran's soothing voice, to which she added her own
assurance that Sally could return very soon and continue the
game.

'It just won't be the same . . .' Sally's voice ended on a petulant
high note.

The women saw a swish of royal blue skirts, which told them
that Sally was submitting to the inevitable.

'Fran, love, would you put the things away for Sally since she
has to leave now?'

'Yes, Mummie. Come *on* now, Marjorie, you can help . . .'

Marjorie blubbered a protest, evoking her privilege as the
youngest in the family.

'If you're big enough to *be* a lady-in-waiting, you're big
enough to help,' Fran said in such an imitation of an adult that
Amy and Mrs Merrion grinned at each other.

Sally's stiff-legged descent of the stairs reminded them of
that young lady's disgruntlement well before they could see her
scowling face. Amy gathered up Sally's school mac and book
bag, quickly deciding that the dirtier of the two school scarves
was not Fran's, and prepared to speed the parting guest.

Sally allowed herself to be helped into her coat, but her seething
resentment dissipated as she babbled to her mother that Mrs
Landon had smashing things to play dress-up in, Mummie, and
when could she come again please, and thank you Mrs Landon
for the tea and Mummie didn't you have to go to the dentist
again soon?

Mrs Merrion, amused by her daughter's effusiveness, smiled
and said all the properly courteous things as she hurried Sally
across the square hall and out of the door. As Amy waited politely
on the steps while the Merrions' green shooting brake was buck-
ing down the pebbled drive, she began to wonder at Sally's
unexpected enthusiasm. What on earth had the girls managed to

find in the 'smashing' category in that blanket chest? What else was in it? Suits of Peter's that she'd put by for his son, the odd blanket or two, a few curtains, some outgrown things of Patricia's, party dresses of hers that she would be unlikely to wear in Dorset, several lengths of fabric. Nothing royal blue in the lot! And she'd never had any occasion to use gauze. Nor headdresses. As far as she could remember, there'd been nothing left behind in the box room by the previous owners, the unfortunate Alderdyces.

'Mum, the milk!' Peter shouted through the pantry door.

'Do put everything back, Fran, won't you?' Amy paused long enough in the stairwell to hear her daughter's assurance before she returned to the kitchen and an urgent affair of pasteurisation.

At supper that night, when Marjorie was safely in bed, Amy remembered the royal blue puzzle.

'Fran, pet, how did you get on as ladies-in-waiting?'

'Oh, Mummie,' and Fran's face glowed unexpectedly, 'we had a super time. Marjorie was in the red wool though we had to pull the skirt up over the belt so she wouldn't trip. She was the junior lady-in-waiting and carried Sally's train. Sally was queen because she was guest, so she had the blue because blue is a royal colour. Isn't it?' Peter had guffawed so Fran turned wide serious eyes on her brother. 'Sally said it was . . .' ('To be sure, it is, Fran, pet,' Amy reassured her, glaring at Peter.) '. . . So that left the green for me. But I think the green was for a man . . . because it only came to my knees. Marjorie's and Sally's dresses dragged on the floor . . .'

'Red? Green? What green?' Amy was mystified.

'Green . . . sort of velvet stuff, I think, and it went from here to here'—Fran measured the length on her small body—'and there was fur along the collar and no buttons so I used another belt . . .'

'I don't recall putting away any belts . . .'

'The fancy dress ones, Mummie, with the belt buckles and sparkly stones . . .'

Fran's pleasure was fading fast in the face of possible maternal disapproval, and her voice wavered as her eyes sought her mother's.

'Oh, those!' Amy said as if her memory had been at fault. 'Those old things. I'd forgotten about them.'

'I don't remember you and Father going to costume do's,' Peter said, gathering his brows just the way his father had.

'You could scarcely remember everything your father and I did, Peter,' Amy said placidly. Peter tended to act the expert. 'There's more Horlicks.' She reached for Peter's glass, smiling to clear the anxiety from her daughter's face. 'Molly's making more and we have to keep up with her production. Peter, time for you to check her while we girls do the supper dishes. Then all of you, off to bed . . .'

She made the school lunches and checked the doors before she could no longer defer the mystery of the fancy clothes. Resolutely she climbed the stairs, looking down into the square hall, as she came to the first landing. The oldest part of the house, the estate agent had said, probably was an old Norman keep, though the stonework was in astonishingly good condition for a structure so old. Doubtless that was why the fifteenth-century architects had incorporated the keep when the cottage was built. Certainly, thought Amy, the house was a continuous production: all periods, rather than one, now combined into a hodgepodgery that had appealed to Peter's sense of the ridiculous.

The heterogeneity had also fascinated the surveyor who had examined the house for Peter and Amy prior to the contract signing. On the way down to Dorset, the man had been frankly suspicious at the asking price and warned Peter and Amy to be forearmed for disappointment in its state of repair. Surprisingly, the surveyor had discovered very few problems, most of which could be put right with a judicious slap of mortar, plaster or paint, and the odd dab of putty or sealer. The cellar was dry, the thick sound walls oozed no damp, the floors were remarkably level, the chimneys, of which there were nine in all, drew, the drains were recent and in good order, the slate roof was undamaged by the storms of the previous winter. And not a sign of woodworm or dry rot. The surveyor reluctantly concluded that the Tower Cottage had been so reasonably priced because, as

advertised, it was genuinely to be sold quickly to settle the Alderdyce estate.

Still, there was a palpable aura in the square hall, which Peter
had chalked up to antiquity. And something almost expectant in
the atmosphere in the box room immediately above the hall, those
two rooms comprising what was left of the old Norman keep.
Amy was not a fanciful person, certainly not superstitious, or she
would never have moved into Tower Cottage at all after Peter's
death. Yet she avoided the box room, sending the children either
to retrieve objects stored there or consign others to its capacious
shelving or the huge, heavy wooden chest that dominated the front
wall under the two slit windows. 'Flemish work,' the surveyor had
called the chest, with the modern addition of a thin veneer of
cedarwood on the inside to make its purpose clear. He had wondered if the chest had been built *in situ*, for he could not see how
it would otherwise have got through the doorway.

Peter had sat on the chest that day, Amy recalled: he'd thumped
the wood, laughing at the hollow echo of the empty chest,
remarking that it would be a good place to hide the body . . .
several bodies by the size of it. Amy had felt the frisson then,
running up her spine to seize her head and jerk it on the neck
with an involuntary force that had astonished her. The surveyor
noticed and solicitously remarked that un-lived-in houses always
chilled him.

Since they'd moved in, she'd made one concession to the
distressing atmosphere of the box room: she'd put the brightest
possible bulb on the landing and had Peter put an equally strong
one in the box room's single socket. (Oddly enough, the children
loved playing in the box room.) Tonight she turned on both lights
and stood for a moment on the threshold, staring at the dark bulk
of the carved wooden chest.

It did not move. The carvings did not writhe or gesture. A
faint odour of lavender and cinnamon was detectable, mingling
with old leather, wool, and camphor: homey smells, compatible
with the room's use. Not a shadow stirred.

With swift steps, Amy crossed the room and tugged up the lid
of the chest. Just as she'd thought. The two torn sheets, rough-

dried, were neatly folded on top, her maxiskirts just below. But one was a check and the other black. Where was royal blue, or red, or green with a fur-trimmed collar? She sat on the edge of the chest and lifted one stack of garments, Patricia's outgrown jumpers and skirts, Peter's shirts and underclothes, socks. She turned in the other direction and sorted through business suits, waistcoats, more jumpers, her crêpe and wool party dresses. At the bottom were two pairs of old curtains and some net curtains, white. Nothing gauzy blue. No ornate headdresses. No costume belts. She delved to the wood of the chest's floor and found only the mundane things she expected.

Fran was a literal child: if she'd said she'd dressed in green with no buttons and a fur collar, she had.

Puzzled, Amy ran her eyes over the contents of the shelves: nothing there surely but Christmas ornaments, boxed games, lampshades, empty jars, young Peter's tenting and backpack frame, oddments of china set aside for a jumble. On the other side of the door, the tea chests containing Peter's business papers, books, the family's suitcases as neatly stacked as they'd been since the day after removal from London.

Yet Sally Merrion had been dressed in royal blue . . . a queen's colour . . . and gauzes!

A flash of colour caught her eye and she turned towards the chest, blinking. She could have sworn that the topmost sheet had been, however fleetingly, a brilliant blue. To reassure herself, she smoothed the sheet, but her fingers told her that it wasn't velvet, just worn linen. She stood up, closing the lid of the chest, almost dropping it the final few inches as the full weight of the wood tore the lid from her fingers' inadequate grasp.

She'd ask Fran in the morning where she'd found those dress-up clothes. Possibly she'd misunderstood.

The frisson caught her by the back of the neck before she'd reached the safety of the door. It was like a hand on the scruff of her neck, pulling her back to the scene of some childhood crime: an injunction against a cowardly retreat.

In spite of herself, Amy turned back into the room and stared around her. The scent of lavender and cinnamon was cut by a sharper smell, vinegarish. Then a sweetish odour, familiar but unnameable, assailed her, an odour as sharp as the previous intangible command to stay. Stiffly, Amy walked back to the chest, set her hand on the lid, imagining, as Sally might have, wondrous costumes in which to be medieval ladies-in-waiting . . . and a queen.

No torn sheets, no dull woollen jumpers now lay exposed, but royal blue velvet, a deep red wool dress, a green surcoat fur-trimmed, and belts, encrusted with rough-cut bright stones set in the dull gleam of gold links.

She let the lid drop and the compressed air smelled of sweat, human and horse, of stale food and spilled, soured wine, heavy perfumed musk mixed with camphor. Weakly, Amy sank to the cold stone floor, impervious to that chill.

'The Alderdyces came into money . . .' Mr Suttle's words came to mind.

Had some Alderdyce child, or adult, dreamed of hidden treasure in the old keep? And found it in the chest?

Amy shook her head, fighting to think rationally. Did the chest grant wishes, then? Pray God it was only one wish and Fran had had the chest's quota for them all, and that was the end of the matter.

She thought of gold and jewels, rich fabrics, Oriental silk and gauzes, of ornate Arabian leather slippers. And opened the chest. Her heart pounded as she dropped the lid on those same imagined riches.

Mrs Mallett? She'd lived in Tower Cottage for years, spry till the day of her death. Hadn't Mr Suttle said so? Wanting for nothing, the house and grounds supplying her requirements.

Amy laughed, a single sound, hard and strained, like her credulity. What had the widowed Mrs Mallett lifted the lid to find? A body? As Peter had whimsically suggested.

The sweetish odour, familiar but unidentifiable, pervaded the box room.

Amy screamed, a soft tortured cry, her hands stifling it to a whisper, lest Peter or Patricia hear her. That same sweetish odour had filled her nostrils as she'd knelt before Peter's coffin in the church. How could the house have killed her Peter in that bombed-out public house? It couldn't have ... Illusions! Her longing for him that day!

'NO!' The single negative was as low as it was firm. She spread her hands, fingers flat on the lid of the chest, denying what could be if she so desired. 'No!'

She spread her arms across the chest in repression, in supplication, in prayer. This was just a chest with old clothes in it, two torn sheets and some dresses waiting for parties, for children to grow up to fill. This was just an ancient tower, used as part of an old house, a house where children could grow up in healthy country air, on fresh vegetables and milk, and where they could pick apples and pears in an orchard and bramble berries from hedges. Just an old house that had served many families in the same way.

The nauseating sweetness dispersed: lavender and cinnamon returned, and the smell of night and rain.

Slowly Amy pulled her arms together, rose to her knees before the chest. She placed the heels of her hands under the lid and, swallowing against the dryness of her throat, pushed upwards. Her body blocked some of the light from the overlight bulb, but she saw the comforting white of old cotton sheeting, caught a whiff of her favourite cologne, impregnated in the dresses stored in the chest, a hint of the cedarwood. It was as she'd wished. She let the lid down gently and leaned her forehead weakly against the edge.

It took her a few moments to gather enough strength to rise. Really, she told herself as she walked towards the door, she ought not to attempt to do so much in one day, though they'd enough bramble jelly to last years, even with the amount Peter slathered on his toast.

She switched off the light and closed the box room door behind her. Her fingers hovered briefly over the key. No, she could not lock out what had apparently happened or lock in whatever it was. That would be superstitious as well as downright useless.

Nonetheless, when she flicked off the hall light, she said 'good night' just as if there were someone waiting to hear.

2

THE LEARNING YEARS

Tales of Schooldays

THE FACE OF EVIL

Frank O'Connor

There are few more poignant accounts of schooldays in Ireland than those described in An Only Child *(1961), the autobiography of Frank O'Connor (1903–1966) who is today acknowledged as 'the Old Master of the Irish short story'. O'Connor's memories of his youth in Cork, where he was born Michael O'Donovan, the son of a domestic servant and an intermittently alcoholic labourer, with the many crises and moments of unexpected humour as the family time and again narrowly escaped from the brink of destitution, make compulsive reading. Young Frank received only an elementary education until he reached the mandatory leaving age of 14, but these were to prove highly influential years because his teacher was the legendary Daniel Corkery (1878–1964), who founded the Cork Dramatic Society and imparted his love of the Gaelic language in his plays and stories as well as to his young pupils. In* An Only Child *Frank O'Connor acknowledges Corkery's influence on his own subsequent career, although after leaving school he had a number of unrewarding jobs before taking up arms in the Irish Civil War. Captured by government troops, he put his imprisonment to good use by completing his education and writing the first of the essays on Gaelic literature and short stories that made him famous and earned him teaching appointments in America, along with the publication of his work in some of the leading magazines of the day.*

Several of the best of Frank O'Connor's short stories about the years of his youth are to be found in his collections Guests of the Nation *(1931),* Bones of Contention *(1936) and* Domestic

Relations *(1957), and they range from 'The Man of the House',*
about a ten-year-old taking on responsibilities when his mother
falls ill, to 'Private Property', concerning an adolescent joining
the revolutionary army. 'The Face of Evil' falls midway between
these two. It describes a boy's struggle to understand the com-
plexities of good and evil, and makes an ideal opener for this
section.

*   *   *

I could never understand all the old talk about how hard it is to
be a saint. I was a saint for quite a bit of my life and I never
saw anything hard in it. And when I stopped being a saint, it
wasn't because the life was too hard.

I fancy it is the sissies who make it seem like that. We had
quite a few of them in school, fellows whose mothers intended
them to be saints, and who hadn't the nerve to be anything else.
I never enjoyed the society of chaps who wouldn't commit sin
for the same reason that they wouldn't dirty their new suits. That
was never what sanctity meant to me, and I doubt if it is what
it means to other saints. The companions I liked were the tough
gang down the road, and I enjoyed going down of an evening
and talking with them under the gaslamp about football matches
and school, even if they did sometimes say things I wouldn't say
myself. I was never one for criticising; I had enough to do criticising myself, and I knew they were decent chaps and didn't really
mean much harm by the things they said about girls.

No, for me the main attraction of being a saint was the way
it always gave you something to do. You could never say you
felt time hanging on your hands. It was like having a room of
your own to keep tidy; you'd scour it, and put everything neatly
back in its place, and within an hour or two it was beginning to
look as untidy as ever. It was a full-time job that began when
you woke and stopped only when you fell asleep.

I would wake in the morning, for instance, and think how nice
it was to lie in bed, and congratulate myself on not having to get
up for another half-hour. That was enough. Instantly a sort of

alarm clock would go off in my mind; the mere thought that I could enjoy half an hour's comfort would make me aware of an alternative, and I'd begin an argument with myself. I had a voice in me that was almost the voice of a stranger, the way it nagged and jeered. Sometimes I could almost visualise it, and then it took on the appearance of a fat and sneering teacher I had some years before at school—a man I really hated. I hated that voice. It always began in the same way, smooth and calm and dangerous. I could see the teacher rubbing his fat hands and smirking.

'Don't get alarmed, boy. You're in no hurry. You have another half-hour.'

'I know well I have another half-hour,' I would reply, trying to keep my temper. 'What harm am I doing? I'm only imagining I'm down in a submarine. Is there anything wrong in that?'

'Oho, not the least in the world. I'd say there's been a heavy frost. Just the sort of morning when there's ice in the bucket.'

'And what has that to do with it?'

'Nothing, I tell you. Of course, for people like you it's easy enough in the summer months, but the least touch of frost in the air soon makes you feel different. I wouldn't worry trying to keep it up. You haven't the stuff for this sort of life at all.'

And gradually my own voice grew weaker as that of my tormentor grew stronger, till all at once I would strip the clothes from off myself and lie in my night-shirt, shivering and muttering, 'So I haven't the stuff in me, haven't I?' Then I would go downstairs before my parents were awake, strip and wash in the bucket, ice or no ice, and when Mother came down she would cry in alarm, 'Child of Grace, what has you up at this hour? Sure, 'tis only half past seven.' She almost took it as a reproach to herself, poor woman, and I couldn't tell her the reason, and even if I could have done so, I wouldn't. How could you say to anybody 'I want to be a saint'?

Then I went to Mass and enjoyed again the mystery of the streets and lanes in the early morning; the frost which made your feet clatter off the walls at either side of you like falling masonry, and the different look that everything wore, as though, like yourself, it was all cold and scrubbed and new. In the winter the lights would still be burning red in the little cottages, and in summer they were ablaze with sunshine so that their interiors were dimmed to shadows. Then there were the different people, all of whom recognised one another, like Mrs MacEntee, who used to be a stewardess on the boats, and Macken, the tall post-man, people who seemed ordinary enough when you met them during the day, but carried something of their mystery with them at Mass, as though they, too, were re-born.

I can't pretend I was ever very good at school, but even there it was a help. I might not be clever, but I had always a secret reserve of strength to call on in the fact that I had what I wanted, and that beside it I wanted nothing. People frequently gave me things, like fountain pens or pencil-sharpeners, and I would sud-denly find myself becoming attached to them and immediately know I must give them away, and then feel the richer for it. Even without throwing my weight around I could help and protect kids younger than myself, and yet not become involved in their quarrels. Not to become involved, to remain detached—that was the great thing; to care for things and for people, yet not to care for them so much that your happiness became dependent on them.

It was like no other hobby, because you never really got the better of yourself, and all at once you would suddenly find your-self reverting to childish attitudes; flaring up in a wax with some fellow, or sulking when Mother asked you to go for a message, and then it all came back; the nagging of the infernal alarm clock which grew louder with every moment until it incarnated as a smooth, fat, jeering face.

'Now, that's the first time you've behaved sensibly for months, boy. That was the right way to behave to your mother.'

'Well, it *was* the right way. Why can't she let me alone, once in a while? I only want to read. I suppose I'm entitled to a bit of peace some time?'

'Ah, of course you are, my dear fellow. Isn't that what I'm saying? Go on with your book! Imagine you're a cowboy, riding to the rescue of a beautiful girl in a cabin in the woods, and let that silly woman go for the messages herself. She probably hasn't long to live anyway, and when she dies you'll be able to do all the weeping you like.'

And suddenly tears of exasperation would come to my eyes and I'd heave the story-book to the other side of the room and shout back at the voice that gave me no rest, 'Cripes, I might as well be dead and buried. I have no blooming life.' After that I would apologise to Mother (who, poor woman, was more embarrassed than anything else and assured me that it was all her fault), go on the message, and write another tick in my notebook against the heading of 'Bad Temper' so as to be able to confess it to Father O'Regan when I went to Confession on Saturday. Not that he was ever severe with me, no matter what I did; he thought I was the last word in holiness, and was always asking me to pray for some special intention of his own. And though I was depressed, I never lost interest, for no matter what I did I could scarcely ever reduce the total of times I had to tick off that item in my notebook.

Oh, I don't pretend it was any joke, but it did give you the feeling that your life had some meaning; that inside you, you had a real source of strength; that there was nothing you could not do without, and yet remain sweet, self-sufficient, and content. Sometimes too, there was the feeling of something more than mere content, as though your body were transparent, like a window, and light shone through it as well as on it, onto the road, the houses, and the playing children, as though it were you who was shining on them, and tears of happiness would come into my eyes, and I would hurl myself among the playing children just to forget it.

But, as I say, I had no inclination to mix with other kids who might be saints as well. The fellow who really fascinated me was a policeman's son named Dalton, who was easily the most vicious kid in the locality. The Daltons lived on the terrace above ours. Mrs Dalton was dead; there was a younger brother called Stevie, who was next door to an imbecile, and there was something about that kid's cheerful grin that was even more frightening than the malice on Charlie's broad face. Their father was a tall, melancholy man, with a big black moustache, and the nearest thing imaginable to one of the Keystone cops. Everyone was sorry for his loss in his wife, but you knew that if it hadn't been that it would have been something else—maybe the fact that he hadn't lost her. Charlie was only an additional grief. He was always getting into trouble, stealing and running away from home; and only his father's being a policeman prevented his being sent to an industrial school. One of my most vivid recollections is that of Charlie's education. I'd hear a shriek, and there would be Mr Dalton, dragging Charlie along the pavement to school, and whenever the names his son called him grew a little more obscene than usual, pausing to give Charlie a good going-over with the belt which he carried loose in his hand. It is an exceptional father who can do this without getting some pleasure out of it, but Mr Dalton looked as though even that were an additional burden. Charlie's screams could always fetch me out.

'What is it?' Mother would cry after me.

'Ah, nothing. Only Charlie Dalton again.'

'Come in! Come in!'

'I won't be seen.'

'Come in, I say. 'Tis never right.'

And even when Charlie uttered the most atrocious indecencies, she only joined her hands as if in prayer and muttered, 'The poor child! The poor unfortunate child!' I never could understand the way she felt about Charlie. He wouldn't have been Charlie if it hadn't been for the leatherings and the threats of the industrial school.

Looking back on it, the funniest thing is that I seemed to be the only fellow on the road he didn't hate. The rest were all terrified of him, and some of the kids would go a mile to avoid him. He was completely unclassed: being a policeman's son, he should have been way up the social scale, but he hated the respectable kids worse than the others. When we stood under the gaslamp at night and saw him coming up the road, everybody fell silent. He looked suspiciously at the group, ready to spring at anyone's throat if he saw the shadow of offence; ready even when there wasn't a shadow. He fought like an animal, by instinct, without judgement, and without ever reckoning the odds, and he was terribly strong. He wasn't clever; several of the older chaps could beat him to a frazzle when it was merely a question of boxing or wrestling, but it never was that with Dalton. He was out for blood and usually got it. Yet he was never that way with me. We weren't friends. All that ever happened when we passed one another was that I smiled at him and got a cold, cagey nod in return. Sometimes we stopped and exchanged a few words, but it was an ordeal because we never had anything to say to one another.

It was like the signalling of ships, or more accurately, the courtesies of great powers. I tried, like Mother, to be sorry for him in having no proper home, and getting all those leatherings, but the feeling which came uppermost in me was never pity but respect: respect for a fellow who had done all the things I would never do: stolen money, stolen bicycles, run away from home, slept with tramps and criminals in barns and doss-houses, and ridden without a ticket on trains and on buses. It filled my imagination. I have a vivid recollection of one summer morning when I was going up the hill to Mass. Just as I reached the top and saw the low, sandstone church perched high up ahead of me, he poked his bare head round the corner of a lane to see who was coming. It startled me. He was standing with his back to the gable of a house; his face was dirty and strained; it was broad and lined, and the eyes were very small, furtive and flickering, and sometimes a sort of spasm would come over them and they flickered madly for half a minute on end.

'Hullo, Charlie,' I said. 'Where were you?'

'Out,' he replied shortly.

'All night?' I asked in astonishment.

'Yeh,' he replied with a nod.

'What are you doing now?'

He gave a short, bitter laugh.

'Waiting till my old bastard of a father goes out to work and I can go home.'

His eyes flickered again, and selfconsciously he drew his hand across them as though pretending they were tired.

'I'll be late for Mass,' I said uneasily. 'So long.'

'So long.'

That was all, but all the time at Mass, among the flowers and the candles, watching the beautiful, sad old face of Mrs MacEntee and the plump, smooth, handsome face of Macken, the postman, I was haunted by the image of that other face, wild and furtive and dirty, peering round a corner like an animal looking from its burrow. When I came out, the morning was brilliant over the valley below me; the air was punctuated with bugle calls from the cliff where the barrack stood, and Charlie Dalton was gone. No, it wasn't pity I felt for him. It wasn't even respect. It was almost like envy.

Then, one Saturday evening, an incident occurred which changed my attitude to him; indeed, changed my attitude to myself, though it wasn't until long after that I realised it. I was on my way to Confession, preparatory to Communion next morning. I always went to Confession at the parish church in town where Father O'Regan was. As I passed the tramway terminus at the Cross, I saw Charlie sitting on the low wall above the Protestant church, furtively smoking the butt-end of a cigarette which somebody had dropped getting on the tram. Another tram arrived as I reached the Cross, and a number of people alighted and went off in different directions. I crossed the road to Charlie and he gave me his most distant nod.

'Hullo.'

'Hullo, Cha. Waiting for somebody?'

'No. Where are you off to?'

'Confession.'

'Huh.' He inhaled the cigarette butt deeply and then tossed it over his shoulder into the sunken road beneath without looking where it alighted. 'You go a lot.'

'Every week,' I said modestly.

'Jesus!' he said with a short laugh. 'I wasn't there for twelve months.'

I shrugged my shoulders. As I say, I never went in much for criticising others, and, anyway, Charlie wouldn't have been Charlie if he had gone to Confession every week.

'Why do you go so often?' he asked challengingly.

'Oh, I don't know,' I said doubtfully. 'I suppose it keeps you out of harm's way.'

'But you don't do any harm,' he growled, just as though he were defending me against someone who had been attacking me.

'Ah, we all do harm.'

'But, Jesus Christ, you don't do anything,' he said almost angrily, and his eyes flickered again in that curious nervous spasm, and almost as if they put him into a rage, he drove his knuckles into them.

'We all do things,' I said. 'Different things.'

'Well, what do you do?'

'I lose my temper a lot,' I admitted.

'Jesus!' he said again and rolled his eyes.

'It's a sin just the same,' I said obstinately.

'A sin? Losing your temper? Jesus, I want to kill people. I want to kill my bloody old father, for one. I will too, one of those days. Take a knife to him.'

'I know, I know,' I said, at a loss to explain what I meant. 'But that's just the same thing as me.'

I wished to God I could talk better. It wasn't any missionary zeal. I was excited because for the first time I knew that Charlie felt about me exactly as I felt about him, with a sort of envy, and I wanted to explain to him that he didn't have to envy me, and that he could be as much a saint as I was just as I could be as much a sinner as he was. I wanted to explain that it wasn't a matter of tuppence ha'penny worth of sanctity as opposed to tuppence worth that made the difference, that it wasn't what you did, but what you lost by doing it, that mattered. The whole Cross had become a place of mystery; the grey light, drained of warmth; the trees hanging over the old crumbling walls, the tram, shaking like a boat when someone mounted it. It was the way I sometimes felt afterwards with a girl, as though everything about you melted and fused and became one with a central mystery.

'But when what you do isn't any harm?' he repeated angrily, with that flickering of the eyes I had almost come to dread.

'Look, Cha,' I said, 'you can't say a thing isn't any harm.

Everything is harm. It might be losing my temper with me and murder with you, like you say, but it would only come to the same thing. If I show you something, will you promise not to tell?'

'Why would I tell?'

'But promise.'

'Oh, all right.'

Then I took out my little notebook and showed it to him. It was extraordinary, and I knew it was extraordinary. I found myself, sitting on that wall, showing a notebook I wouldn't have shown to anyone else in the world to Charlie Dalton, a fellow any kid on the road would go a long way to avoid, and yet I had the feeling that he would understand it as no one else would do. My whole life was there, under different headings—Disobedience, Bad Temper, Bad Thoughts, Selfishness, and Laziness—and he looked through it quietly, studying the ticks I had placed against each count.

'You see,' I said, 'you talk about your father, but look at all the things I do against my mother. I know she's a good mother, but if she's sick or if she can't walk fast when I'm in town with her, I get mad just as you do. It doesn't matter what sort of mother or father you have. It's what you do to yourself when you do things like that.'

'What do you do to yourself?' he asked quietly.

'It's hard to explain. It's only a sort of peace you have inside yourself. And you can't be just good, no matter how hard you try. You can only do your best, and if you do your best you feel peaceful inside. It's like when I miss Mass of a morning. Things mightn't be any harder on me that day than any other day, but I'm not as well able to stand up to them. It makes things a bit different for the rest of the day. You don't mind it so much if you get a hammering. You know there's something else in the world besides the hammering.'

I knew it was a feeble description of what morning Mass really meant to me, the feeling of strangeness which lasted throughout the whole day, and reduced reality to its real proportions, but it was the best I could do. I hated leaving him.

'I'll be late for Confession,' I said regretfully, getting off the wall.

'I'll go down a bit of the way with you,' he said, giving a last glance at my notebook and handing it back to me. I knew he was being tempted to come to Confession along with me, but my pleasure had nothing to do with that. As I say, I never had any missionary zeal. It was the pleasure of understanding rather than that of conversion.

He came down the steps to the church with me and we went in together.

'I'll wait here for you,' he whispered, and sat in one of the back pews.

It was dark there; there were just a couple of small, unshaded lights in the aisles above the confessionals. There was a crowd of old women outside Father O'Regan's box, so I knew I had a long time to wait. Old women never got done with their confessions. For the first time I felt it long, but when my turn came it was all over in a couple of minutes: the usual 'Bless you, my child. Say a prayer for me, won't you?' When I came out, I saw Charlie Dalton sitting among the old women outside the confessional, waiting to go in. I felt very happy about it in a quiet way, and when I said my penance I said a special prayer for him.

It struck me that he was a long time inside, and I began to grow worried. Then he came out, and I saw by his face that it was no good. It was the expression of someone who is saying to himself with a sort of evil triumph, 'There, I told you what it was like.'

'It's all right,' he whispered, giving his belt a hitch. 'You go home.'

'I'll wait for you,' I said.

'I'll be a good while.'

I knew then Father O'Regan had given him a heavy penance, and my heart sank.

'It doesn't matter,' I said. 'I'll wait.'

And it was only long afterwards that it occurred to me that I might have taken one of the major decisions of my life without being aware of it. I sat at the back of the church in the dusk and waited for him. He was kneeling up in front, before the altar, and I knew it was no good. At first I was too stunned to feel. All I knew was that my happiness had all gone. I admired Father O'Regan; I knew that Charlie must have done things that I couldn't even imagine—terrible things—but the resentment grew in me. What right had Father O'Regan or anyone to treat him like that? Because he was down, people couldn't help wanting to crush him further. For the first time in my life I knew real temptation. I wanted to go with Charlie and share his fate. For the first time I realised that the life before me would have complexities of emotion which I couldn't even imagine.

The following week he ran away from home again, took a bicycle, broke into a shop to steal cigarettes, and, after being arrested seventy-five miles from Cork in a little village on the coast, was sent to an industrial school.

THE ROADS

Padraic Pearse

*Padraic Henry Pearse (1879–1916) is probably the most famous
Irish schoolteacher of this century—although he is better
remembered as the first President of the Provisional Republic of
Ireland and the man who, as Commander-in-Chief of the Irish
Republican Brotherhood, led a group of 150 insurgents to the
General Post Office in Dublin on Easter Monday, 1916. Declar-
ing unilateral independence, they thereby accelerated the chain
reaction which led to Irish Home Rule six years later. Pearse,
however, was arrested, court-martialled and executed by a firing
squad in Kilmainham Jail on May 3.*

*The other side of Pearse was the poet, short-story writer and
founder of his own college. Born in Dublin, the son of an English-
man, he was privately educated and went on to University College
(then known as Royal University, Dublin) where he studied law
and developed the interest in Gaelic which inspired his fierce
nationalism. Pearse's dissatisfaction with the Irish education
system—in particular attitudes towards the teaching of Gaelic—
inspired him to write a number of hard-hitting pamphlets, notably*
The Murder Machine *(1912). Earlier, in 1908, he had started
his own school, St Enda's College, where the emphasis was on
pupils learning about their language and heritage. Although his
own life was to end when he was barely 37 years old, the young
founder's work later inspired the famous Summerhill project.*

*Much of Padraic Pearse's work was written in Gaelic, and it
has subsequently earned him a reputation among scholars as
being one of the finest interpreters of the inner lives of the Gael-
tacht people. Apart from his poetry and an unfinished novel,* An

Choill, *he wrote a number of tales of adventure under the name of Colm O Conaire and two collections of short stories,* Íosagán *agus Sgéalte Eile (1907) and* An Mháthair *(1916). 'The Roads' reveals not Pearse the revolutionary but the teacher, in a story about a little girl who cannot go to a dance at the schoolhouse and so determines to run away. It is a tale with the ring of truth about it...*

*   *   *

Rossnageeragh will always remember the night that the Dublin Man threw a party for us in Turlagh Beg Schoolhouse. We never called him anything else except the 'Dublin Man'. Peaitín Pharaic told us that he was a man who wrote for the newspapers.

Peaitín used to read the Gaelic paper that the mistress bought every week and there was little he did not know for the events of the Western World and the happenings of the Eastern World were always described in it, and there was no end to the information he would have for us every Sunday at the chapel gate.

He told us that the Dublin Man had a stack of money for there was £200 a year coming to him for writing that paper every week.

The Dublin Man came to Turlagh to spend a fortnight or month, every year.

One year he sent out word inviting poor and ragged to a party he was throwing for us in the schoolhouse.

He promised that there would be music and dancing and Gaelic speeches at it; that there would be a piper there from Carraroe; that Bríd Ní Mhainín would come to sing 'Condae Mhuigheo'; that Martin the Fisherman would tell a story about Fionn and the Fianna; that old Úna Ní Ghreelis would recite a poem if the creature hadn't got the hoarseness and that Marcuseen Mhíchíl-Ruaidh would do a stepdance if his rheumatism wasn't too bad.

Nobody ever knew Marcuseen to have rheumatism except when he was asked to dance.

'Bedam, but I'm dead with the pains for a week,' he'd always say, when a dance was hinted.

But no sooner would the piper sound up 'Tatther Jack Walsh', than Marcuseen would throw his old hat in the air, say 'hup', and take the floor.

The Col Labhrás family were at tea the night of the party.

'Will we be going to the schoolhouse tonight, daddy,' Cuimin Col asked his father.

'Yes. Father Ronan said that he'd like all the people to go.'

'Won't we have the spree!' Cuimin exclaimed.

'You'll stay at home, Nora,' the mother said, 'to mind the baby.'

Nora made a face but didn't speak.

After tea, Col and his wife went into the bedroom to dress for the party.

'It's a pity that God didn't make me a boy,' Nora said to her brother.

'Why?' Cuimin asked.

'For one reason better than another,' she answered and with that gave a little slap to the child that was half-asleep and half-awake in the cradle. The baby let a howl out of him.

'Will you mind the child, there,' Cuimin said. 'If my mother hears him crying, she'll take the ear off you.'

'I don't care if she takes the two ears off me.'

'What's wrong with you?' Cuimin was washing himself, but stopped to look over his shoulder at his sister, with the water streaming from his face.

'I'm tired of being made a little ass of by my mother and everybody else,' Nora replied. 'I work from morning 'till night while you do nothing. Yet you're all going to the party tonight while I have to stay at home and act as nursemaid to this baby. "You'll have to stay at home, Nora, to mind the baby," says my mother. That is always the way. It's a pity that God didn't make me a boy.'

Cuimin was drying his face in the meantime and 's-s-s-s-s' coming out of him like a person grooming a horse.

'It's a pity all right,' he said, when he was able to speak. He threw the towel away from him, put his head to one side and looked complacently at himself in the glass which was hanging on the kitchen wall.

'All I have to do now is to part my hair, and I'll be tip-top,' he added.

'Are you ready, Cuimin?' his father asked, on his way up from the bedroom.

'Yes.'

'Well come on, then.'

The mother came out. 'If the baby starts to cry, Nora, give him his bottle.'

Nora said nothing. She remained sitting, on the stool beside the cradle with her chin resting in her two hands and her elbows stuck on her knees.

She heard her father, mother and Cuimin going out the door and across the street; she knew by their voices that they were going down the bohereen. The voices soon died away and she knew that they had reached the main road, and had started their journey to the schoolhouse.

Nora began to imagine how things were. She pictured the fine level road, white under the moonlight. The people were walking towards the schoolhouse in little groups.

The Rossnageeragh people were walking on the roadway, the Garumna people were coming round by the mistress's house and the Kilbrickan people and the Turlagh Beg people were crowding down the hillside.

There was a group of people from Turlagh, a few from Glencaha and one or two from Inver walking on the roadway as well.

She imagined that her own people were at the school gate by now, and were going up the pathway. Now they were entering the schoolroom. The schoolhouse was almost full and still the people were coming in. Lamps were hanging on the walls and the house was as bright as though it were the middle of the day.

She could see Father Ronan busily bustling around from person to person, bidding them welcome. The Dublin Man was there . . . as nice and friendly as ever. The schoolmistress was there and so were the master and mistress from Gortmore, and the lace-instructress.

The schoolgirls were sitting together in the front benches.

Weren't they to sing a song? She could see Máire Sean Mor and Máire Pheaitin Johnny and Babeen Col Marcus and the Boatman's Brigid with her red hair and even Brigid Caitín Ni Fhiannachta, with her mouth open as usual. The girls were all looking around, nudging one another and asking where Nora Col Labhras was. The schoolhouse was packed to the door now. Father Ronan was clapping his hands for silence and the whispering and murmuring soon died out.

Father Ronan started to speak to them in a very light-hearted manner. Everybody was laughing. He was calling on the school-girls to give their song. They were getting up and going to the top of the room and bowing to the people.

'O! Why can't I be there,' Nora exclaimed and laying her face in her palms, she began to cry.

Suddenly she stopped crying. She hung her head and rubbed her eyes with her hands.

It wasn't right, she said, in her own mind. It wasn't right, just or fair. Why was she kept at home? Why was she always kept at home? If she was a boy, they'd let her out, but since she was only a girl, they kept her at home.

She was only a little ass of a girl as she told Cuimin herself earlier that evening!

But she wasn't going to put up with it any more. She was going to get her own way in future. She was going to be as free as any boy that ever lived.

She had thought about the deed often before. Tonight she would carry it through.

Several times before Nora had thought of what a fine life she would have as a tramp, independent of everybody! Her face on the roads of Ireland before her, and her back on home and the hardship and anger of her family! To walk from village to village and from glen to glen, the fine level road before her, with green fields on both sides of her and small well-sheltered houses on the mountainslopes around her!

If she should get tired, she could stretch back by the side of a ditch or she could go into some house and ask the woman there for a drink of milk and a place by the fire. To sleep at night under the shadow of trees in some wood, and get up early in the morning and stretch out again under the clear fresh air!

If she should want food (and it was likely that she should) she could do a day's work here and there, and she would be fully satisfied if she was given a cup of tea and crust of bread in payment. Wouldn't that be a fine life, instead of being a little ass of a girl at home feeding the hens and minding the child.

She wouldn't go as a girl but as a boy. Nobody would ever guess that she wasn't a boy. When she would have cut her hair and put on a suit of Cuimin's bawneens who would ever know that she was a girl?

Nora had often thought about doing all this, but she had always been afraid to carry it through. Besides, she never got a proper chance to try!

Her mother was always in the house and no sooner would she be gone than they'd notice that she was missing. But she had the chance now. None of them would be back in the house for another hour, at least. She'd have plenty of time to change her clothes and to slip off unnoticed. She wouldn't meet anyone on the road because everybody was down in the schoolhouse.

She'd have time to get as far as Ellery tonight and sleep in the wood. Then she could get up early in the morning and continue her journey before anyone would be up!

She jumped up from the stool! There was a scissors in the drawer of the dresser. It wasn't long before she had them in her hands and 'Snip! Snap!'

She clipped off her black hair, the fringe that came down over her brow and all her ringlets in the one go. She glanced at herself in the mirror. Her head looked bald and bare.

She gathered her curls from the floor and hid them in an old box. She went over then to the place where a clean suit of bawneens belonging to Cuimin was hanging on a nail. She got down on her knees searching for one of Cuimin's shirts that was in a lower drawer of the dresser. She threw the clothes on the floor beside the fire.

She took off her own clothes in a hurry and threw her dress, and little blouse and her shift into a chest that was under the table. Then she put Cuimin's shirt on herself. She stuck her legs into the breeches and pulled them up.

She remembered then that she had neither braces nor belt, so she made a belt out of an old piece of cord. She put the jacket on herself, looked in the mirror and started!

She thought that Cuimin was in front of her! She looked over her shoulder, but didn't see anyone. It was then she remembered that she was looking at herself and she began to laugh.

But if she did, she was a little scared. If only she had a cap now, she'd be ready for the road. Yes, she knew where there was an old cap of Cuimin's. She got it and put it on her head. 'Goodbye forever now to the old life, and a hundred welcomes to the new!'

When she was at the door, she turned back and tiptoed over to the cradle. The baby was sound asleep. She bent down and gave him a kiss, a light little kiss on the forehead. She crept on the tips of her toes back to the door, opened it gently and shut it quietly after her. She crossed over the street and went down the bohereen. It wasn't long before she came to the main road. She then pressed onward towards Turlagh Beg.

She soon saw the schoolhouse by the side of the road. There was a fine light, shining through the windows. She heard a noise that sounded like the people inside laughing and clapping hands. She climbed over the fence and crept up the school path. She went around to the back of the house.

The windows were high enough but she managed to raise herself up until she could see what was going on inside.

Father Ronan was speaking. He stopped, and O, Lord!—the people began to get up. It was obvious that the party was over and that the people were about to separate and go home. What would she do if she was spotted?

She leapt down from the window. Her foot slipped as she was coming down and she fell on the ground. She very nearly screamed out, but controlled herself in time. She thought that her knee was a little hurt. The people were out in the school yard, by that. She would have to hide until they were all gone. She moved into the wall as close as she could. She heard the people talking and laughing and she knew that they were scattering.

What was that? The voices of people coming towards her; the sound of a footstep on the path beside her!

Suddenly she remembered that there was a short-cut across the back of the house and that there might be some people taking the short way home. It was possible that her own family would be going home that way because it was a little shorter than round by the main road.

A small group of people came near her; she recognised by their voices that they were Peaitin Johnny's family. They passed. Another group; the Boatman's family. They came that close to her that Eamonn walked on her poor bare little foot.

She almost cried out for the second time, but instead she squeezed herself tighter to the wall. Another crowd was approaching; Great God! Her own family!

Cuimin was saying: 'Wasn't Marcuseen's dancing great sport?' Her mother's dress brushed against Nora's cheek as they were passing by; she didn't draw her breath all that time. A few more groups went past. She listened for a while. Nobody else was coming. They must have all gone home, she said to herself.

She came out from her hiding-place and raced across the path. Plimp! She ran into somebody. She felt two big hands around her, and heard a man's voice. It was the priest.

'Who's that?' asked Father Ronan.

She told a lie. What else could she do?

'Cuimin Col Labhras, Father,' she said.

He laid a hand on each of her shoulders and looked down at her. Her head was bent.

'I thought that you went home with your father and mother,' he said.

'I did Father, but I lost my cap and came back to look for it.'

'Isn't your cap on your head?'

'I found it on the path.'

'Haven't your father and mother taken the short-cut?'

'They have, Father, but I am going home by the main road so that I'll be with the other boys.'

'Off with you then, or the ghosts will catch you.' With that Father Ronan let her go from him.

'Good night, Father,' she said. She didn't remember to take off her cap, but she courtesyed to the priest like a girl. If the priest managed to notice that much, he hadn't got time to say a word, for she disappeared very quickly.

As she ran up the main road, her two cheeks were red-hot with shame. She was after telling four big lies to the priest and she was afraid that those lies were a terrible sin on her soul. She got afraid as she travelled that lonely road in the darkness of the night with such a load on her heart.

The night was very dark, but there was a little light on her right hand. This came from the Turlagh Beg lake. Some bird, a curlew or a snipe, rose from the brink of the lake, letting mournful cries out of it.

Nora was startled after hearing the voice of the bird and the drumming of its wings so suddenly. She hurried on, with her heart beating against her breast. She left Turlagh Beg behind her and faced the long straight road that leads to Kilbrickan Cross. She could only barely recognise the shape of the houses on the hill when she reached the cross-roads.

There was a light in the house of Peadar O Neachtain and she heard voices from the side of Snamh Bo. She followed on, drawing near to Turlagh. When she reached Cnocan na Mona, the moon came out and she saw the outline of the hills in the distance. A big cloud passed by the face of the moon then, and it seemed to her that the night was twice as black, at that moment.

She became completely terrorised when she remembered that the Hill of the Grave wasn't too far off and that the graveyard would be on her right, once she passed it. She had often heard that this was an evil place in the middle of the night.

She sharpened her pace and began running. She imagined that she was being followed, that there was a bare-footed woman treading almost on her heels and that there was a child with a white shirt on him, walking before her on the road.

She opened her mouth to scream, but she couldn't utter a sound. She soon broke into a cold sweat. Her legs seemed to bend under her, and she nearly fell in a heap on the road.

By that time she had arrived at the Hill of the Grave. It seemed to her that Cill Eoin was full of ghosts. She remembered the words the priest said: 'the ghosts will catch you'. They were on top of her!

She thought she heard the plub plab of bare feet on the road. She turned to her left and leapt over the ditch. She almost drowned in a blind hole that was unknown to her, between her and the wood. She twisted her foot trying to save herself and felt pangs of pain. She reeled onwards into the fields of Ellery. She saw the light of the lake through the branches. She tripped over the root of a tree and fell to the ground, unconscious.

After a long time, she imagined that the place was filled with a kind of half-light, a light that was between the light of the sun and the light of the moon. She saw very clearly the treestumps, dark against a yellowish-green sky. She never saw a sky of that colour before and she thought that it was very beautiful.

She heard a footstep and she knew that there was somebody coming up towards her from the lake. She knew somehow that a great miracle was about to be shown to her and that someone was going to suffer some dreadful passion there. She hadn't long to wait until she saw a young man struggling wearily through the tangle of the wood.

He had his head bent and he appeared to be very sorrowful. Nora recognised him. It was the Son of Mary and she knew that he was going to his passion all alone.

He threw himself on His knees and began to pray. Nora didn't hear one word he said, but she understood in her heart what He was saying. He was asking His Eternal Father to send somebody to Him to help Him against His enemies and to bear half of His heavy burden. Nora wanted to get up and go to Him, but she couldn't stir from where she was.

She heard a noise and the place was filled with armed men. She saw dark, devilish faces and grey swords and edged weapons.

The gentleman was seized fiercely, His clothes were torn from Him and He was lashed with scourges until His body was a bloody mass and an everlasting wound from head to feet.

Then a crown of thorns was placed on His gentle head, a cross was laid on His shoulders and He slowly commenced His sorrowful journey to Calvary. The chain that was tying Nora's tongue and limbs up to that broke and she exclaimed loudly:

'Let me go with you, Jesus, and carry Your Cross for you.'

She felt a hand on her shoulder. She looked up and saw her father's face.

'What's wrong with my little girl or why did she leave us?' he asked.

He lifted her up in his arms and brought her home. She lay in bed for a month after that. She was out of her mind, half of that time, and sometimes imagined that she was travelling the roads by herself, asking people the way. Other times, she imagined that she was lying under a tree in Ellery, seeing again the passion of that gentleman, and trying to help him but being unable to do so.

Finally she returned to normal and saw that she was at home. And when she recognised her mother's face her heart was filled with gladness and she asked her to put the baby into the bed with her so that she could kiss him.

'O, Mammy,' she said. 'I thought I would never see you, or my father, or Cuimin, or the baby again. Were you here all the time?'

'We were, pet,' her mother replied.

'I'll always stay with you from this out,' she said. 'O, Mammy the roads were very dark . . . And I'll never hit you again,' she said to the baby giving him another kiss.

The baby put his arm around her neck, and she curled herself up in the bed at her ease.

MR COLLOPY

Flann O'Brien

One of the most unforgettable descriptions of an Irish teacher and his class occurs in the opening chapter of An Béal Bocht (The Poor Mouth) *by Flann O'Brien (1911–1966), which mixes remarkable insight with unrestrained comedy. Strangely, this classic novel, which O'Brien originally wrote in Gaelic in 1941, remained untranslated into English until 1973 when its stature was finally acknowledged.*

O'Brien—who was born Brian O Nuallain in Strabane, County Tyrone, and moved with his family to Dublin a couple of years later—has provided glimpses of his spirited and often uproarious days as a schoolboy in several of his novels, as well as in the newspaper column headed 'Cruiskeen Lawn' which he wrote under the pseudonym Myles na Gopaleen for the Irish Times *between 1940 and 1966. His early education was at the Christian Brothers' School in Synge Street, Dublin, followed by Blackrock College, but his love of humour first surfaced while he was a student at University College, taking a BA in modern languages. Here he edited a magazine called, appropriately,* Blather, *in which his mastery of wordplay was one of the outstanding highlights. After taking an MA in modern Irish-language poetry, he joined the Civil Service in 1935 and remained there until 1953. Throughout this period he continued to write and in 1939 published his first novel,* At Swim-Two-Birds, *which was praised by James Joyce but received little attention until the Sixties when it was republished and became an underground classic.*

Apart from his journalism, Flann O'Brien wrote several more novels—notably The Dalkey Archive *(1964) and* The Third

Policeman *(1967), plus a play,* Faustus Kelly, *which was performed at the Abbey Theatre. One of his brothers, Ciaran O
Nuallain, was also a noted editor (of the Irish-language newspaper,* Inniu*) and published several books in Irish, including a
memoir of his brother,* Óige an Dearthár *(1973). Ciaran himself
appears in several of Flann's stories as 'The Brother'.*

*Frequent reprinting of Flann O'Brien's work in paperback in
recent years has firmly established his reputation as one of Ireland's great comic writers. 'Mr Collopy' is a little masterpiece
about the introduction of two brothers, Manus and Finbarr, to
school life. When I add that it is a story peopled with characters
such as Mrs Crotty, Brother Cruppy and Father Kurt Fahrt,
readers familiar with his work will appreciate immediately that
they are in typical O'Brien territory.*

*   *   *

There is something misleading but not dishonest in this portrait
of Mr Collopy. It cannot be truly my impression of him when I
first saw him but rather a synthesis of all the thoughts and experiences I had of him over the years, a long look backwards. But I
do remember clearly enough that my first glimpse of him was,
so to speak, his absence: Mrs Crotty, having knocked imperiously
on the door, immediately began rooting in her handbag for the
key. It was plain she did not expect the door to be opened.

—There is a clap of rain coming, she remarked to Miss Annie.

—Seemingly, Miss Annie said.

Mrs Crotty opened the door and led us in single file into the
front kitchen, semi-basement, Mr Hanafin bringing up the rear
with some bags.

He was sitting there at the range in a crooked, collapsed sort
of cane armchair, small reddish eyes looking up at us over the
rims of steel spectacles, the head bent forward for closer scrutiny.
Over an ample crown, long grey hair was plastered in a tattered
way. The whole mouth region was concealed by a great untidy
dark brush of a moustache, discoloured at the edges, and a fading
chin was joined to a stringy neck which disappeared into a white

celluloid collar with no tie. Nondescript clothes contained a meagre frame of low stature and the feet wore large boots with the laces undone.

—Heavenly fathers, he said in a flat voice, but you are very early. Morning, Hanafin.

—Morra, Mr Collopy, Mr Hanafin said.

—Annie here had everything infastatiously in order, Mrs Crotty said, thanks be to God.

—I wonder now, Miss Annie said.

—Troth, Mr Collopy, Mr Hanafin beamed, but I never seen you looking better. You have a right bit of colour up whatever you are doing with yourself at all.

The brother and myself looked at Mr Collopy's slack grey face and then looked at each other.

—Well the dear knows, Mr Collopy said, I don't think hard work ever hurt anybody. Put that stuff in the back room for the present, Hanafin. Well now, Mrs Crotty, are these the two pishrogues out of the storm? They are not getting any thinner from the good dinners you have been putting into them, Annie, and that's a fact.

—Seemingly, Miss Annie said.

—Pray introduce me, if you please, Mrs Crotty.

We went forward and had our names recited. Without rising, Mr Collopy made good an undone button at the neck of the brother's jersey and then shook hands with us solemnly. From his waistcoat he extracted two pennies and presented one to each of us.

—I cross your hands with earthly goods, he said, and at the same time I put my blessing on your souls.

—Thanks for the earthly goods, the brother said.

—Manus and Finbarr are fine names, fine Irish names, Mr Collopy said. In the Latin Manus means big. Remember that. Ecce Sacerdos Manus comes into the Missal, and that Manus is such an uplifting name. Ah but Finbarr is the real Irish, for he was a saint from the County Cork. Far and wide he spread the Gospel thousands of years ago for all the thanks he got, for I believe he died of starvation at the heel of the hunt on some island on the river Lee, down fornenst Queenstown.

—I always heard that Saint Finbarr was a Protestant, Mrs Crotty snapped. Dug with the other foot. God knows what put it into the head of anybody to put a name the like of that on the poor bookul.

—Nonsense, Mrs Crotty. His heart was to Ireland and his soul to the Bishop of Rome. What is sticking out of that bag, Hanafin? Are they brooms or shovels or what?

Mr Hanafin had reappeared with a new load of baggage and followed Mr Collopy's gaze to one item.

—Faith now, Mr Collopy, he replied, and damn the shovels. They are hurling sticks. Best of Irish ash and from the County Kilkenny, I'll go bail.

—I am delighted to hear it. From the winding banks of Nore, ah? Many a good puck I had myself in the quondam days of my nonage. I could draw on a ball in those days and clatter in a goal from midfield, man.

—Well, it's no wonder you are never done talking about the rheumatism in your knuckles, Mrs Crotty said bleakly.

—That will do you, Mrs Crotty. It was a fine manly game and I am not ashamed of any wounds I may still carry. In those days you were damn nothing if you weren't a hurler. Cardinal Logue is a hurler and a native Irish speaker, revered by Pope and man. Were *you* a hurler, Hanafin?

—In my part of the country—Tinahely—we went in for the football.

—Michael Cusack's Gaelic code, I hope?

—Oh, certainty, Mr Collopy.

—That's good. The native games for the native people. By dad and I see young thullabawns of fellows got out in baggy drawers playing this new golf out beyond on the Bull Island. For pity's sake sure that isn't a game at all.

—Oh, you'll always find the fashionable jackeen in Dublin and that's a certainty, Mr Hanafin said. They'd wear nightshirts if they seen the British military playing polo in nightshirts above in the park. Damn the bit of shame they have.

—And then you have all this talk about Home Rule, Mr

Collopy asserted. Well how are you! We're as fit for Home Rule here as the blue men in Africa if we are to judge by those Bull Island looderamawns.

—Sit over here at the table, Mrs Crotty said. Is that tea drawn, Annie?

—Seemingly, Miss Annie said.

We all sat down and Mr Hanafin departed, leaving a shower of blessings on us.

It is seemly for me to explain here, I feel, the nature and standing of the persons present. Mr Collopy was my mother's half-brother and was therefore my own half-uncle. He had married twice, Miss Annie being his daughter by his first marriage. Mrs Crotty was his second wife but she was never called Mrs Collopy, why I cannot say. She may have deliberately retained the name of her first husband in loving memory of him or the habit may have grown up through the absence of mind. Moreover, she always called her second husband by the formal style of Mr Collopy as he also called her Mrs Crotty, at least in the presence of other parties; I cannot speak for what usage obtained in private. An ill-disposed person might suspect that they were not married at all and that Mrs Crotty was a kept woman or resident prostitute. But that is quite unthinkable, if only because of Mr Collopy's close interest in the Church and in matters of doctrine and dogma, and also his long friendship with the German priest from Leeson Street, Father Kurt Fahrt, SJ, who was a frequent caller.

It is seemly, as I have said, to give that explanation but I cannot pretend to have illuminated the situation or made it more reasonable.

The years passed slowly in this household where the atmosphere could be described as a dead one. The brother, five years older than myself, was first to be sent to school, being marched off early one morning by Mr Collopy to see the Superior of the Christian Brothers' school at Westland Row. A person might think the occasion was one merely of formal introduction and enrolment, but when Mr Collopy returned, he was alone.

—By God's will, he explained, Manus's foot has been placed

today on the first rung of the ladder of learning and achievement, and on yonder pinnacle beckons the lone star.

—The unfortunate boy had no lunch, Mrs Crotty said in a shrill voice.

—You might consider, Mrs Crotty, that the Lord would provide, even as He does for the birds of the air. I gave the bosthoon a tuppence. Brother Cruppy told me that the boys can get a right bag of broken biscuits for a penny in a barber's shop there up the lane.

—And what about milk?

—Are you out of your wits, woman? You know the gorawars you have to get him to drink his milk in this kitchen. He thinks milk is poison, the same way *you* think a drop of malt is poison. That reminds me—I think I deserve a smahan. Where's my crock?

The brother, who had become more secretive as time went on, did not confide much in me about his new station except that 'school was a bugger'. Sooner than I thought, my own turn was to come. One evening Mr Collopy asked me where the morning paper was. I handed him the nearest I could find. He handed it back to me.

—This morning's I told you.

—I think that's this morning's.

—You *think*? Can you not read, boy?

—Well . . . no.

—Well, may the sweet Almighty God look down on us with compassion! Do you realise that at your age Mose Art had written four symphonies and any God's amount of lovely songs? Pagan Neeny had given a recital on the fiddle before the King of Prussia and John the Baptist was stranded in the desert with damn the thing to eat only locusts and wild honey. Have you no shame, man?

—Well, I'm young yet.

—Is that a fact now? You are like the rest of them, you are counting from the wrong end. How do you know you are not within three months of the end of your life?

—Oh my God!

—Hah?

—But——

—You may put your buts back in your pocket. I will tell you what you'll do. You'll get up tomorrow morning at the stroke of eight o'clock and you will give yourself a good wash for yourself.

That night the brother said in bed, not without glee, that some-how he thought I would soon be master of Latin and Shakespeare and that Brother Cruppy would shower heavenly bread on me with his class in Christian Doctrine and give me some idea of what the early Christians went through in the arena by thrashing the life out of me. Unhappy was the eye I closed that night. But the brother was only partly right. To my surprise, Mr Collopy next morning led me at a smart pace up the bank of the canal, penetrated to Synge Street and rang the bell at the residential part of the Christian Brothers' establishment there. When a slatternly young man in black answered, Mr Collopy said he wanted to see the Superior, Brother Gaskett. We were shown into a gaunt little room which had on the wall a steel engraving of the head of Brother Rice, founder of the Order, a few chairs and a table—nothing more.

—They say piety has a smell, Mr Collopy mused, half to himself. It's a perverse notion. What they mean is only the absence of the smell of women.

He looked at me.

—Did you know that no living woman is allowed into this holy house? That is as it should be. Even if a Brother has to see his own mother, he has to meet her in secret below at the Imperial Hotel. What do you think of that?

—I think it is very hard, I said. Couldn't she call to see him here and have another Brother present, like they do in jails when there is a warder present on visiting day?

—Well, that's the queer comparison, I'll warrant. Indeed, this house may be a jail of a kind but the chains are of purest eighteen-carat finest gold which the holy Brothers like to kiss on their bended knees.

The door opened silently and an elderly stout man with a sad face glided in. He smiled primly and gave us an odd handshake, keeping his elbow bent and holding the extended hand against his breast.

—Isn't that the lovely morning, Mr Collopy, he said hoarsely.

—It is, thank God, Brother Gaskett, Mr Collopy replied as we all sat down. Need I tell you why I brought this young ruffian along?

—Well, it wasn't to teach him how to play cards.

—You are right there, Brother. His name is Finbarr.

—Well now, look at that! That is a beautiful name, one that is honoured by the Church. I presume you would like us to try to extend Finbarr's knowledge?

—That is a nice way of putting it, Brother Gaskett. I think they will have to be very big extensions because damn the thing he knows but low songs from the pantomimes, come-all-ye's by Cathal McGarvey, and his prayers. I suppose you'll take him in, Brother?

—Of course I will. Certainly, I will teach him everything from the three Rs to Euclid and Aristophanes and the tongue of the Gael. We will give him a thorough grounding in the Faith and, with God's help, if one day he should feel like joining the Order, there will always be a place for him in this humble establishment. After he has been trained, of course.

The tail-end of that speech certainly startled me, even to tempting me to put in some sort of caveat. I did not like it even as a joke, nor the greasy Brother making it.

—I ... I think that could wait a bit, Brother Gaskett, I stammered.

He laughed mirthlessly.

—Ah but of course, Finbarr. One thing at a time.

Then he and Mr Collopy indulged in some muttered consultation jaw to jaw, and the latter got up to leave. I also rose but he made a gesture.

—We'll stay where we are now, he said. Brother Gaskett thinks you might start right away. Always better to take the bull by the horns.

Though not quite unexpected, this rather shocked me.

—But, I said in a loud voice, I has no lunch ... no broken biscuits.

—Never mind, Brother Gaskett said, we will give you a half-day to begin with.

That is how I entered the sinister portals of Synge Street School. Soon I was to get to know the instrument known as 'the leather'. It is not, as one would imagine, a strap of the kind used on bags. It is a number of such straps sewn together to form a thing of great thickness that is nearly as rigid as a club but just sufficiently flexible to prevent the breaking of the bones of the hand. Blows of it, particularly if directed (as often they deliberately were) to the top of the thumb or wrist, conferred immediate paralysis followed by agony as the blood tried to get back to the afflicted part. Later I was to learn from the brother a certain routine of prophylaxis he had devised but it worked only partly.

Neither of us found out what Collopy's reason was for sending us to different schools. The brother thought it was to prevent us 'cogging', or copying each other's home exercises, of which we were given an immense programme to get through every night. This was scarcely correct, for an elaborate system for 'cogging' already existed in each school itself, for those who arrived early in the morning. My own feeling was that the move was prompted by Mr Collopy's innate craftiness and the general principle of *divide et impera*.

THE POTEEN MAKER

Michael McLaverty

Michael McLaverty (1907–1992) was a schoolmaster all his life—he taught mathematics and physics in Belfast—and it is for his stories about school life that he remains famous, earning this praise from James F. Kilroy in his critical history The Irish Short Story: *'Not surprising, given his career as an educator, McLaverty has used the schoolroom as a setting for his fiction— both schoolmasters and schoolchildren are among his memorable creations.' One story in particular, 'The Poteen Maker', has become almost legendary and when McLaverty died in March 1992,* The Independent *made special reference to it in the opening paragraph of his obituary: 'Michael McLaverty's short story about the country schoolmaster whose only science class is a lesson on distillation is well-known in Ireland even among people who have never read "The Poteen Maker". It matters not that the picture of the schools inspector and the master sampling the illicit brew may have been drawn from a real incident, for McLaverty's telling of the tale remains vivid in the mind ... the characterisation, the dialogue, the attention to detail.'*

Born in Carrickmacross, County Monaghan, McLaverty lived for several years on remote Rathlin Island, off the coast of County Antrim, until the family with its nine children moved to Belfast when he was five. Despite the early death of his mother, he had a happy childhood. Educated at St Malachy's College and Queen's University, he became a teacher in 1924, but soon the outbreak of sectarian violence left him, a Catholic, living in a predominantly Protestant area, in an uneasy situation that contrasted starkly with the tranquillity of his early years. Indeed, his first novels like Call My Brother Back *(1939) were very much a Catholic's response to those troubled times: dealing with issues of family and community loyalty, and with idealism and violence.*

It was, however, his short stories—especially those about school life, the profession in which he remained for 28 years, ending his career as the headmaster of the newly opened St Thomas's Secondary School in West Belfast—that earned Michael McLaverty his enduring fame. Though there are many admirers of his tale about the miserly teacher in 'A School-master', or the schoolboy pigeon fancier caught up in the struggle between the IRA and the Government of Northern Ireland in 'Pigeons', no story is better suited for this collection than 'The Poteen Maker'. I first read it over a decade ago and have read it half-a-dozen times since, and it still makes me laugh aloud.

*   *   *

When he taught me some years ago he was an old man near his retirement, and when he would pass through the streets of the little town on his way from school you would hear the women talking about him as they stood at their doors knitting or nursing their babies: 'Poor man, he's done . . . Killing himself . . . Digging his own grave!' With my bag of books under my arm I could hear them, but I could never understand why they said he was digging his own grave, and when I would ask my mother she would scold me: 'Take your dinner, like a good boy, and don't be listening to the hard backbiters of this town. Your father has always a good word for Master Craig—so that should be enough for you!'

'But why do they say he's killing himself?'

'Why do who say? Didn't I tell you to take your dinner and not be repeating what the idle gossips of this town are saying? Listen to me, son! Master Craig is a decent, good-living man— a kindly man that would go out of his way to do you a good turn. If Master Craig was in any other town he'd have got a place in the new school at the Square instead of being stuck for ever in that wee poky bit of a school at the edge of the town!'

It was true that the school was small—a two-roomed ramshackle of a place that lay at the edge of the town beyond the
last street lamp. We all loved it. Around it grew a few trees, their
trunks hacked with boys' names and pierced with nibs and rusty
drawing-pins. In summer when the windows were open we could
hear the leaves rubbing together and in winter see the raindrops
hanging on the bare twigs.

It was a draughty place and the master was always complaining
of the cold, and even in the early autumn he would wear his
overcoat in the classroom and rub his hands together: 'Boys, it's
very cold today. Do you feel it cold?' And to please him we
would answer: 'Yes, sir, 'tis very cold.' He would continue to
rub his hands and he would look out at the old trees casting their
leaves or at the broken spout that flung its tail of rain against the
window. He always kept his hands clean and three times a day
he would wash them in a basin and wipe them on a roller towel
affixed to the inside of his press. He had a hanger for his coat
and a brush to brush away the chalk that accumulated on the
collar in the course of the day.

In the wet windy month of November three buckets were
placed on the top of the desks to catch the drips that plopped
here and there from the ceiling, and those drops made different
music according to the direction of the wind. When the buckets
were filled the master always called me to empty them, and I
would take them one at a time and swirl them into the drain at
the street and stand for a minute gazing down at the wet roofs
of the town or listen to the rain pecking at the lunch-papers
scattered about on the cinders.

'What's it like outside?' he always asked when I came in with
the empty buckets.

'Sir, 'tis very bad.'

He would write sums on the board and tell me to keep an eye
on the class and out to the porch he would go and stand in grim
silence watching the rain nibbling at the puddles. Sometimes he
would come in and I would see him sneak his hat from the press
and disappear for five or ten minutes. We would fight then with
rulers or paper-darts till our noise would disturb the mistress next

door and in she would come and stand with her lips compressed, her fingers in her book. There was silence as she upbraided us: 'Mean, low, good-for-nothing corner boys. Wait'll Mister Craig comes back and I'll let him know the angels he has. And I'll give him special news about *you*!'—and she shakes her book at me: 'An altar boy on Sunday and a corner boy for the rest of the week!' We would let her barge away, the buckets plink-plonking as they filled up with rain and her own class beginning to hum, now that she was away from them.

When Mr Craig came back he would look at us and ask if we had disturbed Miss Lagan. Our silence or our tossed hair always gave him the answer. He would correct the sums on the board, flivell the pages of a book with his thumb, and listen to us reading; and occasionally he would glance out of the side window at the river that flowed through the town and, above it, the bedraggled row of houses whose tumbling yard-walls sheered to the water's edge. 'The loveliest county in Ireland is County Down!' he used to say, with a sweep of his arm to the river and the tin cans and the chalked walls of the houses.

During that December he was ill for two weeks and when he came back amongst us he was greatly failed. To keep out the draughts he nailed perforated plywood over the ventilators and stuffed blotting paper between the wide crevices at the jambs of the door. There were muddy marks of a ball on one of the windows and on one pane a long crack with fangs at the end of it: 'So someone has drawn the River Ganges while I was away,' he said; and whenever he came to the geography of India he would refer to the Ganges delta by pointing to the cracks on the pane.

When our ration of coal for the fire was used up he would send me into the town with a bucket, a coat over my head to keep off the rain, and the money in my fist to buy a stone of coal. He always gave me a penny to buy sweets for myself, and I can always remember that he kept his money in a waistcoat pocket. Back again I would come with the coal and he would give me disused exercise books to light the fire. 'Chief stoker!' he called me, and the name has stuck to me to this day.

It was at this time that the first snow had fallen, and someone by using empty potato bags had climbed over the glass-topped wall and stolen the school coal, and for some reason Mr Craig did not send me with the bucket to buy more. The floor was continually wet from our boots, and our breath frosted the windows. Whenever the door opened a cold draught would rush in and gulp down the breath-warmed air in the room. We would jig our feet and sit on our hands to warm them. Every half-hour Mr Craig would make us stand and while he lilted *O'Donnell Abu* we did a series of physical exercises which he had taught us, and in the excitement and the exaltation we forgot about our sponging boots and the snow that pelted against the windows. It was then that he did his lessons in Science; and we were delighted to see the bunsen burner attached to the gas bracket which hung like an inverted T from the middle of the ceiling. The snoring bunsen seemed to heat up the room and we all gathered round it, pressing in on top of it till he scattered us back to our places with the cane: 'Sit down!' he would shout. 'There's no call to stand. Everybody will be able to see!'

The cold spell remained, and over and over again he repeated one lesson in Science, which he called: *Evaporation and Condensation.*

'I'll show you how to purify the dirtiest of water,' he had told us. 'Even the filthiest water from the old river could be made fit for drinking purposes.' In a glass trough he had a dark brown liquid and when I got his back turned I dipped my finger in it and it tasted like treacle or burnt candy, and then I remembered about packets of brown sugar and tins of treacle I had seen in his press.

He placed some of the brown liquid in a glass retort and held it aloft to the class: 'In the retort I have water which I have discoloured and made impure. In a few minutes I'll produce from it the clearest of spring water.' And his weary eyes twinkled and although we could see nothing funny in that, we smiled because he smiled.

The glass retort was set up with the flaming bunsen underneath, and as the liquid was boiling, the steam was trapped in a long-necked flask on which I sponged cold water. With our eyes we followed the bubbling mixture and the steam turning into drops and dripping rapidly into the flask. The air was filled with a biscuity smell, and the only sound was the snore of the bunsen. Outside was the cold air and the falling snow. Presently the master turned out the gas and held up the flask containing the clear water.

'As pure as crystal!' he said, and we watched him pour some of it into a tumbler, hold it in his delicate fingers, and put it to his lips. With wonder we watched him drink it and then our eyes travelled to the dirty, cakey scum that had congealed on the glass sides of the retort. He pointed at this with his ruler: 'The impurities are sifted out and the purest of pure water remains.' And for some reason he gave his roguish smile. He filled up the retort again with the dirty brown liquid and repeated the experiment until he had a large bottle filled with the purest of pure water.

The following day it was still snowing and very cold. The master filled up the retort with the clear liquid which he had stored in the bottle: 'I'll boil this again to show you that there are no impurities left.' So once again we watched the water bubbling, turning to steam, and then to shining drops. Mr Craig filled up his tumbler: 'As pure as crystal,' he said, and then the door opened and in walked the Inspector. He was muffled to the ears and snow covered his hat and his attaché case. We all stared at him—he was the old, kind man we had seen before. He glanced at the bare firegrate and at the closed windows with their sashes edged with snow. The water continued to bubble in the retort, giving out its pleasant smell.

The Inspector shook hands with Mr Craig and they talked and smiled together, the Inspector now and again looking towards the empty grate and shaking his head. He unrolled his scarf and flicked the snow from off his shoulders and from his attaché case. He sniffed the air, rubbed his frozen hands together, and took a black notebook from his case. The snow ploofed against the windows, the wind hummed under the door.

'Now, boys,' Mr Craig continued, holding up the tumbler of

water from which a thread of steam wriggled in the air. He talked
to us in a strange voice and told us about the experiment as if
we were seeing it for the first time. Then the Inspector took the
warm tumbler and questioned us on our lesson. 'It should be
perfectly pure water,' he said, and he sipped at it. He tasted its
flavour. He sipped at it again. He turned to Mr Craig. They
whispered together, the Inspector looking towards the retort
which was still bubbling and sending out its twirls of steam to
be condensed to water of purest crystal. He laughed loudly, and
we smiled when he again put the tumbler to his lips and this
time drank it all. Then he asked us more questions and told us
how, if we were shipwrecked, we could make pure water from
the salt sea water.

Mr Craig turned off the bunsen and the Inspector spoke to
him. The master filled up the Inspector's tumbler and poured out
some for himself in a cup. Then the Inspector made jokes with
us, listened to us singing, and told us we were the best class in
Ireland. Then he gave us a few sums to do in our books. He put
his hands in his pockets and jingled his money, rubbed a little
peep-hole in the breath-covered window, and peered out at the
loveliest sight in Ireland. He spoke to Mr Craig again and Mr
Craig shook hands with him and they both laughed. The Inspector
looked at his watch. Our class was let out early, and while I
remained behind to tidy up the Science apparatus the master gave
me an empty treacle tin to throw in the bin and told me to carry
the Inspector's case up to the station. I remember that day well
as I walked behind them through the snow, carrying the attaché
case, and how loudly they talked and laughed as the snow whirled
cold from the river. I remember how they crouched together to
light their cigarettes, how match after match was thrown on the
road, and how they walked off with the unlighted cigarettes still
in their mouths. At the station Mr Craig took a penny from his
waistcoat pocket and as he handed it to me it dropped on the
snow. I lifted it and he told me I was the best boy in Ireland . . .

When I was coming from his funeral last week—God have
mercy on him—I recalled that wintry day and the feel of the
cold penny and how much more I know now about Mr Craig

than I did then. On my way out of the town—I don't live there now—I passed the school and saw a patch of new slates on the roof and an ugly iron barrier near the door to keep the home-going children from rushing headlong on to the road. I knew if I had looked at the trees I'd have seen rusty drawing-pins stuck into their rough flesh. But I passed by. I heard there was a young teacher in the school now, with an array of coloured pencils in his breast pocket.

THE MYSTERY PLAY

Sinéad de Valera

The life of Sinéad de Valera (1878–1975) has been rather over-shadowed by that of her husband, Éamon, the Republican commandant in the 1916 uprising, who later became President of Ireland. However, apart from the unswerving support she gave to her husband, she has also contributed significantly to the promotion of interest in Irish folklore amongst young children, in a series of books in Gaelic and English which she wrote during the Sixties and early Seventies.

Born in Flanaghan, County Dublin, Sinéad de Valera developed a passion for folklore and amateur dramatics during her childhood, but chose the profession of primary school teacher. In the early 1900s, however, she accepted the post of lecturer in Irish language and literature at Leinster College, Dublin. Here she met Éamon de Valera, the American-born son of a Spanish father and Irish mother, who had been brought up on an uncle's farm in County Limerick and would later work as a teacher of mathematics before becoming associated with various republican movements. The couple were married in 1910. Apart from her writing, Sinéad de Valera appeared in a number of amateur dramatic productions, including a remarkable perform-ance of Douglas Hyde's The Tinker and the Fairy *which was performed in the garden of the home of novelist and memoirist, George Moore, in Ely Place, Dublin.*

Among the most popular of Sinéad de Valera's books are Fairy Tales *(1960),* The Stolen Child *(1965) and* The Four-Leaved Shamrock *(1968), which have all run through a number of editions. Several of these contain stories drawn from the author's years as a teacher, including 'The Mystery Play' which focuses on the kind of dramatic production that was close to her heart as a young actress and, later in her teaching career, as a producer.*

* * *

In a town in the centre of Ireland one spring day a group of day pupils were returning home from school. They were talking about a great event which was to take place before the Easter holidays. A mystery play was to be performed in the school.

'Bother the leaving cert.,' said Ita O'Moore. 'It spoils everything. I think it is a shame that none of the sixth year girls will be allowed to take part.'

'I think so too,' said Ethna Burke, 'and indeed you, Ita, would make a beautiful angel with your long, fair hair and blue eyes.'

'I would rather take the part of the Devil,' laughed Nora Blake.

'The part would suit you to perfection,' said Ethna, 'with your height and the glitter in your sparkling black eyes you would be just the thing.'

'What about Mary O'Reilly as the lost soul?' asked Lelia O'Dwyer. 'With her pale cheeks and "the dejected haviour of the visage" she would be wonderful.'

'Oh, Lelia, please leave Shakespeare in the classroom,' said Ita. 'Don't mind her, Mary,' she continued, putting her arms round Mary's shoulders. 'We all know you have more jokes and funny stories than anyone in the class and can quote Shakespeare far more fully than Lelia can.'

'There is no art to find the mind's construction in the face, Lelia,' said Mary, laughing.

By this time Ethna and Mary had reached the street where they lived. As the others walked on Lelia said she was going that night to the Carnival. The Carnival was being held in a field on the outskirts of the town.

'I would like to go too,' said Ita. 'What about you, Nora?'

'Yes, I'll go. I believe the side shows are even better than the merry-go-rounds or swing boats.'

'It is not for any of these things I am going but to have my fortune told by Madame Yvonne. I believe she is wonderful and not difficult to understand though she speaks with a foreign accent.'

'Lelia,' said Ita, 'do you not remember the lecture Mother Lorcan gave us the other day?'

'Oh! I remember all her talk about superstitions, but one can always distinguish between make-believe and reality.'

'Mother warned us particularly about fortune-telling,' said Nora.

Lelia looked quite determined and even stubborn.

'You may stop your preaching. I am going to have my fortune told, and,' she added laughingly, 'see what the future has in store for me. Good bye girls,' she said as she reached her own house.

Nora and Ita lived next door to each other. As they walked on they talked of Lelia's decision to visit the fortune-teller.

'Lelia has been spoiled,' said Nora, 'by reading silly books on second sight, telepathy and a sort of psychology.'

'Yes,' agreed Ita, 'in her case a little learning is a dangerous thing. We cannot reason with her. However, we shall all meet at the Carnival tonight.'

The girls enjoyed the sights and shows as they walked round together. After some time they came to Madame Yvonne's tent. Lelia stopped in front of it.

'Don't go in, Lelia,' urged the other two.

'Don't be silly, girls. I am going to have my fortune told at all costs.'

In she went. In the dim light she saw a small woman whose piercing black eyes looked out from beneath heavy, dark lashes. She was seated on a low stool and had a small table in front of her. Her dress was remarkable. She wore a flowing yellow robe and bright purple cloak or shawl. On her head was a kind of turban.

As Lelia entered the woman took from the floor a large glass bowl and placed it on the table.

'Want your fortune told by Madame Yvonne, young lady?'

Lelia thought Madame's foreign accent very peculiar. It was quite unlike that of Mademoiselle who taught French in school.

'You must cross my hand with silver, two and six, please.'

Lelia gave the necessary fee.

'Show me your hand, young lady. Hah! you are clever and brave. Your beauty will win you many admirers. Wait a moment.'

Madame peered into the glass bowl.

'You will travel much. Hah! what do I see? A handsome rich man will come to this country from abroad and wish to make you his wife.'

Again she looked into the bowl.

'I can tell you how you can see the face of this man, but before doing so I must have more silver. Two shillings.'

Lelia somewhat reluctantly gave the money.

'Now listen carefully. Tomorrow night, when the moon is shining brightly, go alone—mind I say alone—to the heather field at nine o'clock sharp. There behind the clump of bushes on the left hand side you will see the likeness of the man who will soon come and ask you to be his wife. Go now. Good luck.'

As Lelia was leaving the tent she thought she heard Madame chuckling to herself, but when she looked round Madame was gazing intently into the bowl.

Ita and Nora were waiting outside for their friend.

'Well, what did Madame tell you?' was their first question.

'Oh, she said very nice things about me.'

'Oh! she would!' said Ita.

'But really she seemed to understand me very well. It was wonderful how she knew my character.'

'Poor Lelia,' said Nora.

'Poor Lelia indeed? I tell you Madame is very clever. She has told me how I can see a likeness of the man who loves me.'

'Are you mad?' said Ita.

'Not a bit mad. She told me to go alone tomorrow night at nine o'clock sharp to the heather field.'

'You always said there were spirits of some sort in that field,' said Nora.

'Now I am certain of it,' said Lelia.

'Go on please,' said the other two.

'Madame said that among the clump of bushes on the left hand side I will see the face of the man who loves me.'

'I believe,' said Ita, 'that Madame is either crazy or wicked and you will be both, if you follow her directions.'

'Well, it is time for us to go home now,' said Nora. 'We will leave you at your door, Lelia, for in my opinion, you must be still a baby or else a fool to act as you are doing.'

'Thanks, but your warning and advice only make me more determined. Good night.'

As the two friends were on their way home Ita asked:

'Do you think Lelia will really go to the field tomorrow night?'

'Knowing her character as I do,' replied Nora, 'I am sure she will if only to show how daring and sweetly romantic she is.'

Ita suddenly stood still.

'I have an idea, Nora,' she said, 'one that may help to cure Lelia's diseased mind. Kathleen Meagher, one of the boarders, is a great friend of mine. She is in charge of the costumes for the play. There will be no dress rehearsal till next week. I will ask her to lend me Lucifer's get-up.'

'For what, may I ask?'

'For you to put on tomorrow night. When you are dressed in the horned cap and the whole costume you will be a perfect representation of the Devil.'

'Thank you, Ita.'

'I mean,' said Ita laughing, 'you can roll your eyes and look fierce and in the moonlight among the bushes you will appear to Lelia instead of "the man who loves her".'

'Indeed,' said Nora, 'a start or fright might cure her of some of her nonsensical ideas. At present she lives in an unreal world of stupid romance. Still, I would not like to give her a bad shock.'

'Oh,' said Ita, 'we won't keep her long in suspense. It will all be the work of a moment.'

The following night was beautiful in the bright light of the full moon. Shortly before nine o'clock two figures crossed the heather field. One took up a position among the clump of bushes. The other hid behind a big tree.

As the Church clock chimed nine, Lelia appeared. She walked

bravely towards the bushes. As she parted them an awful growl was heard and two claw-like hands stretched out to catch her. At the same time the sinister glare of Satan's eyes came from beneath his horned cap.

She uttered a shriek and fell to the ground. In falling her head touched a stone and she became unconscious.

It was now the other girls' turn to be terrified.

'Oh,' cried Ita, 'we have killed her. Run quickly to the road, Nora, and see if there is anyone who could help us. Fortunately, I have done a little first-aid work.'

Nora ran to the road. In her anxiety she forgot about her 'get-up'.

Two girls on bicycles saw her and pedalled for their lives.

Looking to the other side she saw old Bob Murphy who had just left the bar in the town and was not too steady on his feet. When he saw Nora he went down on his knees shouting 'keep off from me, I'll have nothing to do with you.'

Next came the parish priest in his car. The driver halted a moment and was about to move on when Father Brady told him to stop.

Nora ran quickly towards the priest——

'Oh, Father,' she said, 'come quickly into the field with me.'

'What fool-acting is this. What is the meaning of this interesting costume?' Father Brady asked.

'Oh, Father, I forgot. I'll explain in a minute, but will you please come with me. I'm afraid I have killed Lelia O'Dwyer.'

The bewildered priest followed Nora into the field.

In the meantime Bob Murphy hurried home much more steady on his feet than he had been some time before.

When Father Brady and Nora reached the bushes they found Lelia sitting on the grass terribly shaken, but otherwise not much the worse for her fright or fall.

'Now,' said the priest, 'will you girls kindly explain the meaning of all this. Perhaps we had better get into the car first as you are all three as pale as the moon itself.'

Fortunately the genial priest had a great sense of humour and a sympathetic understanding of young people. When he heard the story from beginning to end he made everything right in the school and homes of the girls.

When Mother Lorcan was told all that had happened she laughed and said:

'Well, Father, we can hardly expect that our mystery play will surpass theirs as a sensational success.'

THE PARTING

Liam O'Flaherty

One of the quintessential twentieth-century Irish novelists, Liam
O'Flaherty (1897–1984) was destined as a child for the priesthood, but instead chose the path of revolution and the call of the
wanderer before achieving recognition as a writer. He was born
on Inishmore, the largest of the Aran Islands, where his father
eked out a precarious existence from the barren soil to support
his family of ten. The older O'Flaherty had a reputation, which
his son inherited, for being a rebel, while his mother was
descended from Plymouth Brethren and saw young Liam's future
in Holy Orders; it was, however, from her that he received his
gift for story-telling.

While growing up in this harsh environment he attended the
Oatquarter School and there became fluent in both Gaelic and
English. The headmaster, sensing the boy's lively intelligence,
recommended him for the priesthood and at the age of 13 Liam
O'Flaherty left Inishmore for Rockwell College seminary, where
he received awards for his studies in the classics and modern
languages, as well as a gold medal for an essay on Gaelic.
However, after a brief period at University College, Dublin, he
decided the priesthood was not for him and enrolled in the Irish
Guards. Shortly afterwards his unit was sent to France and in
1917 he was blown up near Ypres and, badly shell-shocked, was
invalided out of the army. A period of travelling the world as a
hobo, followed by involvement in the Republican cause in Dublin,
provided him with the raw material for his short stories which
were readily accepted by magazines all over the world, and for
the novels that made his reputation. These included The Informer

(1925), which won the James Tait Black Memorial Prize and was filmed by John Ford in 1935, and Famine *(1937), believed by some critics to be his finest achievement.*

The short stories which O'Flaherty wrote throughout his career were heavily influenced by his life and experiences. Several dealt with his formative years, such as 'Spring Sowing' and 'The Reaping Race', about his childhood on Aran, and 'The Parting' which is clearly based on his own departure as a teenager to become a priest. It is a story made all the more relevant by the success of the BBC Television series, Ballykissangel, *about a young priest and the testing of his vows, which was filmed in Avoca, County Wicklow.*

*   *   *

Michael Joyce stood beside his mother against the gable end of the storehouse, down by the head of the pier where the steamer from the mainland lay moored. He was able to leave his native island for the first time, in order to enter the diocesan seminary and study for the priesthood.

Dressed in a new suit of blue serge, with a fawn-coloured raincoat slung across his right shoulder, he looked alert and very much at ease, as if the imminent parting were of no concern to him. Although barely thirteen, he already had a finely proportioned body. He was big and strong for his age. He stood with the assurance of a full-grown man in the prime of condition, balanced lightly on the balls of his feet, with his head thrown back haughtily. His wild blue eyes looked cold and very proud, as they glanced hither and thither. His thin lips were set firmly.

Yet this brave exterior was but a mask to hide the terrible agony he suffered. Indeed, all his strength and pride were necessary to hold back the bitter tears that kept welling up into his throat. He wanted terribly to throw himself on his mother's bosom and weep aloud, as he had so often done in infancy. He longed to feel her loving arms about him, protecting him from the frightening world that was about to make him prisoner. He craved for her soothing words of tenderness, that had until now softened all his woes by their magic power.

Alas! the more he suffered and wanted to surrender, the more his pride of race forced him to remain hard and relentless. Now and again, when the inner struggle almost reached the limit of his endurance and the skin began to contract below his eyes, or about the corners of his mouth, he just gave his head a sudden upward jerk and drew in a deep breath. That helped him to regain control.

This struggle had made his senses painfully acute. From where he stood he could distinctly hear the fireman put coal in the steamer's furnace for the journey back to the mainland. The rasping sound of the shovel against the steel plates of the stoke-hold deck caused his nostrils to twitch. It was like drawing his finger-nails over a smooth stone. On the forecastle head, they were using the donkey engine to hoist cattle on board. Every time the little engine hissed and shot out a jet of steam, as it was about to lift another beast, he had to grit his teeth. The rattle of the chain unfolding from the winch, to lower the hoisted animals into the hold, made him feel that enormous rocks were falling down upon his head.

Worst of all was the smell of burning coal. He belonged to the most remote hamlet on the island, nine miles to the west. His people lived there in primitive simplicity, as their ancestors had lived for thousands of years, using turf and cow dung for fuel. Coal was unknown to them. So that its acrid smell gave him a slight feeling of nausea.

His mother turned towards him, with her head concealed within the hood of her black shawl. She was a tall, slender woman of very dignified carriage, wearing a handsome red frieze skirt that had two deep flounces of black velvet.

'Listen to me, darling,' she whispered. 'Do you remember what I told you about your feet?'

'What's that, Mother?' Michael said without looking at her.

He spoke to her gruffly, in spite of his love for her. Indeed, it was the intensity of his love that forced him to be gruff and almost brutal when he spoke to her. If he allowed any tenderness to creep into his voice, it would mean the collapse of his resistance.

'You must take great care not to get them wet,' she insisted, raising her voice a little and bending close to him. 'Or if you do happen to get them wet, no matter where you are, you must run and change your socks at once. Promise me that now.'

'All right, Mother,' he said.

'Oh! Darling,' she said, 'I'll suffer every night from now until you come back to me on holidays, for fear you might forget about your feet. You are so headstrong and you catch cold so easily. Last spring, you . . .'

'Look, Mother,' Michael interrupted. 'Here's our bullock coming down now. He looks wonderful.'

His mother pushed her shawl back from her head to look at the bullock. Although she was over fifty, her long, pale face was still beautiful. Her hair was very fair. Her eyes were golden.

'Ah! There's our little one, sure enough,' she said. 'The poor little creature! Ah! God help him! The life is frightened out of him.'

'He's not little at all,' Michael said indignantly. 'He's one of the best bullocks on the island this year. He nearly took the sway at the fair today.'

'Ah! the poor little one!' his mother said. 'He'll always be little to me, no matter how big he has grown. I'll always remember him as a little calf. Ah! God help him! He doesn't know where he is. He's mad with the fright.'

The bullock looked a splendid animal. His hide was a deep red colour except for a little white star at the centre of his forehead. His hair was long and curly, of a fine rich texture. He was very fat. He was already sold and the jobber's brand was clearly visible on his massive haunch, as he came charging down the pier. He rushed hither and thither, snorting and tossing foam from his jaws, as he tried to escape from the narrowing circle of young men that shouted and tried to grapple with him. Again and again he swung his powerful head in order to dislodge the hands of some fellow that had managed to grip his horns.

Then Martin Joyce, Michael's eldest brother, got a firm hold that the bullock was unable to dislodge. He was a powerfully built man of twenty-six, wearing grey frieze trousers and a thick blue woollen sweater. Gripping the horns fiercely in his strong hands, he began to turn the beast's head sideways and to bear down on it with all his strength, while his hob-nailed boots slithered over the cobble-stones. Man and beast only came to a halt when they were within a yard of the pier's edge. There the bullock made a supreme effort to free himself. He uttered a wild bellow, tossed his head and reared on his hind legs. Martin was carried off the ground, but he maintained his grip on the horns. When he and the bullock came down again, he deftly shifted his right hand from the horn to the beast's nostrils, into which he thrust his thumb and forefinger. That tamed the bullock. He offered no further resistance. He stood stock still and allowed his head to be twisted right round, until his foaming snout was upturned. Other men then gripped him by the tail and crowded in upon him from all sides.

'Get the slings around him,' Martin said to his father.

Bartly Joyce was a tall, grey-haired man of sixty, with a very red face. He looked half crazy just now, since he was a very neurotic fellow and any excitement caused him to become hysterical. He was barely able to arrange the slings around the bullock's belly, one at either end, because of his agitation. Another man fixed a long halter to the beast's horns. Then Bartly signalled to the mate on the steamer's bridge.

'Lower away there,' the mate yelled to the man at the winch.

Michael shuddered as the unfolding chain began to rattle. He felt an overwhelming pity for the pinioned animal, whose fate he instinctively felt to be somewhat akin to his own. They were both being taken away from their native island to serve the ambition of others, the bullock to be eaten and the boy to become a priest.

'Ah! The poor little creature!' Mrs Joyce said with tears in her eyes as she watched the bullock. 'Look at him standing there and he half dead with fright. The poor dumb creature! How he must be suffering!'

Michael was also very near to tears as he saw his father cross the slings over the animal's back and put the iron hook of the hoist through the loop. He recalled how he had taught the beast to drink milk out of a pail, when it was being weaned from its mother's teats. He used to let it suck his fingers, after having dipped them in the milk. Then he gradually drew the snout down into the pail and kept it there, until the calf finally began to drink the milk of its own accord.

At this moment, more than two years later, the boy vividly remembered the queer, warm pressure of the calf's gums.

'Hoist away there,' the mate shouted.

The engine hissed and shot out steam. The chain began to rattle once more as it rolled back on to the winch. The bullock rose into the air, with his belly forced out to a sharp point on either side by the pressure of the slings. He kept flaying the air with his forelegs and bellowing mightily.

'Get out of my way,' Bartly Joyce shouted as he ran forward to the edge of the pier, holding the guide rope that was attached to the beast's horns. 'Give me room, I say. God blast ye, give me room.'

The excitable fellow struck at those on either side of him with his elbows. It was a simple matter to keep the bullock's head turned towards the pier and to manoeuvre the animal into the correct position above the open mouth of the hold. Yet Bartly made a botch of his task. He slipped on the cobble stones, fell down on his buttocks and lost the rope. The bullock was carried far over to port and then forwards toward the port railing of the passenger deck. There was a wild shout as the animal almost crashed against the iron railing. At the very last moment, the hoist swung back again towards the pier and Martin succeeded in getting hold of the rope. He quickly manoeuvred the bullock into position.

'Lower away now,' the mate yelled.

Bartly had got to his feet in the meantime. He tried to take the rope from Martin as the animal was being lowered gently into the hold.

'Keep back there,' Martin said.

'Give me that rope,' said Bartly. 'Let me handle him.'

Martin swore and pushed his father roughly with his shoulder. Bartly again lost his footing on the slippery cobblestones. He fell down flat on his buttocks. There was a roar of laughter from those present.

'There he is again,' Mrs Joyce said indignantly as she blushed with shame of her husband. 'Making a show of himself.'

Michael bitterly resented the laughter. He particularly resented the laughter of some tourists and cattle-jobbers who were watching the scene from the passenger deck of the steamer. He felt they were laughing in a different way from the islanders. Indeed, he felt that these 'foreigners' looked upon all islanders as savages, whose conduct must always be ludicrous. At the seminary, other 'foreigners' would laugh at everything he himself did and said, because of his humble origin.

'I don't see how he's making a show of himself,' he said angrily to his mother. 'He just fell down. He's not used to wearing boots. That was why he fell. Why don't you side with him, instead of siding with other people?'

'Hush! Little treasure!' his mother said in a forlorn tone. 'Don't say bitter things to me, my little pulse, at the very moment you are going to leave me.'

A wave of remorse overwhelmed the boy for having given pain to his mother. This time he would undoubtedly have burst into tears if his brother had not approached. Horror of letting Martin see him cry enabled him to regain his self-control.

'You'll have a fine trip,' Martin said in a solemn and casual tone, as if he were addressing a grown-up man who was a perfect stranger to him.

'It should be a fine trip, all right,' Michael answered in the same tone, without looking at his brother. 'The sea is dead calm.'

'Whatever wind there is will be with you,' Martin said, 'all the way!'

'We ought to make it in three hours,' Michael said.

'With God's help,' Martin said, 'you should make it easily in that time.'

Mrs Joyce leaned towards Martin and whispered to him.

'You shouldn't have shouldered your father like that,' she said in a reproving though gentle tone. 'Shame on you, treasure, for knocking him down. You made a show of him, darling one, right in front of the whole island. Shame on you, I say.'

Martin turned swiftly towards her. His bronzed face was dark with anger. He looked very strong and virile in his thick blue sweater and grey frieze trousers, that were fouled by the dung of animals he had seized. One of the beasts had cut his right cheek with the sharp point of a horn. A large patch of clotted blood covered the whole centre of the cheek.

'Why didn't he keep out of the way?' he cried roughly. 'He's always interfering and making a mess of things.'

He would get married in the following spring and take command of the homestead. He was already inclined to behave like a master and to be intolerant of his father.

'You shouldn't have shouldered him, all the same, treasure of my heart,' his mother said. 'It wasn't a nice thing to do in front of the neighbours.'

'I tell you he wouldn't get out of my way,' Martin said.

'There were strangers looking on as well,' said Mrs Joyce. 'It was a scandalous thing you did, little one.'

'He might have killed the bullock and myself with his fooling,' said Martin. 'He doesn't know what he's doing when he has the least drop taken. He gets crazy.'

Michael felt very hostile towards his brother, not only for having made his father a laughing stock, but also for a far more personal reason. The boy did not fully understand his other reason. He just felt instinctively that he was chiefly being made a priest in order that he might later help to rear and educate the children that Martin would beget. He now resented the barren destiny that had been planned for him, cut off from the joys of mating and from communion with the earth as a toiler.

His father came over and glanced with hatred at Martin.

'Huh! You blackguard!' he said to his older son. 'You are very free with your shouldering.'

Martin shook hands casually with Michael and then walked away.

'That's enough now, Bartly,' Mrs Joyce said. 'There's no harm done. Forget about it. It was only an accident.'

Bartly's wild eyes became tender as he turned towards Michael. Yet he spoke to the boy gravely and without emotion, as to a stranger.

'You'll have a good crossing,' he said.

'We should,' said Michael. 'The sea is calm.'

'The wind is with you, too,' the father said.

Then he took a paper bag out of his jacket pocket and handed it shyly to the boy. Michael looked into the bag. It contained yellow sticks of candy known as 'Peggy's Leg'. The boy swallowed his breath and wanted to say something tender to his father. Yet his training forbade him to do so.

'May God spare your health,' he said solemnly.

The father also wanted to put his arm about his boy's shoulders and say something tender. The rigid discipline of his life prevented him.

'Well! Here you all are,' cried a flashily dressed young woman who pushed her way through the crowd at that moment. 'I've been looking all over the place for you. Land's sake! This pier is more crowded than Broadway right now.'

She was Barbara Joyce, the oldest surviving daughter of the family. She had been thirteen years in America and was now home on holiday. Although only thirty-two, her once beautiful face had become worn and faded from hard work. She still had a good figure, which a tight red dress showed off to good advantage. A little round hat, surmounted by brightly coloured artificial flowers, was perched jauntily on the side of her head. Her boisterous gaiety was in striking contrast with the grave dignity of the other islanders.

'Hello! Mickey,' she cried, tapping her young brother jocularly on the chin with her knuckles. 'Keep smiling, sonny boy. Don't let it get you. Everybody feels pretty homesick leaving home first time. I know how I felt myself. It was pretty terrible, but I soon got over it. So will you. Just keep that chin up, sonny boy.'

All the surviving children of the family were in America, except Martin and Michael. It was money subscribed by the children in exile and brought home by Barbara that paid Michael's way to the seminary.

Michael loved Barbara very much, because of her gaiety and tenderness. Yet he now felt ashamed of the attention she attracted by her loud voice and her somewhat rowdy manner. So he blushed and looked at the ground.

'Hello! Mary Lydon,' cried Barbara, as she rushed away to greet another woman. 'You look lovely in that new dress. How is your mother? Hello! Bridget. Hello! Johnny Breasail. Land's sake! The whole island is here today.'

The steamer whistle blew suddenly. Michael almost jumped off the ground with fright. The horse reared and whinnied on a shrill note. Mrs Joyce burst into tears.

'It's time to get on board,' Bartly shouted hysterically.

He picked up Michael's suitcase and added:

'Come on now. She'll be going any minute.'

Mrs Joyce threw her arms about her son and began to kiss him frantically all over his face.

'Oh! My little darling!' she muttered as she kissed him. 'My pulse! My lovely little treasure!'

'That's enough now, woman,' Bartly said to her tenderly after a little while. 'He has to go on board.'

He gently disengaged her arms and led Michael towards the gangway. She hid her face in her shawl and continued to weep without restraint. A number of relatives and neighbours pressed forward to shake hands with the boy.

'Make way there,' Bartly shouted at these people. 'There is very little time now. He must go on board.'

Michael felt completely bewildered by the noise as he followed his father on board. Bartly put down the suitcase, shook hands hurriedly with his son and went ashore again. Barbara came on board. She was going with Michael as far as the seminary. She stood for a little while beside him at the rails, talking in a loud voice to those on the pier. Then she joined a group of cattle-jobbers, with whom she entered into a lively conversation. The gangway was pulled ashore. A bell rang on the bridge. The engines began to turn. The mooring ropes were cast loose. The steamer drew away. People began to shout goodbye and to wave handkerchiefs.

The boy was still bewildered as he stood by the rails. Like the poor beasts down in the dark hold, the strangeness of his new environment had made his senses numb. Then the steamer made a wide circuit and headed towards the open sea, with her port bow to the pier. He hurried across to the other side of the deck. The pier was now some distance away. Only a few people stood there watching the steamer. His parents stood alone, side by side, down at the very brink. The steamer gathered speed as it passed them. They were still near enough, as he passed, for him to see the look of anguish on his mother's face.

Then his mind suddenly cleared and pain came to him again with awful bitterness, as he listened to his sister's laughter and watched his parents stand motionless by the brink of the pier wall, beyond the ever-widening white lane that the ship left on the surface of the blue water.

His bitterness was terrible because his young heart knew that dark vows would make this parting final, forever and forever.

WEEP FOR OUR PRIDE

James Plunkett

*Although beatings with the cane or physical punishments of any
kind to children are now banned in schools, punishment meted
out by teachers for misdemeanours real or otherwise will not be
unfamiliar to older readers. It is a theme that a number of Irish
writers have evoked, but few more graphically—or violently—
than James Plunkett (1920–) in this next story. Plunkett, who
was born James Plunkett Kelly in the Dublin suburb of
Sandymount, had a colourful childhood which has inspired several of his short stories and novels. Educated by the Irish Christian Brothers at their Synge Street School, he then went on to
study the violin and viola at the Dublin Municipal School of
Music. A great sportsman, he played Gaelic football at interprov-
incial level, and was briefly a clerk at the Dublin Gas Company
before becoming an official of the Workers' Union of Ireland,
the powerbase of the legendary Labour organiser, 'Big Jim'
Larkin, until his death in 1947. In the early Fifties he came to
public attention with a series of stories about Dublin life in* The
Bell, *a radio drama about Larkin,* The Risen People *(1958), and
several plays for the Abbey Theatre.*

*Inspired by the reception of his tales of Dublin and its people,
in 1969 Plunkett published his first novel,* Strumpet City, *which
became an international best-seller and enabled him to become
a full-time writer. The book was later adapted for RTE television
with Peter O'Toole as Jim Larkin, Peter Ustinov as King Edward
VII and Cyril Cusack as Father Giffley. Plunkett has himself
worked for RTE as a producer while continuing to write
the occasional short story and further popular novels including*

Farewell Companions *(1977), a sequel to* Strumpet City *which encompassed his own youth in Dublin. His work has earned him comparison with O'Flaherty, O'Faolain and O'Connor, while James F. Kilroy in* The Irish Short Story *(1984) described his short stories as 'among the finest Irish achievements in the genre'. 'Weep for our Pride', with its personalised view of some of the less pleasant moments of an Irish childhood, can only add further lustre to his reputation.*

*   *   *

The door of the classroom was opened by Mr O'Rourke just as Brother Quinlan was about to open it to leave. They were both surprised and said 'Good morning' to one another as they met in the doorway. Mr O'Rourke, although he met Brother Quinlan every morning of his life, gave an expansive but oddly unreal smile and shouted his good morning with blood-curdling cordiality. They then withdrew to the passage outside to hold a conversation.

In the interval English Poetry books were opened and the class began to repeat lines. They had been given the whole of a poem called *Lament for the Death of Eoghan Roe* to learn. It was very patriotic and dealt with the poisoning of Eoghan Roe by the accursed English, and the lines were very long, which made it difficult. The class hated the English for poisoning Eoghan Roe because the lines about it were so long. What made it worse was that it was the sort of poem Mr O'Rourke loved. If it was *Hail to thee blithe spirit* he wouldn't be so fond of it. But he could declaim this one for them in a rich, fruity, provincial baritone and would knock hell out of anybody who had not learned it.

Peter had not learned it. Realising how few were the minutes left to him he ran his eyes over stanza after stanza and began to murmur fragments from each in hopeless desperation. Swaine, who sat beside him, said, 'Do you know this?'

'No,' Peter said, 'I haven't even looked at it.'

'My God!' Swaine breathed in horror. 'You'll be mangled!'

'You could give us a prompt.'

'And be torn limb from limb,' said Swaine with conviction; 'not likely.'

Peter closed his eyes. It was all his mother's fault. He had meant to come to school early to learn it but the row delayed him. It had been about his father's boots. After breakfast she had found that there were holes in both his shoes. She held them up to the light which was on because the November morning was wet and dark.

'Merciful God, child,' she exclaimed, 'there's not a sole in your shoes. You can't go out in those.'

He was anxious to put them on and get out quickly, but everybody was in bad humour. He didn't dare to say anything. His sister was clearing part of the table and his brother Joseph, who worked, was rooting in drawers and corners and growling to everybody:

'Where the hell is the bicycle pump? You can't leave a thing out of your hand in this house.'

'I can wear my sandals,' Peter suggested.

'And it spilling out of the heavens—don't be daft, child.' Then she said, 'What am I to do at all?'

For a moment he hoped he might be kept at home. But his mother told his sister to root among the old boots in the press. Millie went out into the passage. On her way she trod on the cat, which meowed in intense agony.

'Blazes,' said his sister, 'that bloody cat.'

She came in with an old pair of his father's boots, and he was made try them on. They were too big.

'I'm not going out in those,' he said, 'I couldn't walk in them.'

But his mother and sister said they looked lovely. They went into unconvincing ecstasies. They looked perfect they said, each backing up the other. No one would notice.

'They look foolish,' he insisted, 'I won't wear them.'

'You'll do what you're told,' his sister said. They were all older than he and each in turn bullied him. But the idea of being made to look ridiculous nerved him.

'I won't wear them,' he persisted. At that moment his brother Tom came in and Millie said quickly:

'Tom, speak to Peter—he's giving cheek to Mammy.'

Tom was very fond of animals. 'I heard the cat,' he began, looking threateningly at Peter who sometimes teased it. 'What were you doing to it?'

'Nothing,' Peter answered, 'Millie walked on it.' He tried to say something about the boots but the three of them told him to shut up and get to school. He could stand up to the others but he was afraid of Tom. So he had flopped along in the rain feeling miserable and hating it because people would be sure to know they were not his own boots.

The door opened and Mr O'Rourke came in. He was a huge man in tweeds. He was a fluent speaker of Irish and wore the gold fáinne in the lapel of his jacket. Both his wrists were covered with matted black hair.

'*Filíocht*,' he roared and drew a leather from his hip pocket.

Then he shouted, '*Dún do leabhar*,' and hit the front desk a ferocious crack with the leather. Mr O'Rourke was an ardent Gael who gave his orders in Irish—even during English class. Someone had passed him up a poetry book and the rest closed theirs or turned them face downwards on their desks.

Mr O'Rourke, his eyes glaring terribly at the ceiling, from which plaster would fall in fine dust when the third year students overhead tramped in or out, began to declaim:

'Did they dare, did they dare, to slay Eoghan Roe O'Neill?
Yes they slew with poison him they feared to meet with steel.'

He clenched his powerful fists and held them up rigidly before his chest.

'May God wither up their hearts, may their blood cease to
flow!
May they walk in living death who poisoned Eoghan Roe!'

Then quite suddenly, in a business-like tone, he said, 'You—Daly.'

'Me, sir?' said Daly, playing for time.

'Yes, you fool,' thundered Mr O'Rourke. 'You.'

Daly rose and repeated the first four lines. When he was half-way through the second stanza Mr O'Rourke bawled, 'Clancy.' Clancy rose and began to recite. They stood up and sat down as Mr O'Rourke commanded while he paced up and down the aisles between the seats. Twice he passed close to Peter. He stood for some time by Peter's desk bawling out names. The end of his tweed jacket lay hypnotically along the edge of Peter's desk. Cummins stumbled over the fourth verse and dried up completely.

'Line,' Mr O'Rourke bawled. Cummins, calmly pale, left his desk and stepped out to the side of the class. Two more were sent out. Mr O'Rourke walked up and down once more and stood with his back to Peter. Looking at the desk at the very back he suddenly bawled, 'Farrell.'

Peter's heart jerked. He rose to his feet. The back was still towards him. He looked at it, a great mountain of tweed, with a frayed collar over which the thick neck bulged in folds. He could see the antennae of hair which sprouted from Mr O'Rourke's ears and could smell the chalk-and-ink schoolmaster's smell of him. It was a trick of Mr O'Rourke's to stand with his back to you and then call your name. It made the shock more unnerving. Peter gulped and was silent.

'Wail . . .' prompted Mr O'Rourke.

Peter said, 'Wail . . .'

Mr O'Rourke paced up to the head of the class once more.

'Wail—wail him through the island,' he said as he walked. Then he turned around suddenly and said, 'Well, go on.'

'Wail, wail him through the island,' Peter said once more and stopped.

'Weep,' hinted Mr O'Rourke.

He regarded Peter closely, his eyes narrowing.

'Weep,' said Peter, ransacking the darkness of his mind but finding only emptiness.

'Weep, weep, weep,' Mr O'Rourke said, his voice rising.

Peter chanced his arm. He said, 'Wail, wail him through the island weep, weep, weep.'

Mr O'Rourke stood up straight. His face conveyed at once shock, surprise, pain.

'Get out to the line,' he roared, 'you thick lazy good-for-nothing bloody imbecile. Tell him what it is, Clancy.' Clancy dithered for a moment, closed his eyes and said:

'Sir—Wail, wail him through the island, weep, weep, for our
  pride
Would that on the battle field our gallant chief had died.'

Mr O'Rourke nodded with dangerous benevolence. As Peter shuffled to the line the boots caught the iron upright of the desk and made a great clamour. Mr O'Rourke gave him a cut with the leather across the behind. 'Did you look at this, Farrell?' he asked.

Peter hesitated and said uncertainly, 'No, sir.'

'It wasn't worth your while, I suppose?'

'No, sir. I hadn't time, sir.'

Just then the clock struck the hour. The class rose. Mr O'Rourke put the leather under his left armpit and crossed himself. '*In ainm an Athar*,' he began. While they recited the *Hail Mary* Peter, unable to pray, stared at the leafless rain-soaked trees in the square and the serried rows of pale, prayerful faces. They sat down.

Mr O'Rourke turned to the class.

'Farrell hadn't time,' he announced pleasantly. Then he looked thunderously again at Peter. 'If it was an English penny dreadful about Public Schools or London crime you'd find time to read it quick enough, but when it's about the poor hunted martyrs and felons of your own unfortunate country by a patriot like Davis you've no time for it. You've the makings of a fine little Britisher.' With genuine pathos Mr O'Rourke then recited:

'The weapon of the Sassenach met him on his way
And he died at Cloch Uachter upon St Leonard's day.'

'That was the dear dying in any case, but if he died for the likes of you, Farrell, it was the dear bitter dying, no mistake about it.'

Peter said, 'I meant to learn it.'

'Hold out your hand. If I can't preach respect for the patriot dead into you, then honest to my stockings I'll beat respect into you. Hand.'

Peter held it out. He pulled his coat sleeve down over his wrist. The leather came down six times with a resounding impact. He tried to keep his thumb out of the way because if it hit you on the thumb it stung unbearably. But after four heavy slaps the hand began to curl of its own accord, curl and cripple like a little piece of tinfoil in a fire, until the thumb lay powerless across the palm, and the pain burned in his chest and constricted every muscle. But worse than the pain was the fear that he would cry. He was turning away when Mr O'Rourke said:

'Just a moment, Farrell. I haven't finished.'

Mr O'Rourke gently took the fingers of Peter's hand, smoothing them out as he drew them once more into position. 'To teach you I'll take no defiance,' he said in a friendly tone and raised the leather. Peter tried to hold his crippled hand steady.

He could not see properly going back to his desk and again the boots deceived him and he tripped and fell. As he picked himself up Mr O'Rourke, about to help him with another, though gentler, tap of the leather, stopped and exclaimed:

'Merciful God, child, where did you pick up the boots?'

The rest looked with curiosity. Clancy, who had twice excelled himself, tittered. Mr O'Rourke said, 'And what's the funny joke, Clancy?'

'Nothing, sir.'

'Soft as a woman's was your voice, O'Neill, bright was your eye,' recited Mr O'Rourke, in a voice as soft as a woman's, brightness in his eyes. 'Continue, Clancy.' But Clancy, the wind taken out of his sails, missed and went out to join the other three. Peter put his head on the desk, his raw hands tightly under his armpits, and nursed his wounds while the leather thudded patriotism and literature into the other, unmurmuring, four.

Swaine said nothing for a time. Now and then he glanced at Peter's face. He was staring straight at the book. His hands were tender, but the pain had ebbed away. Each still hid its rawness under a comfortably warm armpit.

'You got a heck of a hiding,' Swaine whispered at last. Peter said nothing.

'Ten is too much. He's not allowed to give you ten. If he gave me ten I'd bring my father up to him.'

Swaine was small, but his face was large and bony and when he took off his glasses sometimes to wipe them there was a small red weal on the bridge of his nose. Peter grunted and Swaine changed the subject.

'Tell us who owns the boots. They're not your own.'

'Yes they are,' Peter lied.

'Go on,' Swaine said, 'who owns them? Are they your brother's?'

'Shut up,' Peter menaced.

'Tell us,' Swaine persisted. 'I won't tell a soul. Honest.' He regarded Peter with sly curiosity. He whispered: 'I know they're not your own, but I wouldn't tell it. We sit beside one another. We're pals. You can tell me.'

'Curiosity killed the cat . . .' Peter said.

Swaine had the answer to that. With a sly grin he rejoined, 'Information made him fat.'

'If you must know,' Peter said, growing tired, 'they're my father's. And if you tell anyone I'll break you up in little pieces. You just try breathing a word.'

Swaine sat back, satisfied.

Mr O'Rourke was saying that the English used treachery when they poisoned Eoghan Roe. But what could be expected of the English except treachery?

'Hoof of the horse,' he quoted, 'horn of a bull, smile of a Saxon.' Three perils. Oliver Cromwell read his Bible while he quartered infants at their mothers' breasts. People said let's forget all that. But we couldn't begin to forget it until we had our full freedom. Our own tongue, the sweet Gaelic *teanga*, must be restored once more as the spoken language of our race. It was the duty of all to study and work towards that end.

'And those of us who haven't time must be shown how to find the time. Isn't that a fact, Farrell?' he said. The class laughed.

But the clock struck and Mr O'Rourke put the lament regretfully aside.

'Mathematics,' he announced, '*Céimseachta.*'

He had hoped it would continue to rain during lunchtime so that they could stay in the classroom. But when the automatic bell clanged loudly and Mr O'Rourke opened the frosted window to look out, it had stopped. They trooped down the stairs. They pushed and jostled one another. Peter kept his hand for safety on the banisters. Going down the stairs made the boots seem larger. He made straight for the urinal and stayed there until the old brother whose duty it was for obscure moral reasons to patrol the place had passed through twice. The second time he said to him: 'My goodness, boy, go out into the fresh air with your playmates. Shoo—boy—shoo,' and stared at Peter's retreating back with perplexity and suspicion.

Dillon came over as he was unwrapping his lunch and said, 'Did they dare, did they dare to slay Eoghan Roe O'Neill.'

'Oh, shut up,' Peter said.

Dillon linked his arm and said, 'You got an awful packet.' Then with genuine admiration he added: 'You took it super. He aimed for your wrist, too. Not a peek. You were wizard. Cripes. When I saw him getting ready for the last four I was praying you wouldn't cry.'

'I never cried yet,' Peter asserted.

'I know, but he lammed his hardest. You shouldn't have said you hadn't time.'

'He wouldn't make me cry,' Peter said grimly, 'not if he got up at four o'clock in the morning to try it.'

O'Rourke had lammed him all right, but there was no use trying to do anything about it. If he told his father and mother they would say he richly deserved it. It was his mother should have been lammed and not he.

'You were super, anyway,' Dillon said warmly. They walked arm in arm. 'The Irish,' he added sagaciously, 'are an unfortunate bloody race. The father often says so.'

'Don't tell me,' Peter said with feeling.

'I mean, look at us. First Cromwell knocks hell out of us for being too Irish and then Rorky slaughters us for not being Irish enough.'

It was true. It was a pity they couldn't make up their minds.

Peter felt the comfort of Dillon's friendly arm. 'The boots are my father's,' he confided suddenly. 'My own had holes.' That made him feel better.

'What are you worrying about?' Dillon said, reassuringly. 'They look all right to me.'

When they were passing the row of water taps with the chained drinking vessels a voice cried. 'There's Farrell now.' A piece of crust hit Peter on the nose.

'Caesar sends his legate,' Dillon murmured. They gathered round. Clancy said, 'Hey, boys, Farrell is wearing someone else's boots.'

'Who lifted you into them?'

'Wait now,' said Clancy, 'let's see him walk. Go on—walk, Farrell.'

Peter backed slowly towards the wall. He backed slowly until he felt the ridge of a downpipe hard against his back. Dillon came with him. 'Lay off, Clancy,' Dillon said. Swaine was there too. He was smiling, a small cat fat with information.

'Where did you get them, Farrell?'

'Pinched them.'

'Found them in an ashbin.'

'Make him walk,' Clancy insisted; 'let's see you walk, Farrell.'

'They're my own,' Peter said; 'they're a bit big—that's all.'

'Come on, Farrell—tell us whose they are.'

The grins grew wider.

Clancy said, 'They're his father's.'

'No, they're not,' Peter denied quickly.

'Yes, they are. He told Swaine. Didn't he, Swaine? He told you they were his father's.'

Swaine's grin froze. Peter fixed him with terrible eyes.

'Well, didn't he, Swaine? Go on, tell the chaps what he told you. Didn't he say they were his father's?'

Swaine edged backwards. 'That's right,' he said, 'he did.'

'Hey, you chaps,' Clancy said, impatiently, 'let's make him walk. I vote . . .'

At that moment Peter, with a cry, sprang on Swaine. His fist smashed the glasses on Swaine's face. As they rolled over on the muddy ground, Swaine's nails tore his cheek. Peter saw the white terrified face under him. He beat at it in frenzy until it became covered with mud and blood.

'Cripes,' Clancy said in terror, 'look at Swaine's glasses. Haul him off, lads.' They pulled him away and he lashed out at them with feet and hands. He lashed out awkwardly with the big boots which had caused the trouble. Swaine's nose and lips were bleeding so they took him over to the water tap and washed him. Dillon, who stood alone with Peter, brushed his clothes as best he could and fixed his collar and tie.

'You broke his glasses,' he said. 'There'll be a proper rucky if old Quinny sees him after lunch.'

'I don't care about Quinny.'

'I do then,' Dillon said fervently. 'He'll quarter us all in our mothers' arms.'

They sat with their arms folded while Brother Quinlan, in the high chair at the head of the class, gave religious instruction. Swaine kept his bruised face lowered. Without the glasses it had a bald, maimed look, as though his eyebrows, or a nose, or an eye, were missing. They had exchanged no words since the fight. Peter was aware of the boots. They were a defeat, something to be ashamed of. His mother only thought they would keep out the rain. She didn't understand that it would be better to have wet feet. People did not laugh at you because your feet were wet.

Brother Quinlan was speaking of our relationship to one another, of the boy to his neighbour and of the boy to his God. We communicated with one another, he said, by looks, gestures, speech. But these were surface contacts. They conveyed little of what went on in the mind, and nothing at all of the individual soul. Inside us, the greatest and the humblest of us, a whole world was locked. Even if we tried we could convey nothing of that interior world, that life which was nourished, as the poet had said, within the brain. In our interior life we stood without friend or ally—alone. In the darkness and silence of that interior and eternal world the immortal soul and its God were at all times face to face. No one else could peer into another's soul, neither our teacher, nor our father or mother, nor even our best friend. But God saw all. Every stray little thought which moved in that inaccessible world was as plain to Him as if it were thrown across the bright screen of a cinema. That was why we must be as careful to discipline our thoughts as our actions. Custody of the eyes, custody of the ears, but above all else custody . . .

Brother Quinlan let the sentence trail away and fixed his eyes on Swaine.

'You—boy,' he said in a voice which struggled to be patient, 'what are you doing with that handkerchief?'

Swaine's nose had started to bleed again. He said nothing. 'Stand up, boy,' Brother Quinlan commanded. He had glasses himself, which he wore during class on the tip of his nose. He was a big man too, and his head was bald in front, which made his large forehead appear even more massive. He stared over the glasses at Swaine.

'Come up here,' he said, screwing up his eyes, the fact that something was amiss with Swaine's face dawning gradually on him. Swaine came up to him, looking woebegone, still dabbing his nose with the handkerchief. Brother Quinlan contemplated the battered face for some time. He turned to the class.

'Whose handiwork is this?' he asked quietly. 'Stand up, the boy responsible for this.'

For a while nobody stirred. There was an uneasy stillness. Poker faces looked at the desks in front of them and waited. Peter looked around and saw Dillon gazing at him hopefully. After an unbearable moment feet shuffled and Peter stood up.

'I am, sir,' he said.

Brother Quinlan told Clancy to take Swaine out to the yard to bathe his nose. Then he spoke to the class about violence and what was worse, violence to a boy weaker than oneself. That was the resort of the bully and the scoundrel—physical violence—The Fist. At this Brother Quinlan held up his large bunched fist so that all might see it. Then with the other hand he indicated the picture of the Sacred Heart. Charity and Forbearance, he said, not vengeance and intolerance, those were qualities most dear to Our Blessed Lord.

'Are you not ashamed of yourself, Farrell? Do you think what you have done is a heroic or a creditable thing?'

'No, sir.'

'Then why did you do it, boy?'

Peter made no answer. It was no use making an answer. It was no use saying Swaine had squealed about the boots being his father's. Swaine's face was badly battered. But deep inside him Peter felt battered too. Brother Quinlan couldn't see your soul. He could see Swaine's face, though, when he fixed his glasses on him properly. Brother Quinlan took his silence for defiance.

'A blackguardly affair,' he pronounced. 'A low, cowardly assault. Hold out your hand.'

Peter hesitated. There was a limit. He hadn't meant not to learn the poetry and it wasn't his fault about the boots.

'He's been licked already, sir,' Dillon said. 'Mr O'Rourke gave him ten.'

'Mr O'Rourke is a discerning man,' said Brother Quinlan, 'but he doesn't seem to have given him half enough. Think of the state of that poor boy who has just gone out.'

Peter could think of nothing to say. He tried hard but there were no words there. Reluctantly he presented his hand. It was mudstained. Brother Quinlan looked at it with distaste. Then he proceeded to beat hell out of him, and charity and forbearance into him, in the same way as Mr O'Rourke earlier had hammered in patriotism and respect for Irish History.

It was raining again when he was going home. Usually there were three or four to go home with him, but this afternoon he went alone. He did not want them with him. He passed some shops and walked by the first small suburban gardens, with their sodden gravel paths and dripping gates. On the canal bridge a boy passed him pushing fuel in a pram. His feet were bare. The mud had splashed upwards in thick streaks to his knees. Peter kept his left hand under his coat. There was a blister on the ball of the thumb which ached now like a burn. Brother Quinlan did that. He probably didn't aim to hit the thumb as Mr O'Rourke always did, but his sight was so bad he had a rotten shot. The boots had got looser than they were earlier. He realised this when he saw Clancy with three or four others passing on the other side of the road. When Clancy waved and called to him, he backed automatically until he felt the parapet against his back.

'Hey, Farrell,' they called. Then one of them, his head forward, his behind stuck out, began to waddle with grotesque movements up the road. The rest yelled to call Peter's attention. They indicated the mime. Come back if you like, they shouted. Peter waited until they had gone. Then he turned moodily down the bank of the canal. He walked with a stiff ungainly dignity, his mind not yet quite made up. Under the bridge the water was deep and narrow, and a raw wind which moaned in the high arch whipped coldly at his face. It might rain tomorrow and his shoes wouldn't be mended. If his mother thought the boots were all right God knows when his shoes would be mended. After a moment of indecision he took off the boots and dropped them, first one— and then the other—into the water.

There would be hell to pay when he came home without them. But there would be hell to pay anyway when Swaine's father sent around the note to say he had broken young Swaine's glasses. Like the time he broke the Cassidys' window. Half regretfully he stared at the silty water. He could see his father rising from the table to reach for the belt which hung behind the door. The outlook was frightening; but it was better to walk in your bare feet. It was better to walk without shoes and barefooted than to walk without dignity. He took off his stockings and stuffed them into his pocket. His heart sank as he felt the cold wet mud of the path on his bare feet.

SISTER IMELDA

Edna O'Brien

Edna O'Brien (1932–) has been described as one of Ireland's most successful writers—The Mail on Sunday *recently referred to her as having 'the soul of Molly Bloom and the gifts of Virginia Woolf'. Like so many of the other contributors to this collection, she has drawn heavily on her childhood and upbringing as a source of inspiration for her best-selling novels and short stories. Born on a farm in Tuamgraney in County Clare to a 'non-book owning family', she was deeply influenced by the male-dominated world of an Irish farm and a rigorous Roman Catholic training. She went first to the National School at Scarriff and then the Convent of Mercy at Loughrea in County Galway. Later, she trained as a pharmacist, graduating as a Licentiate of the Pharmaceutical Society of Ireland, but already her heart was set on becoming a writer.*

She achieved immediate fame with her first novel, The Country Girls *(1960), about two girls who, like their author, escape from the strict discipline of convent life to more exciting times in Dublin. She received a £50 advance for the book—which she promptly spent—but the novel was an instant success, being published in twelve countries (except Ireland where it was banned for 'smearing Irish womanhood'), and at a stroke established her as a formidable talent. Her output since has resulted in a number of collections of short stories as well as a series of critically acclaimed novels, including* House of Splendid Isolation *(1995), which was awarded the European Prize for Literature by the European Association for the Arts, and* Down by the River *(1996), another controversial story of sexual hypocrisy set in Ireland.*

Recently Edna O'Brien wrote that the 'enclosed, fanatic and fervent world of her childhood was a writer's dream' and this has certainly been reflected in several of her novels and short stories. Notable among these are A Pagan Place *(1970), about the childhood and early adolescence of a nun living in rural Ireland during the last war, of which the critic John Berger said that it 'constitutes a reconstruction of childhood experience which so far as I know is unique in the English language', and 'Come Into the Drawing Room, Doris' (also known as 'Irish Revel') about a young girl attending her first party at the age of 17. 'Sister Imelda', the story that follows, is full of the author's special insight and understanding of the life of young girls in a convent school.*

*   *   *

Sister Imelda did not take classes on her first day back in the convent but we spotted her in the grounds after the evening Rosary. Excitement and curiosity impelled us to follow her and try and see what she looked like, but she thwarted us by walking with head bent and eyelids down. All we could be certain of, was that she was tall and limber and that she prayed while she walked. No looking at nature for her, or no curiosity about seventy boarders in gaberdine coats and black shoes and stockings. We might just as well have been crows, so impervious was she to our stares and to abortive attempts at trying to say 'Hello Sister'.

We had returned from our long summer holiday and we were all wretched. The convent with its high stone wall and green iron gates enfolding us again, seeming more of a prison than ever— for after our spell in the outside world we all felt very much older and more sophisticated, and my friend Baba and I were dreaming of our final escape, which would be in a year. And so, on that damp autumn evening when I saw the chrysanthemums and saw the new nun intent on prayer I pitied her and thought how alone she must be, cut off from her friends and conversation with only God as her intangible spouse.

The next day she came into our classroom to take Geometry.

Her pale, slightly long face I saw as formidable but her eyes were different, being blue-black and full of verve. Her lips were very purple as if she had put puce pencil on them. They were the lips of a woman who might sing in cabaret and unconsciously she had formed the habit of turning them inwards as if she too was aware of their provocativeness. She had spent the last four years—the same span that Baba and I had spent in the convent—at the university in Dublin where she studied languages. We couldn't understand how she had resisted the temptations of the hectic world and willingly come back to this. Her spell in the outside world made her different from the other nuns, there was more bounce in her walk, more excitement in the way she tackled teaching, reminding us that it was the most important thing in the world as she uttered the phrase 'Praise be the Incarnate World'. She began each day's class by reading from Cardinal Newman who was a favourite of hers. She read how God dwelt in light unapproachable, and how with Him there was neither change nor shadow of alteration. It was amazing how her looks changed. Some days when her eyes were flashing she looked almost profane and made me wonder what events inside the precincts of the convent caused her to be suddenly so excited. She might have been a girl going to a dance except for her habit.

'Hasn't she wonderful eyes,' I said to Baba. That particular day they were like blackberries, large and soft and shiny.

'Something wrong in her upstairs department,' Baba said and added that with make-up Imelda would be a cinch.

'Still she has a vocation!' I said and even aired the idiotic view that I might have one. At certain moments it did seem enticing to become a nun, to lead a life unspotted by sin, never to have to have babies and to wear a ring that singled one out as the Bride of Christ. But there was the other side to it, the silence, the gravity of it, having to get up two or three times a night to pray and above all never having the opportunity of leaving the confines of the place except for the funeral of one's parents. For us boarders it was torture but for the nuns it was nothing short of doom. Also we could complain to each other and we did, food being the source of the greatest grumbles. Lunch was either bacon and cabbage or a peculiar stringy meat followed by tapioca pudding; tea consisted of bread dolloped with lard and occasionally, as a treat, fairly green rhubarb jam, which did not have enough sugar. Through the long curtainless windows we saw the conifer trees and a sky that was scarcely ever without the promise of rain or a downpour.

She was a right lunatic then, Baba said, having gone to university for four years and willingly come back to incarceration, to poverty, chastity and obedience. We concocted scenes of agony in some Dublin hostel, while a boy, or even a young man, stood beneath her bedroom window throwing up chunks of clay or whistles or a supplication. In our version of it he was slightly older than her, and possibly a medical student since medical students had a knack with women, because of studying diagrams and skeletons. His advances, like those of a sudden storm would intermittently rise and overwhelm her and the memory of these sudden flaying advances of his, would haunt her until she died, and if ever she contracted fever these secrets would out. It was also rumoured that she possessed a fierce temper and that while a postulant she had hit a girl so badly with her leather strap that the girl had to be put to bed because of wounds. Yet another black mark against Sister Imelda was that her brother Ambrose had been sued by a nurse for breach of promise.

That first morning when she came into our classroom and modestly introduced herself I had no idea how terribly she would infiltrate my life, how in time she would be not just one of those teachers or nuns, but rather a special one almost like a ghost who passed the boundaries of common exchange and who crept inside one, devouring so much of one's thoughts, so much of one's passion, invading the place that was called one's heart. She talked in a low voice as if she did not want her words to go beyond the bounds of the wall and constantly she stressed the value of work both to enlarge the mind and discipline the thought. One of her eyelids was red and swollen as if she was getting a sty. I reckoned that she over-mortified herself by not eating at all. I saw in her some terrible premonition of sacrifice which I would have to emulate. Then in direct contrast she absently held the stick of chalk between her first and second fingers the very same as if it were a cigarette and Baba whispered to me that she might have been a smoker when in Dublin. Sister Imelda looked down sharply at me and said what was the secret and would I like to share it since it seemed so comical. I said 'Nothing Sister, nothing', and her dark eyes yielded such vehemence that I prayed she would never have occasion to punish me.

November came and the tiled walls of the recreation hall oozed moisture and gloom. Most girls had sore throats and were told to suffer this inconvenience to mortify themselves in order to lend a glorious hand in that communion of spirit that linked the living with the dead. It was the month of the Suffering Souls in Purgatory, and as we heard of their twofold agony, the yearning for Christ and the ferocity of the leaping flames that burnt and charred their poor limbs, we were asked to make acts of mortification. Some girls gave up jam or sweets and some gave up talking and so in recreation time they were like dummies making signs with thumb and finger to merely say 'How are you?' Baba said that saner people were locked in the lunatic asylum which was only a mile away. We saw them in the grounds, pacing back and forth, with their mouths agape and dribble coming out of them, like icicles. Among our many fears was that one of those lunatics would break out and head straight for the convent and assault some of the girls.

Yet in the thick of all these dreads I found myself becoming dreadfully happy. I had met Sister Imelda outside of class a few times and I felt that there was an attachment between us. Once it was in the grounds when she did a reckless thing. She broke off a chrysanthemum and offered it to me to smell. It had no smell or at least only something faint that suggested autumn and feeling this to be the case herself she said it was not a gardenia was it. Another time we met in the chapel porch and as she drew her shawl more tightly around her body I felt how human she was, and prey to the cold.

In the classroom things were not so congenial between us. Geometry was my worst subject and indeed a total mystery to me. She had not taken more than four classes when she realised this and threw a duster at me in a rage. A few girls gasped as she asked me to stand up and make a spectacle of myself. Her face had reddened and presently she took out her handkerchief and patted the eye which was red and swollen. I not only felt a fool but I felt in imminent danger of sneezing as I inhaled the smell of chalk that had fallen onto my gym-frock. Suddenly she fled from the room leaving us ten minutes free until the next class. Some girls said it was a disgrace, said I should write home and say I had been assaulted. Others welcomed the few minutes in which to gabble. All I wanted was to run after her and say that I was sorry to have caused her such distemper because I knew dimly that it was as much to do with liking as it was with dislike. In me then there came a sort of speechless tenderness for her and I might have known that I was stirred.

'We could get her de-frocked,' Baba said and elbowed me in God's name to sit down.

That evening at Benediction I had the most overwhelming surprise. It was a particularly happy evening with the choir nuns in full soaring form and the rows of candles like so many little ladders to the golden chalice that glittered all the more because of the beams of fitful flame. I was full of tears when I discovered a new holy picture had been put in my prayer book and before I dared look on the back to see who had given it to me I felt and guessed that this was no ordinary picture from an ordinary girl friend, that this was a talisman and a peace offering from Sister Imelda. It was a pale-blue picture so pale that it was almost grey like the down of a pigeon and it showed a mother looking down on the infant child. On the back, in her beautiful ornate handwriting, she had written a verse:

> Trust Him when dark doubts assail thee,
> Trust Him when thy faith is small,
> Trust Him when to simply trust Him
> Seems the hardest thing of all.

This was her atonement. To think that she had located the compartment in the chapel where I kept my prayer book and to think that she had been so naked as to write in it and give me a chance to boast about it and to show it to other girls. When I thanked her next day she bowed but did not speak. Mostly the nuns were on silence and only permitted to talk during class.

In no time I had received another present, a little miniature prayer book with a leather cover and gold edging. The prayers were in French and the lettering so minute it was as if a tiny insect had fashioned them. Soon I was publicly known as her pet. I opened doors for her, raised the blackboard two pegs higher (she was taller than other nuns) and handed out the exercise books which she had corrected. Now, in the margins of my geometry propositions I would find 'Good' or 'Excellent', when in the past she used to splash 'Disgraceful'. Baba said it was foul to be a nun's pet and that any girl who sucked up to a nun could not be trusted.

About a month later Sister Imelda asked me to carry her books up four flights of stairs to the cookery kitchen. She taught cookery to a junior class. As she walked ahead of me I thought how supple she was and how thoroughbred and when she paused on the landing to look out through the long curtainless window, I too paused. Down below two women in suede boots were chatting and smoking as they moved down the street with shopping baskets. Nearby a lay nun was down on her knees scrubbing the granite steps and the cold air was full of the smell of raw Jeyes Fluid. There was a potted plant on the landing and Sister Imelda put her fingers in the earth and went 'tch tch tch', saying it needed water. I said I would water it later on. I was happy in my prison then, happy to be near her, happy to walk behind her as she twirled her beads and bowed to the servile nun. I no longer cried for my mother, no longer counted the days on a pocket calendar, until the Christmas holidays.

'Come back at five,' she said as she stood on the threshold of the cookery kitchen door. The girls all in white overalls were arraigned around the long wooden table waiting for her. It was as if every girl was in love with her. Because, as she entered, their faces broke into smiles and in different tones of audacity they said her name. She must have liked cookery class because she beamed and called to someone, anyone, to get up a blazing fire. Then she went across to the cast-iron stove and spat on it to test its temperature. It was hot because her spit rose up and sizzled.

When I got back later she was sitting on the edge of the table swaying her legs. There was something reckless about her pose, something defiant. It seemed as if any minute she would take out a cigarette case, snap it open and then archly offer me one. The wonderful smell of baking made me realise how hungry I was, but far more so, it brought back to me my own home, my mother testing orange cakes with a knitting needle and letting me lick the line of half-baked dough down the length of the needle. I wondered if she had supplanted my mother and I hoped not, because I had aimed to outstep my original world and take my place in a new and hallowed one.

'I bet you have a sweet tooth,' she said and then she got up, crossed the kitchen and from under a wonderful shining silver cloche she produced two jam tarts with a criss-cross design on them, where the pastry was latticed over the dark jam. They were still warm.

'What will I do with them?' I asked.

'Eat them, you goose,' she said and she watched me eat as if she herself derived some peculiar pleasure from it whereas I was embarrassed about the pastry crumbling and the bits of blackberry jam staining the lips. She was amused. It was one of the most awkward yet thrilling moments I had lived, and inherent in the pleasure was the terrible sense of danger. Had we been caught she, no doubt, would have to make massive sacrifice. I looked at her and thought how peerless and how brave and I wondered if she felt hungry. She had a white overall over her black habit and this made her warmer, freer, and caused me to think of the happiness that would be ours, the *laissez-faire* if we were away from the convent in an ordinary kitchen doing something easy and customary. But we weren't. It was clear to me then that my version of pleasure was inextricable from pain and they existed side by side and were interdependent like the two forces of an electric current.

'Had you a friend when you were in Dublin at university?' I asked daringly.

'I shared a desk with a sister from Howth and stayed in the same hostel,' she said.

'But what about boys?' I thought, 'and what of your life now and do you long to go out into the world?' But could not say it.

We knew something about the nuns' routine. It was rumoured that they wore itchy, wool underwear, ate dry bread for breakfast, rarely had meat, cakes or dainties, kept certain hours of strict silence with each other, as well as constant vigil on their thoughts; so that if their minds wandered to the subject of food or pleasure they would quickly revert to thoughts of God and their eternal souls. They slept on hard beds with no sheets and hairy blankets. At four o'clock in the morning while we slept, each nun got out of bed, in her habit—which was also her death habit—and, chanting, they all flocked down the wooden stairs like ravens, to fling themselves on the tiled floor of the chapel. Each nun—even the Mother Superior—flung herself in total submission, saying prayers in Latin and offering up the moment to God. Then silently back to their cells for one more hour of rest. It was not difficult to imagine Sister Imelda face downwards, arms outstretched, prostrate on the tiled floor. I often heard their chanting when I wakened suddenly from a nightmare, because, although we slept in a different building, both adjoined, and if one wakened one often heard that monotonous Latin chanting, long before the birds began, long before our own bell summoned us to rise at six:

'Do you eat nice food?' I asked.

'Of course,' she said and smiled. She sometimes broke into an eager smile which she did much to conceal.

'Have you ever thought of what you will be?' she asked.

I shook my head. My design changed from day to day.

She looked at her man's silver pocket watch, closed the damper of the range and prepared to leave. She checked that all the wall presses were locked by running her hand over them.

'Sister,' I called, gathering enough courage at last. We must have some secret, something to join us together, 'What colour hair have you?'

We never saw the nuns' hair, or their eyebrows, or ears, as all that part was covered by a stiff, white guimp.

'You shouldn't ask such a thing,' she said, getting pink in the face, and then she turned back and whispered, 'I'll tell you on your last day here, provided your geometry has improved.'

She had scarcely gone when Baba, who had been lurking behind some pillar, stuck her head in the door and said 'Christ sake save me a bit.' She finished the second pastry, then went around looking in kitchen drawers. Because of everything being locked she found only some castor sugar in a china shaker. She ate a little and threw the remainder into the dying fire so that it flared up for a minute with a yellow spluttering flame. Baba showed her jealousy by putting it around the school that I was in the cookery kitchen every evening, gorging cakes with Sister Imelda and telling tales.

I did not speak to Sister Imelda again in private until the evening of our Christmas theatricals. She came to help us put on make-up and get into our stage clothes and fancy headgears. These clothes were kept in a trunk from one year to the next and though sumptuous and though strewn with braiding and gold they smelt of camphor. Yet as we donned them we felt different and as we sponged pancake make-up onto our faces we became saucy and emphasised these new guises by adding dark pencil to the eyes and making the lips bright orange. There was only one tube of lipstick and each girl clamoured for it. The evening's entertainment was to comprise scenes from Shakespeare and laughing sketches. I had been chosen to recite Mark Antony's lament over Caesar's body and for this I was to wear a purple toga, white knee-length socks and patent buckle shoes. The shoes were too big and I moved in them as if in clogs. She said to take them off, to go barefoot. I realised that I was getting nervous and that in an effort to memorise my speech the words were getting all askew and flying about in my head, like the separate pieces of a jigsaw puzzle. She sensed my panic and very slowly put her hand on my face and enjoined me to look at her. I looked into her eyes which seemed fathomless and saw that she was willing

me to be calm and obliging me to be master of my fears and I
little knew that one day she would have to do the same as regards
the swoop of my feelings for her. As we continued to stare I felt
myself becoming calm and the words were restored to me in
their right and fluent order. The lights were being lowered out
in the recreation hall and we knew now that all the nuns had
arrived, had settled themselves down and were eagerly awaiting
this annual hotchpotch of amateur entertainment. There was that
fearsome hush as the hall went dark and the few spotlights turned
on. She kissed her crucifix and I realised that she was saying a
prayer for me. Then she raised her arm as if depicting the stance
of a Greek goddess and walking onto the stage I was fired by
her ardour.

Baba could say that I bawled like a bloody bull but Sister
Imelda who stood in the wings said that temporarily she had felt
the streets of Rome and had seen the corpse of Caesar as I
delivered those poignant, distempered lines. When I came off stage
she put her arms around me and I was encased in a shower of silent
kisses. After we had taken down the decorations and put the
fancy clothes back in the trunk, I gave her two half-pound boxes
of chocolates—bought for me illicitly by one of the day-girls—
and she gave me a casket made from the insides of matchboxes
and covered over with gilt paint and gold dust. It was like holding
moths and finding their powder adhering to the fingers.

'What will you do on Christmas Day, Sister?' I said.

'I'll pray for you,' she said.

It was useless to say 'Will you have turkey?' or 'Will you
have plum pudding? or 'Will you loll in bed?', because I believed
that Christmas Day would be as bleak and deprived as any other
day in her life. Yet she was radiant as if such austerity was joyful.
Maybe she was basking in some secret realisation involving her
and me.

On the cold snowy afternoon three weeks later when we returned
from our holidays Sister Imelda came up to the dormitory to
welcome me back. All the other girls had gone down to the
recreation hall to do barn dances and I could hear someone

banging on the piano. I did not want to go down and clump around with sixty other girls, having nothing to look forward to, only tea and the Rosary and early bed. The beds were damp after our stay at home and when I put my hand between the sheets it was like feeling dew but did not have the freshness of outdoors. What depressed me further was that I had seen a mouse in one of the cupboards, seen its tail curl with terror as it slipped away into a crevice. If there was one mouse, there was God knows how many, and the cakes we hid in secret would not be safe. I was still unpacking as she came down the narrow passage between the rows of iron beds and I saw in her walk such agitation.

'Tut, tut, tut, you've curled your hair,' she said, offended.

Yes, the world outside was somehow declared in this perm and for a second I remembered the scalding pain as the trickles of ammonia dribbled down my forehead and then the joy as the hairdresser said that she would make me look like Movita, a Mexican star. Now suddenly that world and those aspirations seemed trite and I wanted to take a brush and straighten my hair and revert to the dark gawky sombre girl that I had been. I offered her iced queen cakes that my mother had made but she refused them and said she could only stay a second. She lent me a notebook of hers, which she had had as a pupil, and into which she had copied favourite quotations, some religious, some not. I read at random:

> Twice or thrice had I loved thee
> Before I knew thy face or name.
> So in a voice, so in a shapeless flame
> Angels affect us oft.

'Are you well?' I asked.

She looked pale. It may have been the day, which was wretched and grey with sleet, or it may have been the white bedspreads but she appeared to be ailing.

'I missed you,' she said.

'Me too,' I said.

At home, gorging, eating trifle at all hours, even for breakfast, having little ratafias to dip in cups of tea, fitting on new shoes and silk stockings, I wished that she could be with us, enjoying the fire and the freedom.

'You know it is not proper for us to be so friendly.'

'It's not wrong,' I said.

I dreaded that she might decide to turn away from me, that she might stamp on our love and might suddenly draw a curtain over it, a black crêpe curtain that would denote its death. I dreaded it and knew it was going to happen.

'We must not become attached,' she said and I could not say we already were, no more than I could remind her of the day of the revels and the intimacy between us. Convents were dungeons and no doubt about it.

From then on she treated me as less of a favourite. She said my name sharply in class and once she said if I must cough could I wait until class had finished. Baba was delighted as were the other girls because they were glad to see me receding in her eyes. Yet I knew that that crispness was part of her love because no matter how callously she looked at me, she would occasionally soften. Reading her notebook helped me and I copied out her quotations into my own book, trying as accurately as possible to imitate her handwriting.

But some little time later when she came to supervise our study one evening I got a smile from her as she sat on the rostrum looking down at us all. I continued to look up at her and by slight frowning indicated that I had a problem with my geometry. She beckoned to me lightly and I went up bringing my copybook and the pen. Standing close to her, and also because her guimp was crooked, I saw one of her eyebrows for the first time. She saw that I noticed it and said did that satisfy my curiosity. I said not really. She said what else did I want to see, her swan's neck perhaps, and I went scarlet. I was amazed that she would say such a thing in the hearing of other girls and then she said a worse thing, she said that G. K. Chesterton was very forgetful and had once put on his trousers backwards. She expected me to laugh. I was so close to her that a rumble in her stomach seemed to be taking place in my own and about this she also laughed. It occurred to me for one terrible moment that maybe she had decided to leave the convent to jump over the wall. Having done the theorem for me she marked it 'one hundred out of one hundred' and then asked if I had any other problems. My eyes filled with tears as I wanted her to realise that her recent coolness had wrought havoc with my nerves and my peace of mind.

'What is it?' she said.

I could cry or I could tremble to try and convey the emotion but I could not tell her. As if on cue, the Mother Superior came in, and saw this glaring intimacy and frowned as she approached the rostrum.

'Would you please go back to your desk,' she said, 'and in future kindly allow Sister Imelda to get on with her duties.'

I tiptoed back and sat with head down, bursting with fear and shame. Then she looked at a tray on which the milk cups were laid and finding one cup of milk untouched she asked which girl had not drunk her milk.

'Me, Sister,' I said, and I was called up to drink it and stand under the clock as a punishment. The milk was tepid and dusty and I thought of cows on the fairs days at home and the farmers hitting them as they slid and slithered over the muddy streets.

For weeks I tried to see my nun in private and I even lurked outside doors where I knew she was due, only to be rebuffed again and again. I suspected the Mother Superior had warned her against making a favourite of me. But I still clung to a belief that a bond existed between us and that her coldness and even some glares which I had received were a charade, a mask. I would wonder how she felt alone in bed and what way she slept and if she thought of me, or refusing to think of me if she dreamt of me as I did of her. She certainly got thinner because her nun's silver ring slipped easily and sometimes unavoidably off her marriage finger. It occurred to me that she was having a nervous breakdown.

One day in March the sun came out, the radiators were turned off, and though there was a lashing wind we were told that officially Spring had arrived, and that we could play games. We all trooped up to the games field and, to our surprise, saw that

Sister Imelda was officiating that day. The daffodils in the field tossed and turned and they were a very bright shocking yellow but they were not as fetching as the little timid snowdrops that trembled in the wind. We played rounders and when my turn came to hit the ball with the long wooden pound I crumbled and missed, fearing that the ball would hit me.

'Champ . . .' said Baba jeering.

After three such failures Sister Imelda said that if I liked I could sit and watch, and when I was sitting in the greenhouse swallowing my shame she came in and said that I must not give way to tears because humiliation was the greatest test of Christ's love or indeed *any* love.

'When you are a nun you will know that,' she said and instantly I made up my mind that I would be a nun and that though we might never be free to express our feelings we would be under the same roof, in the same cloister, in mental and spiritual conjunction all our lives.

'Is it very hard at first?' I said.

'It's awful,' she said and she slipped a little medal into my gym frock pocket. It was warm from being in her pocket and as I held it, I knew that once again we were near and that in fact we had never severed. Walking down from the playing field to our Sunday lunch of mutton and cabbage everyone chattered to Sister Imelda. The girls milled around her, linking her, trying to hold her hand, counting the various keys on her bunch of keys and asking impudent questions.

'Sister, did you ever ride a motor bicycle?'

'Sister, did you ever wear seamless stockings?'

'Sister, who's your favourite film star—male!'

'Sister, what's your favourite food?'

'Sister, if you had a wish what would it be?'

'Sister, what do you do when you want to scratch your head?'

Yes, she had ridden a motor bicycle, and she had worn silk stockings but they were seamed. She liked bananas best and if she had a wish it would be to go home for a few hours to see her parents, and her brother.

*

That afternoon as we walked through the town the sight of closed
shops with porter barrels outside and mongrel dogs did not dispel
my re-found ecstasy. The medal was in my pocket and every
other second I would touch it for confirmation. Baba saw a Swiss
roll in a confectioner's window laid on a doily and dusted with
castor sugar and its appeal made her cry out with hunger, and
rail against being in a bloody reformatory, surrounded by drips
and mopes. On impulse she took her nail file out of her pocket
and dashed across to the window to see if she could cut the glass.
The prefect rushed up from the back of the line and asked Baba
if she wanted to be locked up.

'I am anyhow,' Baba said and sawed at one of her nails, to
maintain her independence and vent her spleen. Baba was the
only girl who could stand up to a prefect. When she felt like it
she dropped out of a walk, sat on a stone wall and waited until
we all came back. She said that if there was one thing more
boring than studying it was walking. She used to roll down her
stockings and examine her calves and say that she could see
varicose veins coming from this bloody daily walk. Her legs like
all our legs were black from the dye of the stockings and we
were forbidden to bathe because baths were immoral. We washed
each night in an enamel basin beside our beds. When girls
splashed cold water onto their chests they let out cries, though
this was forbidden.

After the walk we wrote home. We were allowed to write
home once a week; our letters were always censored. I told my
mother that I had made up my mind to be a nun, and asked if
she could send me bananas, when a batch arrived at our local
grocery shop. That evening, perhaps as I wrote to my mother on
the ruled white paper, a telegram arrived which said that Sister
Imelda's brother had been killed in a van, while on his way home
from a hurling match. The Mother Superior announced it, and
asked us to pray for his soul and write letters of sympathy to
Sister Imelda's parents. We all wrote identical letters, because
in our first year at school we had been given specimen letters
for various occasions, and we all referred back to our specimen
letter of sympathy.

Next day the town hire-car drove up to the convent and Sister Imelda, accompanied by another nun, went home for the funeral. She looked as white as a sheet with eyes swollen and she wore a heavy knitted shawl over her shoulders. Although she came back that night (I stayed awake to hear the car) we did not see her for a whole week, except to catch a glimpse of her back, in the chapel. When she resumed class she was peaky and distant, making no reference at all to her recent tragedy.

The day the bananas came I waited outside the door and gave her a bunch wrapped in tissue paper. Some were still a little green, and she said that Mother Superior would put them in the glasshouse to ripen. I felt that Sister Imelda would never taste them; they would be kept for a visiting priest or bishop.

'Oh Sister, I'm sorry about your brother,' I said, in a burst.

'It will come to us all, sooner or later,' Sister Imelda said dolefully.

I dared to touch her wrist to communicate my sadness. She went quickly, probably for fear of breaking down. At times she grew irritable and had a boil on her cheek. She missed some classes and was replaced in the cookery kitchen by a younger nun. She asked me to pray for her brother's soul and to avoid seeing her alone. Each time as she came down a corridor towards me I was obliged to turn the other way. Now, Baba or some other girl moved the blackboard two pegs higher and spread her shawl, when wet, over the radiator to dry.

I got 'flu and was put to bed. Sickness took the same bleak course, a cup of hot senna delivered in person by the head-nun who stood there while I drank it, tea at lunch-time with thin slices of brown bread (because it was just after the war food was still rationed, so the butter was mixed with lard and had white streaks running through it and a faintly rancid smell), hours of just lying there surveying the empty dormitory, the empty iron beds with white counterpanes on each one, and metal crucifixes laid on each white, frilled, pillow-slip. I knew that she would miss me and hoped that Baba would tell her where I was. I counted the number of tiles from the ceiling to the head of my bed, thought of my mother at home on the farm mixing hen food, thought of my father, losing his temper perhaps and stamping on the kitchen floor with nailed boots and I recalled the money owing for my school fees and hoped that Sister Imelda would never get to hear of it. During the Christmas holiday I had seen a bill sent by the head-nun to my father which said, 'Please remit this week without fail.' I hated being in bed causing extra trouble and therefore reminding the head-nun of the unpaid liability. We had no clock in the dormitory, so there was no way of guessing the time, but the hours dragged.

Marigold, one of the maids, came to take off the counterpanes at five and brought with her two gifts from Sister Imelda—an orange and a pencil sharpener. I kept the orange peel in my hand, smelling it, and planning how I would thank her. Thinking of her I fell into a feverish sleep and was wakened when the girls came to bed at ten and switched on the various ceiling lights.

At Easter Sister Imelda warned me not to give her chocolates so I got her a flashlamp instead and spare batteries. Pleased with such a useful gift (perhaps she read her letters in bed), she put her arms round me and allowed one cheek to adhere but not to make the sound of a kiss. It made up for the seven weeks of withdrawal, and as I drove down the convent drive with Baba she waved to me, as she had promised, from the window of her cell.

In the last term at school studying was intensive because of the examinations which loomed at the end of June. Like all the other nuns Sister Imelda thought only of these examinations. She crammed us with knowledge, lost her temper every other day and gritted her teeth whenever the blackboard was too greasy to take the imprint of the chalk. If ever I met her in the corridor she asked if I knew such and such a thing, and coming down from Sunday games she went over various questions with us. The fateful examination day arrived and we sat at single desks supervised by some strange woman from Dublin. Opening a locked trunk she took out the pink examination papers and distributed them around. Geometry was on the fourth day. When we came out from it, Sister Imelda was in the hall with all the answers, so that we could compare our answers with hers. Then she called me aside and we went up towards the cookery kitchen and sat on the stairs while she went over the paper with me, question for question. I knew that I had three right and two wrong, but did not tell her so.

'It is black,' she said then, rather suddenly. I thought she meant the dark light where we were sitting.

'It's cool though,' I said.

Summer had come, our white skins baked under the heavy uniform and dark violet pansies bloomed in the convent grounds. She looked well again and her pale skin was once more unblemished.

'My hair,' she whispered, 'is black.' And she told me how she had spent her last night before entering the convent. She had gone cycling with a boy and ridden for miles, and they'd lost their way up a mountain and she became afraid she would be so late home that she would sleep it out next morning. It was understood between us that I was going to enter the convent in September and that I could have a last fling too.

Two days later we prepared to go home. There were farewells and outlandish promises, and autograph books signed, and girls trudging up the recreation hall, their cases bursting open with clothes and books. Baba scattered biscuit crumbs in the dormitory for the mice, and stuffed all her prayer books under a mattress. Her father promised to collect us at four. I had arranged with Sister Imelda secretly that I would meet her in one of the summer houses around the walks, where we would spend our last half-hour together. I expected that she would tell me something of what my life as a postulant would be like. But Baba's father came an hour early. He had something urgent to do later and came at three instead. All I could do was ask Marigold to take a note to Sister Imelda.

> Remembrance is all I ask,
> But if remembrance should prove a task,
> Forget me.

I hated Baba, hated her busy father, hated the thought of my mother standing in the doorway in her good dress, welcoming me home at last. I would have become a nun that minute if I could.

I wrote to my nun that night and again next day and then every week for a month. Her letters were censored so I tried to convey my feelings indirectly. In one of her letters to me (they were allowed one letter a month) she said that she looked forward to seeing me in September. But by September Baba and I had left for the university in Dublin. I stopped writing to Sister Imelda then, reluctant to tell her that I no longer wished to be a nun.

In Dublin we enrolled at the college where she had surpassed herself. I saw her maiden name on a list, for having graduated with special honours, and for days was again sad and remorseful. I rushed out and bought batteries for the flashlamp I'd given her, and posted them without any note enclosed. No mention of my missing vocation, no mention of why I had stopped writing.

One Sunday about two years later Baba and I were going out to Howth on a bus. Baba had met some businessmen who played golf there and she had done a lot of scheming to get us invited out. The bus was packed, mostly mothers with babies and children on their way to Dollymount Strand. We drove along the coast road and saw the sea, bright green and glinting in the sun and because of the way the water was carved up into millions of little wavelets its surface seemed like an endless heap of dark green broken bottles. Near the shore the sand looked warm and was biscuit-coloured. We never swam or sunbathed, we never did anything that was good for us. Life was geared to work and to meeting men and yet one knew that mating could only but lead to one's being a mother and hawking obstreperous children out to the seaside on Sunday. 'They know not what they do' could surely be said of us.

We were very made up and even the conductor seemed to disapprove and snapped at having to give the change of ten shillings. For no reason at all I thought of our make-up rituals before the school play and how innocent it was in comparison

because now our skins were smothered beneath layers of it and
we never took it off at night. Thinking of the convent I suddenly
thought of Sister Imelda and then as if prey to a dream, I heard
the rustle of serge, smelt the Jeyes Fluid and the boiled cabbage
and saw her pale shocked face in the months after her brother
died. Then I looked around and saw her in earnest and at first
thought that I was imagining things. But no, she had got on
accompanied by another nun and they were settling themselves
in the back seat nearest the door. She looked older but she had
the same aloof quality and the same eyes and my heart began to
race with a mixture of excitement and dread. At first it raced
with a prodigal strength and then it began to falter and I thought
it was going to give out. My fear of her and my love came back
in one fell realisation. I would have gone through the window
except that it was not wide enough. The thing was how to escape
her. Baba gurgled with delight, stood up and in the most flagrant
way looked around to make sure that it was Imelda. She recognised the other nun as one with the nickname of Johnny who
taught piano lessons. Baba's first thought was revenge, as she
enumerated the punishments they had meted out to us and said
how nice it would be to go back and shock them and say 'Mud
in your eye, Sisters', or 'Get lost', or something worse. Baba
could not understand why I was quaking no more than she could
understand why I began to wipe off the lipstick. Above all I
knew that I could not confront them.

'You're going to have to,' Baba said.

'I can't,' I said.

It was not just my attire, it was the fact of never having written
and of my broken promise. Baba kept looking back and said they
weren't saying a word and that children were gawking at them.
It wasn't often that nuns travelled in buses and we speculated as
to where they might be going.

'They might be off to meet two fellows,' Baba said, and visual-
ised them in the golf club getting blotto and hoisting up their
skirts. For me it was no laughing matter. She came up with a
strategy and it was that as we approached our stop and the bus
was still moving I was to jump up and go down the aisle and

pass them without even looking. She said most likely they would not notice us as their eyes were lowered and they seemed to be praying.

'I can't run down the bus,' I said. There was a matter of shaking limbs and already a terrible vertigo.

'You're going to,' Baba said, and though insisting that I couldn't I had already begun to rehearse an apology. While doing this I kept blessing myself over and over again and Baba kept reminding me that there was only one more stop before ours. When the dreadful moment came I jumped up and put on my face what can only be called an apology of a smile. I followed Baba to the rear of the bus. But already they had gone. I saw the back of their two sable, identical figures with their veils being blown wildly about in the wind. They looked so cold and lost as they hurried along the pavement and I wanted to run after them. In some way I felt worse than if I had confronted them. I cannot be certain what I would have said. I knew that there is something sad and faintly distasteful about love's ending, particularly love that has never been fully realised. I might have hinted at that but I doubt it. In our deepest moments we say the most inadequate things.

3

THE PAINS OF YOUTH

Stories of Adolescence

THE LIVING DEAD

Roddy Doyle

*Roddy Doyle (1958–) is the current phenomenon of Irish litera-
ture. His novels have been compared to those of James Joyce
and have brought him fame, fortune and the Booker Prize. Writing
in the* Daily Telegraph Magazine *shortly after the appearance of
the prize-winning novel* Paddy Clark Ha Ha Ha *(1993), which
describes the life of a ten-year-old in Dublin and is obviously
drawn from Doyle's own memories, Mick Brown said, 'It has
taken Roddy Doyle a little under a year to make the transition
from schoolteacher, to novelist, to the stuff of urban myth.' He
was indeed for 14 years a teacher of English and Geography at
the Greendale Community School, Kilbarrack, in northern
Dublin, and now finds himself the subject of countless stories by
adolescent boys who claim to have been in his class where he
was nick-named 'Punk' Doyle (because he wore an earring) and
allegedly used swear-words in his lessons (which he strongly
denies).*

*Doyle was himself born and grew up in Kilbarrack where his
father taught printing at the local college of technology. The
third of four children, he was educated at the Christian Brothers'
school, and he remembers his childhood as comfortable and
happy, interspersed with pranks and dreams of being, first, a
professional footballer, and later a rock musician. His parents
wanted him to make a career in banking but instead, after studying at University College, Dublin, he 'drifted' into teaching. Even
so, he enjoyed the work, proved to be a good teacher, and quickly
developed a rapport with his pupils. At home in the evenings he
wrote, and in 1987 self-published his novel* The Commitments

*in which the Rabbitt family made their appearance. This story
of a group of youngsters in 'Barrytown' (a thinly disguised Kilbarrack) who form a soul band, became a cult success in Dublin
before being brought to the attention of a London publisher.
The rest is history. Doyle has subsequently written two more
'Barrytown' books,* The Snapper *(1990) and* The Van *(1991),
which also focus on the Rabbitt family and especially their teenage son and daughter, Jimmy and Sharon. The ribald humour
and stoical attitude of the family has made the books irresistible.*

*As a teacher, Doyle says he always got on best with the 'hard
cases' in his class and, believing that there is very little contemporary 'working class' literature in Ireland, he set out to write
stories that would emphasise the spirit, humour and energy of
such adolescents. He also captures their bad language, their
tendency to casual violence and their love of drink. Several of
the 'Barrytown' characters appear in this episode about the open
warfare between Jimmy Rabbitt senior, the owner of a burger
stall, and a bunch of young tearaways. It vividly demonstrates
Roddy Doyle's unique understanding of teenagers.*

*   *   *

That was easily their biggest problem though: young fellas.
Jimmy Sr liked kids, always had; Bimbo loved them as well but,
Jaysis Christ, they were changing their minds, quickly. Everyone
loved bold kids. They were cute. There was nothing funnier
than hearing a three-year-old say Fuck. This shower weren't cute
though. They were cunts, right little cunts; dangerous as well.

There was a gang of them that hung around the Hikers carpark,
young fellas, from fourteen to maybe nineteen. Even in the rain,
they stayed there. They just put their hoodies up. Some of them
always had their hoodies up. They were all small and skinny
looking but there was something frightening about them. The
way they behaved, you could tell that they didn't give a fuck
about anything. When someone parked his car and went into the
pub they went over to the car and started messing with it even
before the chap had gone inside; they didn't care if he saw them.

Jimmy Sr once saw one of them pissing against the window of the off-licence, in broad daylight, not a bother on him. Sometimes they'd have a flagon or a can of lager out and they'd pass it around, drinking in front of people coming in and out of Crazy Prices, people that lived beside their parents. It was sad. When they walked around, like a herd migrating or something, they all tried to walk the same way, the hard men, like their kaks were too tight on them. But that was only natural, he supposed. The worst thing though was, they didn't laugh. All kids went through a phase where they messed, they did things they weren't supposed to; they smoked, they drank, they showed their arses to oul' ones from the back window on the bus. But they did it for a laugh. That was the point of it. It was part of growing up, Jimmy Sr understood that; always had. He'd seen his own kids going through that. If you were lucky you never really grew out of it; a little bit of kid stayed inside you. These kids were different though; they didn't do anything for a laugh. Not that Jimmy Sr could see anyway. They were like fuckin' zombies. When Jimmy Sr saw them, especially when it was raining, he always thought the same thing: they'd be dead before they were twenty. Thank God, thank God, thank God none of his own kids was like that. Jimmy Jr, Sharon, Darren—he couldn't have had better kids. Leslie—Leslie had been a bit like that, but—no.

The Living Dead, Bertie called them.

Himself and Vera had had problems for a while with their young lad, Trevor, but Bertie had sorted him out.

—How?

—Easy. I promised I'd get him a motorbike if he passed his Inter.

—Is that all?

—Si, said Bertie. —Gas, isn't it? We were worried sick about him; Vera especially. He was—ah, he was gettin' taller an' he never washed himself, his hair, yeh know. He looked like a junkie, yeh know.

Jimmy Sr nodded.

—All he did all fuckin' day was listen to tha' heavy metal shite. Megadeath was one, an' Anthrax. I speet on them. I told her not to be worryin', an' I tried to talk to him, yeh know—

He raised his eyes.

—Man to man. Me hole. I wasn't tha' worried meself, but he was too young to be like tha'; tha' was all I thought.

—So yeh promised him the motorbike.

—Si. An' now he wants to stay in school an' do the Leavin'. First in the family. He's like his da, said Bertie. —A mercenary bollix.

They laughed.

—He'll go far, said Bimbo.

—Fuckin' sure he will, said Bertie. —No flies on our Trevor.

—Leslie passed his Inter as well, said Jimmy Sr.

—That's righ'.

—Two honours, said Jimmy Sr. —Not red ones either; real ones.

Anyway, the Living Dead gave Jimmy Sr and Bimbo terrible trouble. It was like that film, Assault on Precinct 13, and the van was Precinct 13. It wasn't as bad as that, but it was the same thing. Jimmy Sr and Bimbo could never really relax. The Living Dead would rock the van, three or four of them on each side. The oil poured out of the fryer, all the stuff was knocked to the floor, the cup for the grease under the hot plate went over and the grease got into the Mars Bars. It was hard to get out of the van when it was rocking like that, and it was fuckin' terrifying as well. There wasn't much weight in it at all; they could have toppled it easily enough. The second time they did it Jimmy Sr managed to catch one of them and he gave him a right hiding, up against the side of the van; clobbered every bit of him he could reach. He thought he was teaching him a lesson but when he stopped and let go of him the kid just spat at him. He just spat at him. And walked away, back to the rest of them. They didn't care if they were caught. They didn't say anything to him or shout back at him; they just stared out at him from under their hoodies. He wasn't angry when he climbed back into the van. He was frightened; not that they'd do it again, not that—but that there was nothing he could do to stop them. And, Jesus, they were only kids. Why didn't they laugh or call him a fat fucker or something?

They lit fires under the van; they robbed the bars that held up the hatch; they cut through the gas tubes; they took the bricks from under the wheels.

Jimmy Sr was looking out the hatch, watching the houses go by, when he remembered that the houses shouldn't have been going anywhere. The fuckin' van was moving! It was before they got the engine. Himself and Bimbo baled out the back door but Sharon wouldn't jump. The van didn't crash into anything, and it wasn't much of a hill. It just stopped. The Living Dead had taken the bricks from behind the wheels, that was what had happened. It was funny now but it was far from fuckin' funny at the time.

Jimmy Sr knew them, that was the worst thing about it. The last time he'd walked across O'Connell Bridge he'd seen this knacker kid, a tiny little young fella, crouched in against the granite all by himself, with a plastic bag up to his face. He was sniffing glue. It was terrible—how could his parents let him do that?—but at least he didn't know him. It was like when he heard that Veronica's brother's wife's sister's baby had been found dead in the cot when they got up one morning; it was terrible sad, but he didn't know the people so it was like any baby dying, just sad. But he knew the names of all these kids, most of them. Larry O'Rourke's young lad, for instance; Laurence, he was one of them. It depressed him, so it did. Thank God Leslie was out of it, working away somewhere.

The ordinary kids around, the more normal ones, they were always messing around the van as well. But at least you could get a good laugh out of them, even if they got on your wick. One of them—Jimmy Sr didn't know him, but he liked him—told Bimbo to give him a fiver or he'd pretend to get sick at the hatch every time someone came near the van. And he did it. There was a woman coming towards them, looking like she was making her mind up, and your man bent over and made the noises, and he had something in his mouth and he let it drop onto the road, scrunched-up crisps or something. And that made the woman's mind up for her. Jimmy Sr went after him with one of the bars from the hatch but he wasn't interested in catching him. The ordinary bowsies robbed the bars from the hatch, and messed with the gas and rocked the van as well, but it was different. When they legged it they could hardly run cos they were laughing so much. Jimmy Sr and Bimbo nearly liked it. These kinds fancied Sharon as well so they came to look in at her. It would have been good for business, only they never had any fuckin' money. Sometimes, Fridays especially, they were drunk. He didn't like that. They were falling around the place, pushing each other onto the road. They were too young. They got the cider and cans from an off-licence two stops away on the DART; Darren told him that. Jimmy Sr was going to phone the guards, to report the off-licence, but he never got round to it.

One night the kids went too far. They started throwing stones at the van; throwing them hard. Bimbo, Jimmy Sr and Sharon got an almighty fright when they heard the first bash, until they guessed what was happening. They were flinging the stones at the hot plate side. When he saw the dints the stones were making, fuckin' big lumps like boils, Jimmy Sr nearly went through the roof. That was real damage they were doing. He grabbed one of the hatch bars and let an almighty yell out of him when he jumped out the back door. They weren't going to throw any stones at him, he knew that; it was only the noise they were enjoying. So he knew he wasn't exactly jumping to his death, but he still felt good when he landed, turned at them and saw the fear hop into their faces. Then he went for them. They legged it, and he kept after them. A kick up the hole would teach these guys a lesson. They weren't like the Living Dead. There were five of them and when they turned and went up the verge onto the Green there were more of them, a mixed gang, young fellas and young ones, little lads sticking to their big brothers. Jimmy Sr wasn't angry any more. He'd keep going to the middle of the Green, maybe catch one of the little lads or a girlfriend and take them hostage. He was closing in on one tiny kid who was trying to keep his tracksuit bottoms up. Jimmy Sr could hear the panic in the little lad's breath. He'd just enough breath left himself to catch him, and then he'd call it a day.

Then he saw them.

He stopped and nearly fell over.

The twins. He barely saw Linda but it was definitely Tracy, nearly diving into the lane behind the clinic. Grabbing a young fella's jumper to stay up. Then she was gone, but he'd seen enough.

The treacherous little bitches. Wait till he told Sharon.

He turned back to the van. He found the bar where he'd dropped it.

His own daughters, sending young fellas to throw stones at their da. With their new haircuts that he'd fuckin' paid for last Saturday.

He'd scalp the little wagons.

—You've no proof, said Linda.

—I seen yeh, said Jimmy Sr, again.

—You've no witnesses.

—I fuckin' seen yeh.

—Well, it wasn't me annyway, said Tracy.

—Or me, said Linda.

—It was youse, said Jimmy Sr. —An' if I hear anny more lies an' guff ou' o' yis I'll take those fuckin' haircuts back off yis. And another thing. If yis go away before yis have this place cleaned properly—properly now, righ'—I'll ground yis.

He climbed out of the van.

—The floors an' the walls, righ'. An' if yis do a good job I might let yis off from doin' the ceilin'.

He looked in at them.

—An' that'll fuckin' teach yis for hangin' around with gangsters.

Linda crossed her arms and stared back at him.

—I didn't spend a fortune on your hair, said Jimmy Sr,—so yis could get picked up by snot-nosed little corner boys.

He loved watching the twins when they were annoyed; they were gas.

—Next time yis are lookin' for young fellas go down to the snobby houses an' get off with some nice respectable lads, righ'.

—Will yeh listen to him, he heard Linda saying to Tracy.

—He hasn't a clue, said Tracy.

—Righ', said Jimmy Sr. —Off yis go. The sooner yeh start the sooner yis'll be finished. Mind yeh don't get your flares dirty now.

—They're not flares, righ'! They're baggies.

He closed the door on them.

They'd do a lousy job, he knew that. It served them right though; it would give them something to think about, that and the hiding Sharon had given them last night. Veronica had had to go into the room to break up the fight.

He listened at the door. He held the handle. He couldn't hear anything. He opened it quickly.

Linda was wiping the walls, kind of. Tracy was pushing a cloth over the floor with her foot.

—Do it properly!

—I am!

—PROPERLY!

—Jesus; there's no need to shout, yeh know.

—I'll fuckin'—

—Can we get the radio? said Linda.

—No!

—Ah, Jesus—

Jimmy Sr shut the door.

WE MIGHT SEE SIGHTS!

Julia O'Faolain

Julia O'Faolain (1933–) grew up with two of the foremost names in modern Irish literature for parents and it is no surprise that she herself has proved to be a major talent. Born in Dublin, she spent her childhood surrounded by some of the leading writers of the time and has vividly recalled her parents' relationships with these men and women, especially James Joyce who featured her mother, Eileen, in Ulysses. *It was the way her father wrote and her mother's skill as a storyteller that has remained in her memory from childhood: 'My mother was a clever anecdotalist and collector of raw material which she used to work up for her own purposes—into a yarn—but would also offer to my father and Frank O'Connor. She saw the storytelling possibilities of events, and it was often she who ignited my father's imagination.'*

Julia O'Faolain's early work was translating histories and novels from the Italian, but she went on to write her own short stories and novels such as No Country For Young Men *(1980), about three generations of the O'Malley and Clancy families set against the background of the twentieth century, and* The Irish Signorina *(1984) which is full of childhood memories. 'We Might See Sights' is one of several stories about young people to be found in her collections. In it a girl in the first year of her teens senses village prejudice and glimpses one of the mysteries that adolescence holds in store for her . . .*

*   *   *

Under a furze bush one day—they were taking a pee—Madge

broke with Rosie Fennel. She was ashamed—which was why she chose such a moment.

'Look, Rose,' she said, 'I'm afraid I can't play with you any more. I might *catch* something from you. It's not your fault and I like you still, but ... it's the way your family lives. You see that, don't you?'

'Yeah,' said Rosie.

They both crawled from under the bush and stood up. Rosie had blonde, naturally curly hair, abundant as an aureole and alive with lice. She had a mouthful of bossy teeth and a foamy laugh. Madge had been her friend for three years—since they were ten. Rosie was good gas to play with: game, a tease, a liar. She went bare-legged in winter, to bed, swimming or to the movies at whatever hour she chose, and was free from the rules that plagued Madge who stood before her now, feeling ridiculous in her gym slip, woolly bloomers that—she had just noticed—snapped pink welts on her stomach, and childish-looking pigtails.

Rosie laughed. 'Well!'

'Well, goodbye, Rosie.'

'Cheero.'

Madge ran down the hill, her laced boys' shoes clattering like hooves. ('Like a horse!' said the nuns in school. 'Hoyden!' 'Lice!' they had said. 'Aren't you ashamed? A doctor's daughter! You should have your head shaved!')

Madge ran in her own gate, down the path, up the stairs and burrowed under the bed where she gibbered to herself in the dark for maybe half an hour, scrawling the springs above with her nails, gabbling that she had been awful. Awful! A filthy stinker! She hated herself! And the worst of all was that Rosie hadn't seemed to mind. But she could never look her in the eye again. Never.

She kept away from the village all day, but next morning her mother sent her up to the pub for cigarettes and there was Rosie outside the lounge door, watching the men play pitch-and-toss. (Rosie laughed at their cheek, knew how to give back as good as she got.) She waved at Madge:

'Howaya doin'?'

'Fine,' said Madge and fled. She had to pass Rosie's house where three younger sisters sat scrabbling in the dust—there was no real floor, just earth—and Joe, the father, neither drunk nor sober, hands on knees, stared before him with eyes like wet pebbles. He called something but Madge pretended not to hear.

She rushed down the street for fear of being hailed and maybe questioned about what she had said to Rosie by one of 'the village'. ('The village' were people who lived in houses like Rosie's; others were what Madge's mother called 'people like ourselves'.) They would think her stuck up. 'I'm not really stuck-up at all,' thought Madge. 'Not really. Not inside.' But felt branded.

She moped for weeks after that; read a school book in the bus for fear someone might talk to her and, in the end, struck up with Bernie O'Toole whose father owned the village pub and who, like herself, attended the private convent school in the nearest town. They were the only two kids from round about who did. ('Kids' was Rosie's word who liked Americanese. '*You*', the class nun told Madge when she heard her use it, 'may like to fancy yourself as related to goats! *We* prefer to believe our charges are at least human!')

Bernie was a bit of a stick. She was from the country and shy, but there was a free flow of raspberryade from the pub to the O'Toole kitchen so Madge took to doing her homework there.

The O'Tooles weren't quite 'people like ourselves' either. They didn't visit Madge's parents or their friends. ('Though they could buy and sell us,' said Madge's mother.) Mrs O'Toole flapped about her dark kitchen like a downcast bird in flowered aprons, made cakes and chatted endlessly with her skivvy—none other than Rosie's elder sister, Bridie, whom Madge, of course, knew well. She and Madge eyed each other and talked over-politely for a week after Madge had started coming to the O'Tooles', then one evening Bridie—she had been handing Madge a glass of lemonade—bounded backwards and shouted in a very grand voice:

'Eugh! *Deugh* excuse me! I wouldn't want you to *catch* anything!'

Madge went red—she could feel herself—to the tips of her ears. After that it was war to the knife between her and Bridie. Which was more comfortable really. You knew where you were.

'Here's Miss Madge,' Bridie would yell when Madge arrived. 'Her ladyship has come!'

'Bridie's got a tootsie,' said Bernie slyly, being on Madge's side, and giggled till her pale eyes watered. They were like raw eggs at the best of times. Wettish. Slightly loose. 'The milkman's her fella!'

'A tootsie! A tootsie! Hee, hee, hee!' The little girls giggled while Bridie banged saucepans about. Bernie's brother, Pat, giggled too and clattered his spoon on the tray of his high chair. He was strapped into it though he was too big and his thighs bulged against the sides. 'Gloughgh!' he howled, and slobber fell on his bib. 'Gluggle!' He had a pale, plump face so peppered with freckles that they formed a small saddle on the bridge of his round-nostrilled nose. His eyes were slanted and he had a puffy look like a stuffed cloth doll. He might have been eight or nine.

'What is it, Pat? Now what set him off?' Mrs O'Toole ran in to wipe off the slobber. 'Tell Mummy, pet! Gluggle,' she said too for she claimed to be able to make out what the child said, and talked back to it with the same noises. 'Pat's my boy,' said she and wiped off his saliva.

'Can she really make out what he says?' Madge asked Bernie when her mother had gone.

'Seems.'

'Listen, what's he like—the tootsie?'

'Hee, hee,' said Bernie. 'You jealous?'

'Silly galoot! What I mean is: what do they do anyway?'

Bernie shrugged. 'Go for walks on the beach. Ma saw them go into the cave.'

'Jeez, that's dangerous. Did you know that was an old copper mine? My Daddy says they had to stop working it because of earth slides. There are passages going right under our hill and . . .'

'Well *they* don't explore any passages you may be sure!' Bernie was contemptuous. 'They just neck!'

And then—being unavowably inquisitive—the girls said no more.

Bridie was a fattish girl with an enormous bosom that shook like clotted milk inside her overall. She wore no bra and, from standing over the O'Tooles' cooking stove, gave off a stew of heavy odours. There was, Madge remembered, only a yard tap for her and Rosie to wash at.

''S a wonder she hasn't creepiecrawlies!'

'She *had*! Ma combed them out with a finecomb!'

'Phew!' said Madge. Then—for hadn't she caught them herself from Rosie?—'Poor thing!'

'That Bob Cronin didn't mind!' Bernie sniggered. 'Nor the milkman. Ma says she's man-mad!'

'Seven o'clock! Jeepers, I've got to fly!'

'See you tomorrow.'

'Bye.'

Rump uppermost in the O'Toole yard, Bridie was washing clothes in a bucket. Her thick thighs and glossy pink knickers struck Madge as offensive.

'I'm off,' she told the rump.

'Eugh, Madam Madge! *Good*bye!' came from the bucket.

A group of ratty-looking youths held up the pub wall, sharing a cigarette butt and staring, it seemed to Madge, with foolish insolence before them. She sprayed them all with her imaginary water-pistol, containing, she decided, sour milk. But felt unassuaged. Like a volley of spittle from her mouth, the one word 'BOYS!' crackled with sudden ringing scorn.

They gaped and the next thing she was racing down the macadam, ears burning, eyes blurred with shame.

'Cretin!' she scolded herself. 'Half-wit! Dope!' Inside her own gate, she flopped against the post. 'Jeez,' she gasped. 'You're a real loony! They'll have to tie you up, Madge Heron!'

Saturday was Bridie's half-day and Mrs O'Toole said the girls would have to take Pat for a walk. *She* had things to do. Madge was fed up the minute she saw him. He was pinned into an enormous scarf, snotty as per usual and looking like—well like what he was. By now, however, she'd accepted too much O'Toole raspberryade to protest. Still she promised herself, they could at least avoid the main roads. She wasn't going to let anyone she knew see her walking out with *that*!

'What about going to the beach?' she proposed to Bernie.

'Bet Bridie's there with her heart-throb! We might see sights!'

'You've a dirty mind, Bernie O'Toole!'

'Go on! Pretend that wasn't what you were thinking of yourself!'

Madge scrabbled at the loose plaster in the O'Toole yard wall. A colony of albino insects raced. 'That's right,' she said. 'It wasn't.'

Flies patrolled the veil Mrs O'Toole had thrown on her meat-safe. Who else used outdoor meatsafes any more? The O'Tooles were that stolid! Bernie had the same round nostrils as her brother: punctures in a boneless nose. 'Her whole face is like his,' Madge noticed, 'all puffs!' In school the nuns never had a thing on her. Slyboots! 'If she giggles now,' Madge thought, 'I'll hit her.'

'I'm fed up with double-meaning talk!' she told Bernie.

'Oh yeah?'

'*Yeah*! What's it to us if Bridie smooches or runs after fellows? If you want to know why we're going to the beach, it's' —Madge, on impulse, dredged up a half-shelved dream—'to explore that cave! No boys have done it. Nobody. How many kids our age have a chance like that? All those passages. Empty for years! Centuries maybe. Anything could be hidden there. We'll need,' she recalled, 'a bicycle lamp and candles to test the oxygen.'

'What about Pat?'

'He can wait outside.'

'I'm going into no dirty old cave,' said Bernie. 'You know as well as I do that trippers use it for a lav!'

'*You* can wait outside if you want. That way if I get into some scrape you can give the alert.'

This echo from the *Girls' Crystal* began to work on Bernie.

'I don't mind cadging lamps and stuff,' she wavered. 'Though if anything happens to *you* I'll be the one to be blemt!'

'Pooh! They'll all know it couldn'ta been *your* idea!'

All the way down hill they discussed the cave, astonished suddenly that they had never tackled it before. Madge said she wouldn't be surprised if the Germans—who were known to have landed money and radio equipment along this coast—hadn't hidden stuff there during the war. Most had been caught the minute they landed but you never knew.

'Or there might be an unexploded mine,' said Bernie.

'Nothing venture, nothing win!' Madge communed with the spirits of blunt men, irked by etiquette, who had kicked their heels in court antechambers when obliged to sue for cavalry of brigs. Old salts, untroubled by subtleties, she summoned them with some remorse for they had once animated her dreams and, lately, she had been neglecting them for fantasies of a soppy, vaguely shaming sort which she refused right now to consider.

'Supposing,' Bernie was whining, 'the passages are all blocked?'

'In for a penny, in for a pound,' Madge declared. 'We'll dig!'

The cave, hidden by a curve in the cliff, had to be reached by scrambling past rocks and rock-pools where slime and algae covered dormant crabs. The girls took turns carrying Pat and were puffed by the time they reached the great cleft itself. It was fringed by a growth of greyish marine vegetation and its base was moist with rivulets of reddish ooze.

'*I*'m going no further!' Bernie, an image of country caution, plonked herself on a rock.

'You can *look* in, can't you? Jeez, you might come to the *opening*!'

'That's the stinky part!'

'Not now it isn't! The tides wash right in at this time of year!'

Placing their feet on dry spots among the issuing scum, the two approached.

'Pat,' his sister told him, 'you stay where you are!'

He had settled on an apron of dry pebbles between two rocks. Crooning to himself, his flabby, starfish fingers clutched, dropped and again clutched at smooth pastel stones. Sandy-haired, freckled and pale, he was almost invisible among the mica glints of the brownish-whitish rock: a dappled animal returned to its own habitat.

The girls stepped some way into the cave. Its upper vaulting was lost in darkness; the black gullet, piercing the interior of the hill they had just descended, presented no contour. Under the beam of Madge's lamp, a stretch of inner wall sweated a red liquid which gathered in darker trickles.

'Blood!' Bernie whispered.

'Copper!' Madge reminded her. 'It's a *copper* mine!'

Growing used to the dark, they were able to make out boulders and, in the far end, a slit of richer, velvety black.

'The passage!'

'Shshsh! There's someone there!'

To one side of the passage were two shapes. On a spread macintosh, a man and a woman lay with their heads tilted towards the interior of the cave. Madge was astonished that she should have missed them before for they were pitching and surging in a repetitious undulation, disagreeably similar to the agony of grounded fish. The woman lay uppermost and her skirt, rucked up to her waist, showed a patch of shiny pink.

Madge felt a rush of nausea. 'Let's get out of here.'

'What do you bet it's Bridie and the milkman! The dirty things! I'm telling Ma!'

'Come out, willya!' Madge began to back away.

Bernie caught her arm. 'Half a mo'! Look at Pat!' she whispered. 'Jeepers *look* at him! Pat!' she whispered urgently. 'Come here!'

The child had crept in behind and around them. Now he was half-way across the cave, making for the still jouncing couple.

'Blawchlee!' he gurgled happily. 'Blawdee!'

'Leave him,' Madge whispered. 'They'll have fits if they think *we* saw them! Bridie's fond of him,' she reassured Bernie when they were outside. 'We'll pretend we didn't see him mooching off.'

'We could call him!'

'OK!'

'Pa-a-at!'

'Now give them time to send him out.'

The girls sat on a rock. 'Pa-a-at!' Bernie yelled again.

Madge found a linty twist of paper in her pocket with a bull's-eye and acid drop welded together. She tried to prise them apart but they fell, bounced off the rock and rolled into a scummy pool. 'Hell!' she cried. 'Everything's the same today! Spoilt! Everything!' Biting her nails, she stared into the water where a sea anemone waved delicate fretted tendrils, enfolding its flower-like heart against the danger. 'Stupid slow thing!' said Madge. 'If those sweets had been something dangerous it would be dead by now!'

'Don't they shoot poison?' Bernie wondered. 'Pat!' she began to call again. 'Pa-a-at!'

With a yelp and a scutter of pebbles, Pat appeared at the mouth of the cave; he stumbled on the scum, picked himself up, collected his clumsy body for a last rush and threw himself on Bernie, hugging her knees and gobbling.

She stroked his large, cropped head. 'Whatsa matter, Pat? It's OK now. It's all OK!'

There was a man behind him. Madge stared at him and he stopped to stare back. He had a muddled aghast look. His mouth was like a hole burnt in cloth: unformed, struggling as she had often seen Pat's. Indeed he had a look of Pat: clumsy, bulbous-faced and as if, when he made a noise, it too might be a meaning-less gobble. One hand held up his trousers while the other groped inside them to tuck in the tail of his shirt. He was making a poor fist of it and was not, it occurred to Madge to notice, the milkman. At last he managed to bring out some words: 'Tan his arse for him!' he shouted in an English accent. A tripper. 'Little Peeping Tom . . .' But he looked uncertainly around.

'He's afraid,' Madge guessed, 'that we've got grown-ups with us!' She was enraged by the man's language and appearance. Her throat was knotted with anger and it was some seconds before she managed to yell: 'Mister, you leave that kid alone! He's not right! He gets fits!'

'Shsh! Madge!' Bernie begged.

'I'll say he's not right!' the man muttered. 'My God!' He

began to button his pants and glanced at Pat whose face was buried in Bernie's lap. 'You don't know what he was doing . . .'

'And what were *you* doing, Mister? We could get the guards after you!'

'Dickie!' a woman's voice called from the cave. Another English voice. Not Bridie's. 'They're only kids. No need to get your dander up.'

'Oh hell!' The man turned back. 'Delights of Nature!' He was muttering as he went into the cave. 'Have to run into the blooming village idiot . . .'

'Dickie!' the woman's voice called.

'The guards!' Madge yelled after him. 'Cheek!' She was boiling with disgust and fury. 'Chasing Pat like that! Who does he think . . .'

'Shut up, will you!' Bernie whispered. '*I*'m going! Come on, Pat, I'll give you a piggyback!'

Madge followed them. Half-way up the hill she took Pat from Bernie. He was heavy. 'Gee,' she gasped. 'That fellow was worried!'

Bernie pondered. 'I wonder what Pat saw? Sights I'll bet! The English are terrible dirty!'

When they reached the end of the grassy slope, Madge eased Pat off her back and flopped down between two bushes. 'Got to rest!' she groaned. 'I'm puffed!' She found another bull's-eye and gave it to Pat. He sat sucking it, his round face further distent by its bulge, his eyes inflamed. The girls looked at him with interest. The afternoon had been a wash-out. They felt cheated.

'Think he saw *everything*?'

'Must have!'

'Well, there's no getting it out of *him*!' Madge spoke with a mixture of relief and regret.

Bernie began to giggle. 'I dunno about that! He might *do* it for us!'

Madge stood up. '*Now* you're talking!' She began to unbuckle Pat's belt. 'Pat,' she soothed, 'show the game the man was playing! Show us, Pat!' She gurgled encouragingly. 'Let's play, Pat!' She peeled down the stiff, stained short trousers until she was confronted by his little boy's body: yellowish, smelling of pee, with bits of fluff tucked under the loose skin.

'*Madge*! He'll tell! My Ma understands him! Madge!'

Madge ignored her. 'Whose idea was it anyway? Spoil-sport!' She whispered to Pat: 'Come on! Show us! What were they doing? Show!'

Bernie smirked. 'OK then. *I*'ll show you something!' She began tickling the loose flesh between the little boy's legs.

The child let out a wail, pushed her violently from him and began to shiver again.

'OK,' his sister told him. 'OK! So you don't want to today! Hold your hair on!'

But Pat was down on his back now kicking with frenzy. Bernie stared at him with wet eye orbs. 'Oh Madge! He's having a fit!' She began to cry. 'He'll tell, Madge!' she moaned. 'My Ma understands what he says and my Da'll crease me! It's all your fault. It's a mortal sin.'

Madge was indignant. 'It's *not* my fault!'

'It is so!'

'Oh for Pete's sake! There's a *pair* of you!' Madge tried to seize Pat who was writhing. Maybe it *was* a fit? His face was crab-red and there was spittle on his lips. 'Pat,' she begged. 'Can't you *do* anything?' she shouted to Bernie. 'At least shut up crying yourself! You're only encouraging him!'

But Bernie just wept. 'He'll go off his head for good!' she sobbed. 'The doctor told Ma. If he's excited. And it'll be your fault, Madge Heron! All your fault! And what'll me mother do? Uuughhuu!' She joined her high shrill wail to Pat's.

'SHUT UP!' Madge was distracted. 'Both of you! Pat!' His mouth was more than ever like a black hole burnt in his face. He was slobbering but had stopped howling. She picked him up. 'Quiet,' she told him. He peed on her. He must have felt it happening for he began to wail once more. She put him down. 'Oh God, the filthy thing . . .' She felt like crying herself. 'WILL YOU AT LEAST QUIT CRYING!' she roared. 'If anyone comes they'll think we're killing the little beast! STOP!' He wouldn't. She smacked his face. For a moment he did stop and stared at her, wall-eyed, too much white showing. Then he began to yell worse than ever. She picked up his belt—a proper man's leather one cut down—and gave him a lash across the legs with it. 'Now will you stop? Will you, will you?' She had given him three or four cuts with it and was staring in horror at the pink welts on his poor pale idiot's body before Bernie got to her. 'What a beast I am,' she thought. 'All beasts!' Bernie was upon her.

'You stop that, Madge Heron, you . . .'

She gave Bernie a shove with her knee that caught her in the stomach and sent her rolling. 'Beast,' she thought, 'but I won't stop for her! Not for her! I am a beast, I . . .' and again she raised the belt but the child had crawled away and Bernie was on her again.

'You're out of your mind, Madge Heron!' She tore the belt from Madge's hand and, pulling one of Madge's feet from under her, sent her flat on her face on the grass. Madge lay where she had fallen, not listening to Bernie's shouting, not listening to the child who was now quieted and snuffling gently to itself a few yards off. 'I can't,' she thought but couldn't think what it was she couldn't do. 'Grass,' she thought and buried her face in it. 'Blot it out. Grow over it, let me forget it. Grass, nothing but grass . . .'

SEDUCTION

Neil Jordan

Neil Jordan (1950–) is one of the new generation of Irish writers and has enjoyed outstanding reviews for his novels and short stories. He has also had huge success as a film-maker, in particular with The Crying Game *(1992), a powerful story about the relationship between an IRA man and a black British soldier, for which he received an Oscar; the Gothic thriller* Interview With the Vampire *(1995), based on the novel by Anne Rice; and the controversial biopic,* Michael Collins *(1996), starring Liam Neeson.*

Born in County Sligo, but raised in Dublin where his father was a teacher, Jordan was exposed to Irish literature and supernaturalism from an early age. 'My father was always telling me ghost stories, superstitious stories,' he recalls, 'and I was introduced to Beckett and Joyce at a very early age. I was also the victim of every sort of educational theory as a child.' He studied medieval Irish history at University College (his thesis was on the lives of the saints) and wanted to become a teacher, but was unable to find a job. Instead he turned to writing, and with the success of his first book, Night in Tunisia *(1976), which won the Guardian Fiction Prize, he soon found work writing plays and scripts for the theatre and Irish television. His 1980 novel,* The Past, *focused on a Dublin childhood, and his most recent work,* Sunrise with Sea Monster *(1994), is about growing up in Ireland during the years of the Second World War, when the country was neutral.*

A strongly personal Irish sensibility about Republicanism runs through several of Jordan's films and books. 'It's part of my

*history,' he says. 'Most people of my generation had grand-
mothers smuggling guns or whatever. Everybody is on one side
or the other of the civil war divide, and that aspect of Irish
history is never far from the surface.' Childhood memories have
also surfaced in stories like 'Sand', in which a young boy is
offered a donkey ride by a tinker trying to get off with his sister,
and 'Seduction', about two boys in a seaside town dreaming of
the girls they desire. It represents a universal adolescent feeling
and deserves to be filmed—by Jordan himself, of course.*

*　　　*　　　*

'You don't believe me, do you,' he said, 'you don't believe
anything, but I've seen her'—and he repeated it again, but I
didn't have to listen this time, I could imagine it so vividly. The
naked woman's clothes lying in a heap under the drop from the
road where the beach was clumsy with rocks and pebbles, her
fat body running on the sand at the edge of the water, the waves
splashing round her thick ankles. The imagining was just like
the whole summer, it throbbed with forbidden promise. I had
been back in the town two days and each day we had hung around
till twilight, when the hours seemed longest, when the day would
extend its dying till it seemed ready to burst, the sky like a
piece of stretched gauze over it, grey, melancholy, yet infinitely
desirable and unknown. This year I was a little afraid of him,
though he was still smaller than me. I envied and loved his
pointed shoes that were turned up and scuffed white and his hair
that curled and dripped with oil that did its best to contain it in
a duck's tail. I loved his assurance, the nonchalant way he let
the vinegar run from the chip-bag onto the breast of his off-white
shirt. But I kept all this quiet knowing there were things he envied
about me too. I think each of us treasured this envy, longing to
know how the other had changed but disdaining to ask. We loved
to talk in monosyllables conscious of the other's envy, a hidden
mutual delight underneath it like blood. Both of us stayed in the
same guest-house as last year. My room faced the sea, his the
grounds of the convent, the basket-ball pitch with the tennis-net

running through it where the nuns swung racquets with brittle, girlish laughter. We sniffed the smell of apples that came over the town from the monastery orchard behind it and the smell of apples in late August meant something different to me this year, as did the twilight. Last year it would have meant an invitation to rob. I wondered did it mean the same to him. I concluded that it must, with his hair like that. But then he was tougher, more obscene.

'Look, she's coming out now.' He nodded his head sideways towards the chip-shop and I stared in through the dripping steamed glass. It looked warm inside, warm and greasy. I saw the woman coming out of the tiny corridor in which the chips were fried, leaning against the steel counter. Some older boys waiting for orders threw jibes at her. She laughed briefly, then took out a cigarette, put it in her mouth and lit it. I knew that when the cigarette came out its tip would be covered in lipstick, the way it happens in films. When she took the coins from them two gold bangles slipped down onto her fat wrist. There was something mysterious, hard and tired about her, some secret behind those layers of make-up which those older boys shared. I watched them laughing and felt the hard excitement of the twilight, the apples. And I believed him then, though I knew how much he lied. I believed him because I wanted to believe it, to imagine it, the nakedness of this fat blonde woman who looked older than her twenty-five years, who sang every Saturday night at the dance in the local hotel.

'Leanche's her name. Leanche the lion.'

'Lioness,' I said, being the erudite one. He looked at me and spat.

'When'll you ever dry up.' I spat too. 'Here.' He held out the chip bag.

I took one. It was like when I came to the guest-house and he had already been there a day. He stood in the driveway pulling leaves off the rhododendron bush as we took things off the rack of our Ford car. I looked over at him, the same as last year, but with a new sullenness in his face. I hoped my face was even more deadpan. He turned his face away when I looked but stayed still, pulling the oily leaves till the unpacking was finished. Then I went over to talk to him. He said that the town was a dump this year, that there was an Elvis playing in the local cinema. He said that Ford cars with high backs had gone out since the ark. I asked him had his people got a car yet and he said no. But somehow it seemed worse to have a car with a high back and rusted doors than no car at all. He said 'Come on, we'll go to the town' and we both walked to the gate, to the road that ran from the pier towards the town where every house was painted white and yellow and in summer was a guest-house.

'Let's go inside,' he said, just as it was getting dark and the last of the queue filed from the chipper. 'We've no money,' I said. 'Anyway, I don't believe you.' I hoped my fright didn't glare through. 'It's true,' he said. 'The man in the cinema told me.' 'Did he see her,' I asked. 'No, his brother did.' There was disdain in the statement that I couldn't have countered.

We pushed open the glass door, he took out a comb as he was doing so and slicked it through his hair. I went over to the yellow jukebox and pushed idly at the buttons. 'Are ye puttin' money in it son,' I heard. I turned and saw her looking at me, the ridiculously small curls of her hair tumbling round her large face. Her cheeks were red and her dress was low and her immense bosom showed white through it, matching the grease-stains on her apron. 'No,' I said and began to blush to the roots, 'we just wanted to know . . .'

'Have you got the time,' Jamie burst in. 'Have you eyes in your head,' she countered. She raised her arm and pointed to a clock on the wall above her. Twenty past ten.

We had walked past the harbour and the chip-shop and the Great Northern Hotel that were all the same as last year. The rich hotelier's son who had left the priesthood and had gone a little mad was on the beach again, turning himself to let his stomach get the sun now that his back was brown. Jamie told me about the two Belfast sisters who wore nylons and who were protestants, how they sat in the cinema every night waiting for something. He asked me had I ever got anything off a girl that wore nylons. I asked him had he. He said nothing, but spat on the ground and stirred the spittle with the sole of his shoe. The difference in the town was bigger now, lurid, hemming us in. I borrowed his comb and slicked it through my hair but my hair refused to quiff, it fell back each time on my forehead, incorrigibly flat and sandy-coloured.

The woman in the chip-shop smiled and crooked her arm on the counter, resting her chin on her fist. The folds of fat bulged round the golden bangles. 'Anything else you'd like to know.' I felt a sudden mad urge to surpass myself, to go one better than Jamie's duck-tailed hair. 'Yeah,' I began, 'do you . . .' Then I stopped. She had seemed a little like an idiot to me but something more than idiocy stopped me. 'Do I!' she said and turned her head towards me, looking at me straight in the eyes. And in the green irises underneath the clumsy mascara there was a mocking light that frightened me. I thought of the moon with a green mist around it like the Angel of Death in the Ten Commandments. I saw her cheeks and heard the wash of the sea and imagined her padding feet on the sand. And I shivered at the deeper, infinite idiocy there, the lurid idiocy that drew couples into long grass to engage in something I wasn't quite sure of. I blushed with shame, with longing to know it, but was saved by her banging hand on the silver counter. 'If you don't want chips, hop it.' 'Don't worry,' said Jamie, drawing the comb through his hair. 'Don't worry,' I said, listening to his hair click oilily, making for the glass door. 'I still don't believe you,' I said to him outside. 'Do you want to wait up and see then.' I didn't answer. Jamie drew a series of curves that formed a naked woman in the window-dew. We both watched them drip slowly into a mess of watery smudges.

We had gone to the cinema that first night, through the yellow-emulsioned doorway into the darkness of the long hall, its windows covered with sheets of brown paper. I smelt the smells of last year, the sweaty felt brass of the seats and the dust rising from the aisle to be changed into diamonds by the cone of light above. There was a scattering of older couples there, there was Elvis on the screen, on a beach in flowered bathing-trunks, but no Belfast sisters. 'Where are they' I asked him, with the ghost of a triumphant note in my voice. He saved himself by taking out a butt, lighting it and pulling harshly on it. We drank in Elvis silently. Later the cinema projectionist put his head between both our shoulders and said 'Hey boys, you want to see the projection-room?' His breath smelt the same as last year, of cigarettes and peppermint. But this year we said no.

Later again I sat in my room and watched the strand, where two nuns were swinging tennis-racquets on a court they had scrawled on the sand. It was ten past nine and the twilight was well advanced, the balance between blue and grey almost perfect. I sat on my bed and pulled my knees to my chest, rocking softly, listening to the nuns' tinkling laughter, staring at the billows their habits made with each swing of their arms. Soon even the nuns left and the strand was empty but for the scrawled tennis-court and the marks of their high-heeled boots. But I watched on, hearing the waves break, letting the light die in the room around me, weeping for the innocence of last year.

We pressed ourselves against the wall below the road, trying to keep our feet from slipping off the large round pebbles. My father was calling my name from the drive of the guest-house. His voice seemed to echo right down the beach, seeming worried and sad. Soon even the echo died away and Jamie clambered up and peeped over the top and waved to me that no one was there. Then we walked down the strand making a long trail of footsteps in the half-light. We settled ourselves behind an upturned boat and began to wait. We waited for hours, till Jamie's face became pinched and pale, till my teeth began to chatter. He stared at the sea and broke the teeth from his comb, one by one, scattering them at his feet. I spat in the sand and watched how my spittle rolled into tiny sandballs. The sea washed and sucked and washed and sucked but remained empty of fat women. Then Jamie began to talk, about kisses with the mouth open and closed, about the difference between the feel of a breast under and over a jumper, between nylons and short white socks. He talked for what seemed hours and after a while I stopped listening, I knew he was lying anyway. Then suddenly I noticed he had stopped talking. I didn't know how long he had stopped, but I knew it had been some time before I noticed it. I turned and saw he was hunched up, his face blank like a child's. All the teeth were broken from his comb, his hand was clutching it insensibly and he was crying softly. His hair was wild with curls, the oil was dripping onto his forehead, his lips were purple with the cold. I touched him on the elbow and when his quiet sobbing didn't stop I took off my coat and put it gingerly round his shoulders. He shivered and moved in close to me and his head touched my chest and lay there. I held him there while he slept, thinking how much smaller than me he was after all.

There was a thin rim of light round the edge of the sea when he woke. His face was pale, although not as grey as that light, and his teeth had begun to chatter. 'What happened,' he asked, shaking my coat off. 'You were asleep,' I said, 'you missed it,' and began a detailed account of how the woman had begun running from the pier right up past me to the end of the strand, how her breasts had bobbed as the water splashed round her thick ankles. 'Liar,' he said. 'Yes,' I said. Then I thought of home. 'What are we going to do?' I asked him. He rubbed his eyes with his hand and drew wet smudges across each cheek. Then he got up and began to walk towards the sea. I followed him, knowing the sea would obliterate his tears and any I might have. When he came near the water he began to run, splashing the waves round him with his feet and I ran too, but with less abandon, and when he fell face down in the water I fell too. When I could see him through the salt water he was laughing madly in a crying sort of way, ducking his head in and out of the water the way swimmers do. I got to my feet and tried to pull him up but his clothes were clinging to every bone of his thin body. Then I felt myself slipping, being pulled from the legs and I fell in the water again and I felt his arms around my waist, tightening, the way boys wrestle, but more quietly then, and I felt his body not small any longer, pressing against mine. I heard him say 'this is the way lovers do it' and felt his mouth on my neck but I didn't struggle, I knew that in the water he couldn't see my tears or see my smile.

RED JELLY

Eithne Strong

Few Irish writers have had a more varied and intimate knowledge of the adolescent mind at work than Eithne Strong (1923–). She has raised nine children, and yet still found time to write several acclaimed books of poetry, a novel, Degrees of Kindred *(1978), and a number of highly original stories of which 'Red Jelly', first published in* Winter's Tales From Ireland: Two *(1972), has been cited by some of her fellow writers and critics as one of the best short stories of recent years. Born Eithne O'Connell in Glensharrold, West Limerick, she remembers a childhood amidst the beautiful scenery of that part of Ireland, contrasting starkly with the hardship which, for many families, was never far away. A bright and intelligent teenager, she studied psychology at Trinity College, Dublin, which later helped to give her poetry and fiction a special sense of insight into the human predicament. She worked as a civil servant until her marriage to Rupert Strong and the start of their family in 1943.*

Eithne Strong has written a good deal of journalism as well as an increasing amount of poetry in Gaelic. 'Red Jelly' is a compelling picture of the agonies of growing up and the uneasy relationship of a teenage girl with her mother and father.

*   *   *

Molly tells me today about the room. She got the thing all fixed for me so I can move in straight away. So when I get home I tell them. It's more or less as I expected from them only maybe not so bad. The worst was over already I suppose when there was that show-down the first night, that night I said it's either Sucker or me. Anyway, when I tell them my father's face tightens and all the little lines on it get a bit deeper. I don't like looking at either of them although on principle I stare at them just to let them see it's costing *me* nothing. SHE doesn't say anything at all only she has that ridiculous look that comes over her when she's feeling sorry for herself; what did I do to deserve this, life's so painful, ogodgivemethestrength look. Max painted a picture of it once—shiny reds, all different kinds of bloody sweat reds in a sort of huge egg shape and he said,

'That's HER in agony.'

and I said,

'It looks sort of like red jelly.'

'Right,' he said, 'yes. That's what we'll call it—RED JELLY—*an agony.*'

He's keeping it for his exhibition in the spring. Walter says he'll buy it to hang, title and all, in his Bistro and I said it'll put the people off eating if they have to sit under that. But Walter has it that you should always play up your bad point, make a big thing of it, communicate to people the idea of your belief in yourself. He needs a bit of that since he took on the Bistro and as the food in the place is hardly likely to improve—not with *his* wife's dab hand—maybe his notion about the picture is not so bad. Then he thought a bit and said he might change the name, make it maybe *Mélange Rouge*—he digs this French antic—and Max said he could once he'd bought it. Max is holding out for a tenner; Walter has offered him five but Max said he'd had more than a tenner's worth of trouble in our house to get all those shades of agony. I mean all the brats and everything.

As I'm telling them about the room SHE'S crying, no noise of course. That silent suffering effort. But I despise her for it. Too far late in the day now for crying, as I told her the first time we had the row about the carry-on. I don't know what she expects—that I'm going to smile and grin and fair weather to her trukking around with that Sucker. My father is another kind of fool giving fancy names to what they are up to, himself, herself and the Sucker and blazes knows who else. It's all an excuse for whoring. I'm staying around no more. So I tell them about the room.

I say it stubborn and angry so they'll get no ideas about stopping me, not that I think they will—they want me willing, it seems, or not at all—but just in case. There's not much they can really do. That first night I threatened to tell everywhere about . it all if they made any fuss about me clearing out. I'll say though SHE was able for me over that. She said:

'Go ahead. Do your worst. Shout it from the housetops if you want to—you jolly well know, Maryjane, I won't be bullied by that sort of tantrum. We are living our life the best we can: I've never not done anything, anything at all for you I could. Full well you know it. You have been an—an adored child in this house.'

I didn't go for all that soft bit.

'You can do more,' I shout. 'I don't want that filthy Sucker nosing around here. I've copped on, make no mistake. Either that stops or I get out.'

'It's up to yourself now,' she says, 'it's blackmail what you're doing. You know your standing with us, I don't have to prove anything to you about it. In seventeen years you certainly know it.'

She was looking at me with that fierce kind of look, her eyes all drawn together and this groove between her eyebrows and although she was red she didn't look like jelly I must say. I know what she meant too, 'tis just I can't stand this mucking around: she's my—my—my mother isn't she? The thought of a thing like the Sucker . . . God it makes me just heave vomit PUKE. Inside out.

That was all the time we had the first row. But although I know she means what she says and that she'll stick to it to the last, she—they—won't do anything much about stopping me.

'It's up to you,' she had said. '*You* are separating *your*self from us. This is your home. You feel what you are feeling and I don't know that it's helping you anyway to grow up more by letting that feeling dominate over what we believe to be—right.'

So pie oh my so holy pie!

I tell them a friend will be sharing the room with me. I don't, naturally enough, breathe a word about Molly, that she's moving in with me only because she has to leave the place she and Walter have been sleeping in—his wife will be back soon and he won't be able to stay away from home every night. That's the thing about the parents that's so disgusting: so *pie* about it all as if it's something special they are doing; holy of holies. No such thing as calling a spade. I'd rather any day the lark Molly and Walter are up to. They certainly are not making any grand act out of it. Makes me want to throw up: all that high-pie talk.

I have to get my stuff moved in. Although he must hate to like cancer my father says he'll do it. Then he is working when I am ready to shift so SHE does it. They are handy still for this kind of thing, there's that sloppy obliging streak that you see at the most peculiar times—this is a peculiar time. Anyway it all— the obligingness, the slop—goes with the high-pie.

'Omygod,' she says as we go up past the dustbins on the first landing. It is a very close heavy sort of a day. The smells don't get any better as we go further on up to the door of the room that is to be mine. I have to knock to get the key from the tenant opposite. He's hairy, I mean about two yards of hair, and not exactly clean. She doesn't say it any more but I can hear her thinking 'omygod' all the time. What's *she* so choosy about? The mess at home is a fright most of the time although she's always saying 'omygod' about that too. Her face is red from crying. She's been at it fit to make me retch all the time she was driving me to the place. What she meant to be that silent suffering. No sound much except an odd snort. Maybe it was giving her some soppy satisfaction but if it was supposed to stir me up, I was like a stone.

The room smells of sour dish-cloths and dead air. She goes to the window but does nothing about opening it. She hates bad smells but it is my room and she isn't going to interfere. She is learning the hard way. Outside the glass there are clogged gutters and broken black slates and a filthy backyard belonging to the dump opposite, all nicely in view. I know it looks bad and I am glad. At home my room looked out on trees and a bit of a river

and grass and all that. It is her fault I am here. 'Nympho' I had
shouted at her the night it came to a show-down.

After she had put down the stuff she was carrying she went
away and I didn't watch her going. Before all this whatever, I
nearly always kissed her if I were going anywhere. Even in the
crazy rush for the bus to school in town. And we'd say 'god
bless'. It's a kind of thing they say all the time in the family like
'hello' or 'goodbye'. No more of that sop now.

I'm earning for myself and I won't have to touch them for
anything—well maybe some things here and there if I just absolutely have to. They certainly owe it to me—it's too easy if my
clearing out means there is that bit more to spend on the rest of
the pack. But I'd really rather not to have to risk for anything.
I'm off their hands young that's one thing. Their own fault it is
if they have to struggle and scrape: who asked them to have all
that lot that wasn't exactly pleading to be born I know *I* never
asked it and now that I'm there I'm mucked up already at seventeen. A good job they did on me surely. Well they'll see. I'll
drag their name maybe. Serve them.

Max comes in to paint up the place a bit. Not much, for we have
hardly anything to spend on it but he had a few odd pots left from
the time he was painting up his own studio in the summer. He has
it nearly finished when I come in from work and then he stays on.
Molly doesn't come till next week to halve the rent for me. But I'm
OK for now, for the first week anyway, with the few extra quid my
father gave me. He said he'd give me nothing, not that I asked
him: he was just saying it to let me know he was giving no helping
finances to what I was doing. Bullying, he said. Maybe so. But they
know. Either a change from them or I stay away. In the end he gives
me these few quid. He's always soft to us about money, struggling
and all. SHE never has any. I've already decided I'll never be like
that, waiting in hope for money. I'll take it where it will come from.
I think anyway.

The room looks fairly all right now and we put *red* see-through
paper in the lower part of the window to rich the view. Today
though it makes me think of red jelly.

*

Now that Molly is here the place seems very cramped, SHE was forever ticking me off for keeping my room at home in a mess. She'd sometimes go through it all when I was out and make it tidy, hanging up my clothes, taking away the dirty ones and fixing it all up. When I'd see it that way, for a few days I might maybe keep it straight. Then I'd let it all slide. It was too much effort and I'd often be down in the dumps with the noise of the brats that you couldn't get away from and the rotten lot of home-work and worrying about what was wrong with the way I looked. There are a lot of things I'd like different with the way I look although SHE was always saying I was lovely. Of course coming from her it meant nothing. Couldn't take any notice of that. I was in no way convinced. For Max to say it would be altogether another story. But he doesn't say it, nothing like that, only snide bits. I often cry about the things he says that way. It only matters coming from a guy, really, the praise bit. Bitches will *always* chew you up behind your back however smarmy to your face. Myself I don't much see the point of the praise bit from one woman to another so I say nothing to their face. I don't see the point. I often *think* they look great of course, but mostly the real good-lookers are stinkers. There's nothing can be done about bitchiness.

Now SHE wouldn't ever do the chewing-up bit I *know*—about me, that is. But she says the nice things because I'm HER child, taking the credit to herself, you see. That's how it used to be anyway. Maybe she just gets some consolation from the drag thinking her bunch is just great. It wouldn't be surprising in a way. I mean forcing the consolation part. Give her due, she'd never hurt my feelings that way. It is the other carry-on, the Sucker thing and that being with her a matter of principle— *principle* mind you—as she put it the night I slammed cards on the table. I said me or the Sucker which is it to be? So I'm here in this room and that was the answer. I wouldn't be here if . . .

I think I'll go up to Walter's Bistro for a drink.

Molly is untidy. Even I am better at sorting things out. And I'm cleaner. At least I scrubbed down all the old sink and draining board with disinfectant and I put down rat-poison. There were two rats in the dustbins the other night. Molly doesn't care. And I only buy stuff that won't go bad. I don't like bad smells either. But I was glad of the smell that day when SHE first came. Just to lay the whole misery on.

Walter came back with Molly the other night and he stayed on and on—till morning. So Max stayed too. It was a crush four to the bed.

I think I'll go for a drink up to the Bistro.

I'm back at home today. I was out this way anyway on a job for my manager and it was handy to drop in to use the phone here. Calls to do with the job. I said to HER I'd leave money for the calls—keeping up the independence bit, but she'll forget or I can pretend I forgot although I kind of meant it when I said it.

SHE is looking a bit of a wreck I must say. She wears everything out to the last possible, I mean acres of darns and patches up the leg. Shoes like boats. Clean of course, but the patchwork— god the clothes! I wouldn't be seen dead! She can look about passable sometimes. Going out, say. Only she must be finding it a stretch these days to keep looking anything. She hasn't much clothes and there's always this mess everywhere that she fusses so much about cleaning up. Don't slop; don't spill; pick up this, that and the other; keep the place decent, I can't do it all—HELP ME. That's the way she goes on, always struggling, cleaning, giving out about messes. All the fault of those grotty brats.

Christ I get mad when I'm trying to phone and they all start off a racket. Now that I'm not living here any more I don't want to screech and yell at them the way I used to, I don't want to let them see I'd be bothered, you know. But they drive me crazy and I can't hear a word on the phone and so I give a *small* roar at them. Not *too* much off my dignity, Will you PLEASE keep quiet, and then when they take no notice I put the phone down and give them a few belts. Stephen is the worst. He goes yah yah yah back at me and runs away outside so I know I don't have a hope about catching him and I leave it at that. Anyway I think I've got rid of him, but I've no sooner started on the

phone again when back he's in to make more racket with the
rest. This time I don't pretend to notice until he is right up to
me and then I grab him by the hair and give him what he's
looking for. Then of course he goes screeching off to HER where
she's trucking round in the basement trying to fix up some of
the grot. She comes up the stairs all red in the face.

'Maryjane,' she says, 'if you come back here you take us as
you find us. We are as we always were. You were the same at
his age. I'm not saying he's right but don't take it on yourself
to wallop him like that. You come and tell me about him. I'll
stop him.'

Don't make me laugh. Stop him. She will like fun. He's grinning now from one ear to the other. She says prim and posh as
she always is when she's ticking off,

'Stephen, have manners. Don't you know when a person is on
the telephone—I'm always telling you all when a person is on
the phone . . . to be . . . to be quiet.'

He's still grinning away and she takes him by the shoulder
and rattles the daylights out of him. It's not hitting, you see, and
so it's all right to do it—that's the way she thinks. He sees she's
getting mad and pretends to try to straighten his face, but the
whole business now is too funny for him. Back comes the grin.
He's mocking her and it really gets her. Anyone mocking her
always gets her. I know she's hard put not to strike him but for
one thing it wouldn't do in front of me. She's supposed to be
showing me how to handle the situation. She suddenly spreads
out her arms and sweeps them all out the door and locks it. They
stay for a bit looking back in through the glass sniggering and
not too sure whether to start off again, but they have seen her wild
before now and it seems they decide they've gone far enough. She
comes back to me very stiff.

'You can go ahead with your calls. I daresay we are still some
convenience. Handy not to have to pay in a box outside.'

She gives me a stare and I stare her back and she goes off
down, her eyes red as well as her face by this. She looks a sight.
If the boyfriend saw her now. But come to think of it she wouldn't
be too put out—in all the years he must have seen her a sight

many a time. She used to say to me when I'd be crying over the way I looked or over something Max had said about it, 'Ah child, if he only likes the way you look 'tis a poor story.' It was never any comfort, for what *is* there to like in me? I wish someone did like whatever it might be; it's such a drag always having to think about glamming up.

As luck would have it while I'm still here busy with phoning the doorbell goes and it's the Sucker at the other side of the glass. Harvey is really his name but I always call him the Sucker. He can't work his key for she has of course locked the door that time. I never could stand the way he has been hanging around her for years. You could say I don't exactly love him. And the hanging around was bad but on top of it he'd try to jam up to us kids. Especially myself and Peg, us two being the older ones. Trying to put himself in our good books, trying to have us believe he was what he wasn't—kindhearted. As far as Peg and me and him were concerned there was no trust lost. He has a stinking temper really. One of those poisonous polite-spoken smarmies, every so often making a sad hand out of a poor joke for our nothing-doing benefit.

Well I let him in. I'm pretty sure he knows the latest on me— he's always in on the big news and my move-out is BIG—but I couldn't care less what he knows. Force of habit he sets his head in that pompous way—mock-jolly-good-fellow pompous it's meant to be—and it's the way he used to try out on me when I was a kid about a century ago. And now suddenly, it seems to strike him what he's doing and that he's on to the wrong tack, for he starts the poisonous polite bit:

'And how are *you*, Maryjane?'

He cares damn all. Anyway I don't answer him. Just stare at him with the phone to my ear. The brats come bursting back in—I never locked the door the second time—and they start prancing around Harvey the Sucker. I see him trying the buttery bit but he is hard put to to keep the smooth for they are galloping over his suede shoes and you can see he's dead afraid they'll mark them. He starts trying to be frolicsome, doing a bit of a dance, pretending to be enjoying their carry-on but it's killing him. I know I stand a chance to make them behave after what has just happened with Stephen and my mother but I'm not all that pushed now any more. I've really finished the phoning so their blasted noise doesn't bother me all that much and I'm getting a kick out of watching Harvey's fix.

'Children, children, please,' says the Sucker. The temper could be warming up there. Stephen falls over the young brat and bashes his own ear on something sharp and, true to form, he starts yelling like a stuck pig.

'You see I warned you,' Harvey's voice is like a preacher's and you can see he is glad to be able to say it. He's pulling Stephen up off the floor and rubbing his ear the way SHE might rub the bottom of the ninety-ninth saucepan—there are about a hundred dirty for washing-up every day. I'm not exactly grief-stricken for Stephen. Pity he didn't fall so as to hit his two ears.

SHE comes up the stairs wondering about the new fuss. 'Hello,' she says to Harvey and she was red again, but this time it's a blush for Sucker. She starts simpering although Lord knows she's had to do with the Sucker long enough to give over that jazz. She simpers in that put-on way with some people trying to take their mind off the wreck. The idea is they'll be so charmed by the sweet sweetness they'll overlook the jungle. She hopes. But it's a losing game, no one is fooled and anyway why use it on the Sucker? He must know the worst by now.

'Please excuse the chaos,' she had no other tune to start with. She dreams it, and when people stay the night and come down to the breakfast wilderness she begins the day with 'please excuse the chaos'.

'I don't see it', is what he mostly says. A stinking hypocrite. He knows I see through him and that is why he always goes out of his way to do the earnest sincere bit with me. I get the message that he doesn't exactly love me either.

'Would you like a cup of something?' She'll always ask him that, knowing well enough she's only going to get more bogged if she starts making a cup of anything with the swarm around. She isn't asking me though. I'm dying for a cuppa as it so happens. And anyway just to let her see I'm a free agent whatever

about the Sucker being around and all that, I follow the troop
down the stairs. As they go down he has an arm across her
shoulders. What does he see in her? She's gone off so much.
Since the last baby she's a real drag.

Down below, with me there, the style is cramped. The two of
them make *nice* conversation while I just hump against the wall
and watch. The rabble are pelting things around the floor and the
Sucker gets tangled up in roller skates that come flying at his
ankles. He's worrying about his shoes again. The oil off the
skates is his trouble. Sure enough the trendy suede has a streak,
a lovely, dirty, greasy smudge.

'Oh Patricia, what shall I do?'

He is in real agony. Like a helpless baby. 'What shall I do,'
mind you. Take off your sock and pee in your shoe that's what
I've a mind to call. The thought of calling that out to him just
now, sets me off laughing. The kids see me and start off too.
They think I'm laughing *with* them, but damn their eyes the
whole bunch make me *puke*. The only reason I'm down here is
to be a nuisance, just to be a nuisance in the way of a cuppa. I
can always go on in to Walter at the Bistro if I'm not getting
one here. Or maybe he'd stretch to a small brandy. I could,
actually, even pay for it. But I'll have to bum a few bob at the
club tonight.

Harvey's hanging around with the smudged shoe in his hand
and she's dabbing away with some stuff out of a bottle and a
piece that she's torn off the baby's napkin—not hard to do, that,
the napkins are in ribbons this long day. Even those she makes
last. Mending them. Mending *napkins*!

The kettle is steaming away like mad, but they're too busy
with the shoe to do anything so I saunter over towards the stove,
but then I think I won't bother. Serve her right if the bottom
burns out: she's bound to have put on only a small drop, seeing
I wasn't included.

The young brat is sitting on the floor beside the stove, dabbling
in a pool of milk that's probably been lying there since the last
lot for the baby boiled over. Anyway there's always some pool
of milk by the stove because of the dip in the lino. 'Twas a yawk

of a country yob (SHE has a soft spot for country yobs) put it down for her and he hadn't a clue. All lumps and bumps all over the floor that was uneven in the first place anyhow. He told her he was putting boards down to even it out for her. He put boards down all right, trudging in and out between the old shed that had fallen down and the kitchen. He used every sort of a board out of that old shed, all bits and pieces, so that you can imagine the floor was a real glory after him.

I'm watching that brat washing his filthy paws in the slop of milk and then he begins to pick at the lino, breaking it back in little pieces from the leg of the stove. Then he starts to squawk:

'Yuoooo mammeee, eeuch, eeuch, look at 'gusting spiders.'

'Yes,' she says, not really listening, and she half turns round and tells him 'now you naughty little boy, stop that dabbling. Omygod Harvey the mess gets me down.'

It's the first real thing she has said since he came. I mean there is no simpering now and no *nice* air. She really means that bit about it getting her down. She takes a full turn around and with the piece of napkin she's been using on the shoe she stoops to mop up the milk. Then she gives a shriek and her face gets red as red and she clutches herself away from the stove and squeezes her eyes up.

'What is it daaarling?' He loves the drama bit always, 'Daarling, whatever is it?'

'Omygod don't even look at them the revolting things.' She's still clutching herself and squeezing her face up. She is a proper sight.

But he looks anyway.

'Oh Gawd,' he is horror-struck and his pulpit voice is all tragic in the drama of it.

The mob gathers round and they are all shrieking and gabbling and doing a jig around the stove. I push a bit closer to have a dekko. In the hole where the lino is picked away there's about a trillion maggots; they all look as if they're standing on one end and waving the other end up at us. There they are, about a couple of trillion maggots like nothing I've ever seen before in my life, different from blue-bottle ones, all standing on their heads and

waving their one leg at us. It makes your back shrivel and your
ankles give.

'They're from the milk,' says SHE when she gets around to
saying anything. 'It's always getting boiled over. I'm always
telling you all not to let the milk boil over.'

She's glaring at Stephen and the NEXT ONE—the two of
them are always making slops on the stove. Give her due she's
not the only slopper, but they all grew out of her. They didn't
have to be there at all did they? She has only herself to blame.

'There's a special sort of fly,' she goes on flapping around,
'I've been seeing them all over the kitchen lately a lot and I've
been wondering—so that's what they've been up to, Omygod.'

She says herself 'tis a free world. Multiplication. Everybody's
twistin'.

Stephen takes down the toasting fork that's never used except
to grow cobwebs and he starts poking back the lino. The more
he pokes the more maggots. Then there is this awful sudden
smell, but that's only the kettle burnt black.

Harvey the Sucker has gone far back to the middle of the
kitchen and he's bending over from the stomach in the direction
of the stove. It's the big sympathy stance, making out he's tied
up in her trouble, safe distance and all, but the way he's standing,
it looks like he's ready to throw up any minute and is trying for
his chance to make off in a way least likely to rile her. Maybe,
though, she is glad enough for him to clear off at the moment:
this, on top of, or under, all the other mess is hardly the memory
of her he'll most treasure. Anyhow, for now he's yabbering away,

'Patricia I—I—don't quite see what use I can be at this
moment; in fact though, even if I did, I have to be at that meeting
I was telling you about, in five minutes. So—so—if you'll excuse
me—'

He was backing to the door waving his body at her from the
waist up. His face was a sight. A mixture of a Sucker agony and
a Sucker smile. He showed her his front and back teeth in the
sympathy effort.

'Oh of course, Harvey, of course. Forgive me if I don't come
up.'

That's the way they always go on, so fecking polite to make you vomit.

Now for some real business. There are all the little grey slugs waving away at her, the little pets, not to be given the go-by.

'Godogod,' she starts off, 'you'll all have to go out. I can't tackle this with all of you crowding around me. Get away from me, right away and let me at it.'

But no one budges and she roars GET BACK ALL OF YOU FOR THE LORD'S SAKE. So they move a bit. About an inch.

'Now this is one instance when you'll get a good wallop, I'm warning you. Even though I don't believe in walloping I'm no saint, and I'm stretched to the limit.'

She turns on Stephen and the NEXT ONE, her hand lifted ready for it—she'd not touch the small ones I'll say.

'Get out, Stephen, d'you hear? And take them all with you. Lift up that child,' she says to the NEXT ONE, meaning for her to take the small one who picked the hole, 'and keep him outside till I say not.'

Stephen sees she means business but his love of the maggots, the dear little creatures, makes him brave.

'Ah Ma,' he says—he says 'Ma' sometimes and mostly it gets her goat, but this time she doesn't notice, 'I'll keep them all back over there,' he points to the far corner, 'I promise, if you'll let us stay.'

'Did anyone—don't CALL me Ma—' (she noticed all right) 'ever have such a family? Morbid little brutes. Other mothers get far more result—they belt and wallop all the time—I'm far too soft with you all, far too soft.' But she has put her hand down, so she's not going to wallop, it seems. And she's looking sideways at the squirming multiplication. She can't face it square yet. Maybe she doesn't know which way she'd best turn.

'You can stay, but don't budge out of that corner.' She hooshes them all into the corner, where they start pinching and kicking just to keep in form. 'Oh God I need help. I NEED help. So will you lot help me by just staying quiet? It's not too much to ask is it and it's the most help I can expect, I suppose.'

All the time I am standing there she acts as if I amn't around.

I wish she might just chance asking me something so I could refuse or be lousy someway.

First she makes this ton of strong, boiling Jeyes' fluid stuff and pours a flood of it over the maggots. There's that army of them the odd kick's left in them even after that. She keeps clapping her hand up to her nose and mouth as if she's afraid to breathe. Then she gets these miles of newspaper—she always keeps the things for lighting fires 'and you never know how they'll be handy'. Now she knows like she never knew before— nor me either. She hauls out this old galvanised bath full of holes and starts wadding paperfuls of maggots and Jeyes' into it. She's nearly dying for the want of breath and keeps going over to the window for a fresh gulp. She's not breathing while she does each separate bit of wadding. Every go she uses about twenty layers of paper as a kind of a scoop. Now if 'twere me I'd just get the mallet and shovel from the old shed and pound the lot to hell, rotten boards and all, and then shovel the whole mess into the bath. But she has no head like that. All fluster and squeam. Still 'tis hardly the job you'd exactly pick, especially with the crowd in the corner laughing their silly nuts off.

They are reasonable enough apart from that, I'll say, but if it goes on too long they are likely to break out. They can't stand anything for long and this looks like it could go on till kingdom come.

My father is due home soon for his meal. Appetising welcome.

Ah well I'll go on up and out. There's just time to stop off at the Bistro. Imagine *tea* after that.

'See you,' I kind of call.

But she doesn't answer even a syllable. It's just about possible she didn't hear me. Maybe she's forgotten I'm there. I didn't exactly put my helpful presence forward since the maggot racket. Ah well . . .

Still it's her own fault. Who asked them to have all the brats? Now with only me and Peg, with only me . . . Peg's gone anyway, couldn't wait to spring the joint—

Well if it isn't the Sucker rushing against me back down to her. I hear him inside the kitchen.

'Patricia, I've rung them up to say I'm not coming. Look I'll fix it up for you. Hang on, take it easy—there must be something in the shed—hang on.'

He gallops off out to the back, suede shoes and all, and he's back in a minute with a shovel and a bucket of sand. I never thought of the sand.

I'll have to go now, no time even for Walter's. Maybe Max might run to some brandy later.

And it's my father coming up the front steps.

'*Maryjane*, you're *back*!' and he stands looking at me all lines and puzzles in his face, and then he puts this kiss on my forehead.

But I'm not back.

I'm not so sure I like RED JELLY as a name for what Max painted. I don't know if I even *like* that picture. In fact it's a lousy picture.

THE WAY OF THE WHITE COW

Peter Tremayne

Peter Tremayne (1943–) is one of the country's leading Celtic historians, as well as the author of a number of Irish-based fantasy novels and the unique Sister Fidelma series, about a seventh-century crime-solving nun. Born Peter Berresford Ellis, he is the third generation of his family to have entered journalism. His father was from Sunday's Well, Cork City, and worked on the Cork Examiner, *and he himself was the deputy editor of the* Irish Post *before turning to full-time authorship. One of his forebears, Hercules Ellis, stood as a Tenants' Rights prospective parliamentary candidate in County Cavan; while another, Tom Ellis, was a member of the revolutionary socialist Irish Citizens' Army and fought in the War of Independence in 1919–21.*

Peter Tremayne earned a first class honours degree in Celtic Studies and a master's degree, and his first book on Ireland, History of the Irish Working Class *(1972), published under his own name, is now considered a classic and is still in print. He has subsequently used much of his extensive research material— a great deal of it derived from contemporary sources previously untapped—as the basis for his novels, including* Raven of Destiny *(1984),* Island of Shadows *(1991) and the Sister Fidelma series which began with* Absolution by Murder *(1994) and is now several volumes strong and attracting an ever-increasing readership on both sides of the Atlantic.*

Childhood travels in Ireland first opened Tremayne's eyes to the country's rich mythology and he returns regularly to under-take research and to lecture about his work. He also serves in senior positions in organisations such as the Celtic League and at Scrif-Celt, the Celtic Languages book fair. As he admits, the course of his life might have been very different but for a strange and moving experience he had as a fifteen-year-old at Dunboy Castle near Castletownbere on the Beara Peninsula. 'The Way of the White Cow' is based on that incident—a moment of truth for one young man when the future became not a puzzle but an objective.

*   *   *

I shall never forget that summer in Cork. I was fifteen years old and had been allowed to travel from London to Ireland by myself for the very first time. I suppose it could be argued that there were several things which made me remember that particular holiday. The death of my aunt, for one thing. But I do not think it was that alone which has fixed the events so clearly in my mind. First love, that heart-thumping, stuttering adolescent encounter, also impinges on the memory. No, it was not that either. Something else makes me remember that summer. Something more poignant to the maturity of my impressionable youth. Something that I cannot really explain—even after all these years.

To be able to travel alone from London to Cork was, I had thought, the very proof of my new-found adulthood: fifteen was surely a 'grown up' age. In those days, and it was only in the 1950s, when children were fifteen years old, the law allowed them to leave school if they wanted to, and get a job. I recall being dismayed, having suggested the idea to my parents, at their horror. They instructed me to forget such ridiculous notions, for I would stay on at school and, hopefully, go on to higher education.

But to put that journey in perspective, my mother had ensured that I was placed safely on the train for Fishguard, in Wales. Following the crowd from the train onto the ferry, the *Innisfallen*, was not a hard task to accomplish. In my youthful exuberance, the ferry appeared as a gigantic ocean-going ship. I suppose, in reality, it was just a small boat which, in those days, took one from Fishguard directly into Cork City. It was the pride of the old City of Cork Steam Packet Company. The crossing seemed to take an eternity before the boat rounded the frowning granite of Roche's Point, through the great inlet of Cork Harbour, and steamed by Passage West to make its confident way along the River Lee into the heart of the city where its passengers were deposited on Penrose Quay.

And there, on the quay, stood Aunt Rhoda, anxiously scanning the disembarking crowd, waiting to take charge of me. She was elderly, or so it seemed to me then. In fact, she was only in her late fifties. Streaked grey hair in a flattened bun at the back, protruding under a dark, broad-brimmed flat hat. Her pale eyes glinted behind spectacles. She appeared a forbidding lady to those who did not notice the creases at the corners of her mouth, the laughter lines about her eyes.

'Well now, *a mhic*, you are safe come and welcome,' she greeted me, in that curious sing-song accent of Cork people. She was not an Irish speaker, but like many who came from the prosperous middle classes and had lost the language after independence, she affected several Irishisms. A *mhic* (O son!) was a favourite of hers when addressing me.

'And were you sick on the boat?' she continued solicitously.

I denied that I had been, but to be truthful I had felt queasy for most of the long journey and unable to look at the meals brought by the sympathetic steward.

'And could you stand an immediate train journey, *a mhic*? If you're up to it, we can catch the train in half-an-hour.'

While Aunt Rhoda lived in the city of Cork, it had been arranged that she would take me to the country where she had rented a small cottage for the summer.

I nodded politely, trying not to show my reluctance because my balance was not all it should be. I felt as if I were walking on cotton wool and not the concrete slab of the quay.

'Then we'll walk up to the station. I've already deposited my suitcase there. By the time you get there, you'll have recovered your land legs.' Aunt Rhoda seemed to know exactly how I felt.

Dutifully, I followed her, clutching at my own suitcase in

which I had packed my things, under mother's supervision, for the holiday. We walked up the hill to Glanmire Road Station and on the way I found we were bound for Bantry Bay. This, of course, was some years before the CIÉ, the Irish transport system, announced their plans to close all the rail services in West Cork and replace them with bus routes. That didn't happen until 1960. You could still get a four-carriage steam train, with black carriages and broad yellow stripe, which would snort and hiss its way through Ballinhassig, through Bandon, down to Drimoleague and Bantry.

The childhood memories are as clear today as if that journey were made yesterday.

I should explain that my Aunt Rhoda was unmarried and still lived in Sunday's Well, in Cork City, where my father was born. She had been born in the year of Victoria's Jubilee, when the British Empire spanned a third of the globe, and was in her mid-twenties when Ireland won its independence.

In my eyes she was the fountain of all knowledge and full of wise sayings. I learned much from her. To be truthful, her name was not Rhoda at all but Rúadnat, which was an old Irish name. Her father had been a great admirer of Douglas Hyde, who was to become first President of Ireland in 1937. Some years before Aunt Rhoda's birth, Dr Hyde had delivered a famous address on 'The Necessity for De-anglicising the Irish Nation'. Aunt Rhoda's father had thought he would contribute his bit to restoring Irish culture by naming his daughter Rúadnat. But Irish names were not so fashionable in the pre-independence period as they have become today. So my aunt had adopted Rhoda as the nearest anglicised equivalent. Rúadnat was the name of an ancient Irish saint and I found it more fascinating than Rhoda. However, I could never quite summon up courage to call her Aunt Rúadnat though I would have liked to. It would have implied a shared secret, an expression of belonging to a place apart.

Alas, I did not know then that it would be the last such holiday I would spend in Ireland; nor that Aunt Rhoda had so little time to live.

We arrived in Bantry where Aunt Rhoda had booked rooms

at the Anchor Hotel for the night. It was exciting to be staying in the hotel, which seemed crowded with cigarette and pipe-smoke, the curious bitter-sweet odours of alcohol and fishermen: fishermen intent on angling for salmon and trout in the neighbouring streams; more adventurous fishermen who were planning to head off on boats out into the wild seas of Bantry Bay and beyond for deep-sea fishing. And controlling all the cacophony which erupted from the guests in the bar was a kindly, broad-faced man named O'Donnell who ran the hotel. How proud I was to be able to sit in the bar lounge, too interested to take more than a cursory sip of the ice-cold lemonade from the glass placed before me, while Aunt Rhoda nipped sedately at her sherry as we waited for the evening meal to be prepared.

The next morning we were off on a ramshackle bus along the hedge-bordered road down the Beara Peninsula, the most south-westerly of Ireland's long peninsulas, hemmed in by red fuchsias and evergreen trees with glimpses of the rounded tops of the bald mountains appearing now and then above the hedge line. Through Glengarriff and Adrigole, past the tall peaks of the Caha Mountains, until finally we came to Castletownbere— Castletown Berehaven, to give it its correct name—where the bus could go no farther. Yet there was more distance to go before we completed our journey.

This time we transferred to an ancient pony and trap, driven by an old man named O'Sullivan, gnarled and browned by the weather, who smoked a foul-smelling pipe and whose accent I never began to understand. And so eventually, in the early afternoon sun, we arrived at the whitewashed cottage that my aunt had rented. It no longer exists, or rather there is just a pile of stones where once it stood. Brackcloon Cottage, overlooking a wild stretch of sea and the mountains of Slieve Miskish rising behind, with the constant cry of the seabirds all around.

I remember running round the cottage, examining it, and calling to my aunt: 'At last, we can start the holiday now.'

Aunt Rhoda smiled as she opened the cottage door with a key taken from under a plantpot by the portal: 'It is not always the arriving, *a mhic*, but the journey which is the most interesting part of life.' I only realised later in life that the comment was not so simple as it then sounded to my youthful ears.

It took me a few days to adjust myself and then, like most boys loose in a strange and foreign (for all my father's connection with Ireland) land, I was off exploring. Provided that I told my aunt where I was going, provided that I did not swim unless I was with someone who knew the devious tides and currents of the waters around the coast, provided I returned when I said I would, my aunt allowed me free rein to do as I willed. She even hired a bicycle for me at a place in Castletown called MacCarthy's, which was both pub, shop and a focus for the social life of the town.

I first saw Dunboy Castle from the inlet. To be more precise, I first saw the gaunt, charred ruins of Puxley Mansion, which is often mistaken for the castle by visitors who have just arrived in the area. Puxley Mansion rises up with its gaping windows as a roofless shell which dominates the area. Dunboy Castle itself is hardly more than a mound of stones on a low headland in front of the house. It stands on a small, low finger of land, thrust into a fairly enclosed but large inlet opposite the broad passage into the turbulent seas of the Atlantic beyond. You could see at once why the castle was placed in that position: it dominated the seaway into the quiet waters of the inlet.

The inlet was spectacular that summer, an area of serene beauty whose shoreline was surrounded by oaks. Their green canopy rose in ridges fringed with varied evergreens. It was a place of gentle silence, with the sunlight creating a blue, shimmering surface on the stretch of its waters. Red fuchsias appeared everywhere beyond the grey-green shoreline of seaweed and here and there were strawberry trees and shrubs whose colours created a kaleidoscopic vista of shades. Now and again an inquisitive seal would plop up out of the water to stare at our boat. Herons swooped in the sky to be scolded now and then by the protesting gulls and guillemots.

It was an O'Sullivan who took me out into the inlet to fish. Not the same O'Sullivan who had driven the cart when we arrived. In fact, to my ears, every other person on the Beara seemed to be named O'Sullivan. That was because this is O'Sullivan clan territory.

'What place is that?' I demanded, jerking my free hand towards the exquisite headland on which the ruins stood, while making sure I kept firm hold of my line with the other.

The fisherman's eyes narrowed as he followed my gesture.

'That's Puxley Mansion. Bad cess to it!' And the man spat into the water. I would have been cuffed on the ear by my father if I had done as much. The fisherman went on: 'The Puxleys drove out the O'Sullivans, confiscated their estates and tried to steal everything that they owned. They would have stolen their souls if they could. 'Twas a Puxley that built that great house. 'Twas Copper John Puxley who opened the mines around these parts and worked people to death in them. Wild Copper John!' He spat again. 'He it was who built that pile of brick on his ill-gotten profits. They tell me that an English writer wrote a book about Wild Johnny Puxley and the copper mines hereabouts and named it *Hungry Hill*. You would pass a big mountain as you came through Adrigole. That's Hungry Hill.'

I knew by now that he was referring to the ruined shell of a house rising behind the more exciting remains of the older fortress on the headland. It was this old place that I was more keen to know about. But the fisherman was into his story and I could not deflect him.

'Well, an O'Sullivan did for John Puxley. Shot him dead at the gates of his own estate. That was Morty Óg O'Sullivan. God's forgiveness be on him for he already has mine.'

I was not sure what he meant but I felt that I should make some contribution.

'How did it get like that? The big house, I mean? Did the owners move away?'

The fisherman laughed. It was not a humorous sound; more of a harsh, vibrating noise.

'Yes, they moved away. At the time of what we call ''The Troubles'', Henry Puxley succeeded to the manor. A fine Ascendancy gentleman he was, an officer of the British Navy. Castletown Berehaven was then the anchorage of the British Atlantic Fleet and remained so right up until 1937, even after we became a Free State. During the war of independence Puxley allowed the house to be used by the British military as an headquarters. The boys attacked it one night, one night in 1921 it was, and burnt it down.'

'The boys?' I queried.

'The Irish Volunteers, the republicans. They burnt it down. Since when it has stood as you see it. A blackened shell. The Puxleys left and never returned.'

'But what about that ruined fortress in front there? What is that?'

The fisherman swallowed slowly.

'That's a shrine, boy,' he said solemnly. 'A holy shrine. Tread softly there, for you tread on ground sanctified by blood.'

He glanced up at the sky, saw the day was drawing to a close and brusquely told me to reel in my line before bending to the oars to row back to shore.

It wasn't until the next afternoon that I remembered about the place and took my bike with some sandwiches for a snack. I cycled towards the towering remains of Puxley Mansion, following the cow tracks beyond the crumbling gatehouse, where a rusty gate presented no impediment to my journey along an overgrown driveway which led to the gaunt ruins themselves. All along the way were luxuriant rhododendron bushes and scrub trees with flourishing evergreen oaks.

The house stood cold and bleak. It seemed in contrast to the beauty of the inlet which stretched behind it. I had a feeling of sorrow as I gazed upon that shell. It did not seem to me to have been a place which had contained much happiness. Windowless, roofless, blackened timbers and scorch-marked walls—it appeared like a monument to the dead. I could not articulate the feelings at the time yet I believe I was thinking that man was a vain creature to have attempted to build such a vast monstrosity and call it 'home'.

I was standing there, leaning on my bike and examining the remnants of the house, when I heard her before I saw her.

'You are the English boy staying at Brackcloon.' The voice was low, sweet and feminine.

I turned and stared at a girl, scarcely older than myself, standing on a slight rise of ground a few yards away. She had long golden tresses, a fair skin and eyes that appeared to be deep green, glittering like the sun sparkling on the sea. She was clad in a bright emerald green dress with white cuffs. It was the sort of dress that is often worn by girls engaged in Irish folk dancing. She had a soft accent but her tone came almost like a humming song, the phraseology was one that, even then, I associated with someone whose first language was Irish.

'My father is from Cork City.' I don't know why I was suddenly so defensive at being called English.

She laughed disarmingly. 'It matters more who *you* are,' she countered, placing the accent on the 'you'. 'You are staring at the house. What are you thinking?'

I swallowed hard, for I was immediately smitten by the girl's beauty and her easy manner. My sudden perplexity made me stammer a little.

'I was thinking that if I became rich I should buy that place and rebuild it.'

'And then do what with it?' She was mocking me.

I blushed and said: 'I'd like to invite all my friends to stay and enjoy this beautiful spot.'

'Would you like to be so rich? Would you want to be a great lord of the manor?' There was a jeering note in her voice.

I thought a moment and then shrugged.

'It was just a notion. Anyway, the place seems so . . .' I shrugged for I could not quite articulate the feelings I had. 'I was going on to see the old fort,' I ended lamely.

'Ah, that is more interesting than this sorrowful pile of bricks.'

It seemed curious that she seemed to share my thoughts about the house. She was right, of course: the folly of the great ruined house began to oppress me the more I examined it.

'No good came to the Puxleys in this land,' she cut in on my thoughts. 'Death and misery ever haunted them. Come, I'll take you down to the old fort.'

She turned with a jaunty swing and I followed, pushing my bike obediently at her side.

We moved along an overgrown paved stretch by the inlet which had probably been a quay many years before, and then out to the headland which thrust towards the opening to the sea. The air here was mild, almost balmy and soft. It caressed one with its warm breath. Sea birds darted lazily across the waters.

'Is it an old castle?' I asked curiously as we approached the sprawl of grey granite stones.

'Older than you could ever dream. This is Dunboy.'

'I know that *dun* is a fort but what does the name mean?'

'The fortress of the Cow Goddess, *Dun Baoí*, in Irish. The cow goddess, Baoí, was sometimes called *Cailleach Beara*, the Old Woman of Beara. This was her fort in the time before time. She was one of the ancient goddesses who dwelt in this land.'

'Goddesses!' I sneered. 'I do not believe in gods and goddesses!'

The girl turned solemn eyes upon me. She peered deeply into my eyes. Then she smiled softly. It captivated my heart again and I felt all the troubled, unfamiliar and confusing passions of one who stands at the threshold of manhood—neither innocent nor mature.

'At night, look up at the sky. You will see the *Bealach na Bó Finne*, what you call the Milky Way. That will show you the passing of the Cow Goddess through the great universe.'

'*Bealach na Bó Finne?*' I tried to pronounce the words as carefully as I could. 'What does that mean?'

'The Way of the White Cow, the path of the Cow Goddess. The Way of the White Cow is the radiant path of stars which leads to heaven, a path that we must all tread eventually. It is our fate, our future.'

'I don't believe in gods, goddesses or in heaven,' I declared stoutly. It was a fad in my class during the last term that we had all decided to profess to be atheists. The previous term it was Buddhism which had been the fashion.

'We all have a personal heaven,' the girl insisted.

I thought she was joking with me and turned away in disgust.

It was then I noticed a small plaque on the stone wall beside me. It seemed that it had only recently been placed there. It was in old Irish script and all I could make out were the dates '1602' and '1952'. I overcame my pride.

'Can you translate this?' I asked the girl.

'Of course.'

When she said nothing else, I swallowed more of my pride.

'*Will* you translate it? Please?'

'It is in memory of the heroes who fell in the siege of Dunboy in June 1602. It was placed here a few years ago.'

'Do you know anything about that siege?' I demanded excitedly. 'Is that when the castle was destroyed?' I was fond of such tales.

'The story is simple enough. This was the chief fortress of Donal Cam O'Sullivan Beare—Crooked Donal the English called him, on account that he had one shoulder higher than the other. He was chieftain of this land and bowed the knee only to the MacCarthy Mór, King of Desmond. When the English attempted to conquer Ireland, they knew they had to reduce Dunboy which was the most important stronghold in the south-west. They sent Sir George Carew, a man of great obsession to destroy all things Irish, to take the castle. He came by sea with shipload after shipload of soldiers and surrounded Dunboy.

'By chance O'Sullivan Beare had left the fortress with a small party to go across the mountains behind us, to Ardea, to meet a Spanish ship landing arms for the Irish. The man placed in charge during his absence was Risteárd Mac Geoghegan into whose care O'Sullivan had entrusted his niece, Féthnat. Mac Geoghegan gathered the people inside with a herd of 500 milch cows to feed them.'

I was partially aware that her voice had become animated with the telling of the story, its tones rising and falling with fierce yet musical cadences. The inflections were hypnotic and I peered about me, imagining the scene of those exciting events.

'See there,' she suddenly pointed across the inlet to an adjacent headland, 'there on a June Sunday the foreigners, with two big guns and two regiments of men, marched up and began to fire on this place. Then more transports and soldiers landed on the opposite side. Mac Geoghegan tried to beat off the attack on the shoreline but soon had to retire inside the castle, sending one of his wounded men to alert O'Sullivan. Ten days later at four o'clock, as dawn was breaking, the big guns were drawn up a hundred and forty yards from these walls . . . there and there . . .'

She swung her hand dramatically. I could see them in my mind's eye; see them as I stood looking from the point of view of those who were defending Dunboy.

'One demi-cannon, two whole culverins and one demi-culverin began to fire into this fortress.'

I did not understand what these names meant, and the extent of her knowledge surprised me, but the sound of her voice drove me along with the tale.

'The south-west turret of the fortress was hit. Down it came, its falling masonry crashing down and burying many of the defenders where they had stood. See there . . .'

I stared at the spot, imagining men, choking on white masonry dust, seeing the blood and hearing the screams and cries of the wounded; hearing the roar of the massive cannons just a short distance away.

'The defenders sent a messenger to Carew to offer a surrender. Mac Geoghegan knew it was only a short time before the guns destroyed them all. Carew promptly had the envoy hanged so those inside the fortress could see. Still his cannons poured shot at them. Before the day was out, a great breach was made in the wall. Carew sent his soldiers in, driving the defenders back by musketry and hand-to-hand fighting. Back they were driven until the survivors of the garrison were forced to take refuge in the cellars below us.

'Forty of the defenders managed to break away. They scrambled over the wall and ran down to the sea shore to avoid capture by attempting to swim across to that wooded headland. Carew had boats out and they rowed about firing or hurling lances at each swimmer, or simply striking at them with swords, until every one of those forty men was slaughtered and the inlet was running red with blood.'

She paused, her face still animated.

I muttered: 'Go on, go on!'

'The defenders were now reduced to a hundred souls, grouped in the cellar where they had been driven . . . you can see the remnants of the cellar, look through here . . . see it . . . smell the stench of death?'

I felt a curious fear as I gazed inside the black entrance to which she had pointed. It seemed so real as the girl told it. I almost saw the mass of bodies below me, smelt the sickly stink of dead and dying, heard the groaning and muttered prayers.

'The survivors again asked to be allowed to surrender and were again refused. All through the night the survivors huddled there, among the groaning wounded and dying, among the dead. Mac Geoghegan himself lay wounded and unable to command any defence. He realised that Carew planned to slaughter every-one—continuing his cannonade—killing or burying the remaining defenders alive in the rubble.'

I realised from the turmoil of her features that the girl was living the story, and her vitality and passion in the telling of it were making me live it too.

'At dawn, an attack came. Covered with wounds, Mac Geoghegan managed to rise from his deathbed and stagger with a lighted candle towards an open powder keg, intent on taking his enemies with him rather than see the survivors die like slaugh-tered cattle. But one of Carew's officers had chosen that moment to launch a raid into the cellars to see if he could capture O'Sullivan Beare, who he thought was hiding there. The officer seized Mac Geoghegan just as he was about to torch the powder and he held him fast while his soldiers stabbed him to death. It was then that Carew had a change of mind, perhaps after hearing that O'Sullivan was not in the fortress. He announced that he would allow the survivors to surrender. Some ninety-nine souls surrendered and came out of that terrible cellar. Carew immedi-ately hanged fifty-eight just there, on the lawn before the Puxley Mansion, only at that time it was the marketplace for the fortress. Twenty-six were executed shortly after, while fifteen others were taken and executed elsewhere.'

'So there were no survivors?'

'Only one. The young girl named Féthnat, O'Sullivan's niece.

She had been hidden in the cellar under the bodies of the dead defenders. She managed to climb out at nightfall, escaped into the woods and eventually joined O'Sullivan Beare.'

'And did O'Sullivan Beare return and avenge himself on Carew?' I demanded indignantly, my blood stirring against the evil pitilessness of the man.

The girl gave a sad grimace.

'Life is never so simple. Hardly ever does right triumph over might. Carew had reduced O'Sullivan's stronghold and executed its defenders. There was now a price on the head of the last chieftain of the south to defy the English armies. He knew that he and his people could expect no mercy at the hands of Carew. So in the dark, cold days after Christmas 1602, O'Sullivan Beare took a thousand of his immediate retinue and set off towards the north, to Leitrim Castle where Irishmen were still holding out against the conquest. Leitrim was the castle of Brían O Ruairc. O'Sullivan hoped to join forces with him. A thousand set out, including women and children. In fifteen days, through the height of the freezing winter, they marched 300 miles, avoiding the English when possible, fighting them when they had to. Out of those thousand souls, only thirty-five survived and one was a woman.'

'What happened to them after they reached O Ruairc?' I demanded, intrigued.

'Then the surrender of Ireland had been completed. But they eventually escaped to a life of exile in Spain. And since that day the O'Sullivan castle has stood desolate. The last of the native princes of Ireland had fled into exile.'

'Was the woman who survived the winter march the same one who escaped from here? From Dunboy?'

The girl sighed and shook her head.

'No. O'Sullivan's niece died of winter chill and fever after eight days on that awesome march.'

'You know an awful lot about it,' I conceded with admiration. 'I would like to be able to tell stories like that. It is difficult to remember all those facts from stuffy old history books.'

The girl spread her hands expressively.

'But history is all around you, living and breathing. It is here in these poor stones, in the lapping of the water on the pebbles, in the sighing of the wind in the trees. Open your heart, listen to the voices of the past. Unless we open our minds to the past we cannot understand our present and not understanding we shall have no future.'

I frowned. 'I am not sure that I understand you.'

In fact, I had no understanding at all for I found what she was saying totally beyond my fifteen-year-old capability. I did not want to press her for, to be truthful, I was slightly ashamed that she had so much more knowledge than I did; not knowledge of facts but of words and the strange concepts she was attempting to convey to me.

'Sometimes you have to just follow the Way of the White Cow without understanding.'

In following her upward glance to the heavens, I suddenly realised that the sun was low in the sky. It was later than I had thought. I had promised Aunt Rhoda that I would be home by supper time. I had been carried away by the girl's fascinating story of the siege of Dunboy and lost track of time.

'I have to go,' I said reluctantly. 'Will I see you again? I would like to see you again,' I corrected hurriedly.

The girl chuckled softly.

'Then you will find me once you have followed the Way of the White Cow. Look for that path in the sky at night and recognise where it might lead.'

Still laughing she began to trot away.

'Hey!' I called. 'What is your name? Your name!'

She paused and glanced back, smiling over her slender shoulder.

'O'Sullivan. What else would it be?' she called.

'Your first name,' I cried as she turned and continued to hasten towards the nearby woods.

I am sure it was the name Féthnat which floated back to me on the evening air.

I never saw her again, even though, throughout the rest of my holiday, I searched and even asked at local farmhouses for her.

But everywhere I was told that no Féthnat O'Sullivan lived in the district. One old lady assured me, indignantly, that no one would be called Féthnat in a good Christian country. It was an ancient name. Surely, wasn't Féthnat the storyteller and musician to the Ever Living Ones, the ancient gods and goddesses of Ireland? Féthnat, indeed! The woman sniffed and then, taking pity on me, suggested that I had surely been wrong in my understanding of the name! Perhaps I was. And O'Sullivan was such a common name so there was no telling who the girl might have been.

Even asking Aunt Rhoda to make some inquiries produced no result. No one recognised the girl from my description.

One evening, before bed, after Aunt Rhoda had lit the oil lamp (for there were places not yet fitted with electricity in the area) and we were sitting at the kitchen table to have a cup of cocoa, I asked her if she knew what the White Cow was. To my surprise, for I thought she knew everything, she initially shook her head. I explained that it was supposed to be the Milky Way. Then she smiled brightly.

'Oh, you mean the "Way of the White Cow", which is the meaning of the Irish name for the Galaxy. Is that it, *a mhic*?' She paused and reflected. 'In the old days they said that it was the brilliant path which led to heaven or, perhaps, to our individual heavens. Now I come to think of it, there is an old saying that each of us has a cow-path to follow. Did you know that the Irish word for a road, *bóthar*, means a cow-path?'

I shook my head.

'Well, they say that the universe of each of us is but what each of us desires and that the way to achieve our desire is to find a star and follow the cow-path to it.'

'I still don't understand,' I protested.

'Time enough,' she sighed. 'But the secret of success in life is constancy of purpose. The soul that has no established aim and does not follow the cow-path will soon lose itself. It all depends on you. The Way of the White Cow, so the old ones say, is not a friendly route, nor is it hostile. It is simply indifferent and how you tread the path is up to you.'

I went to bed that night to dream of sieges and battles but with no real understanding of Aunt Rhoda's explanation.

For the rest of that summer I haunted the desolate woodlands, the coves and hills around the ruins of Dunboy. It was strange, yet I grew to feel a curious affinity with the area. Not with the gaunt Puxley Mansion but with that smaller heap of grey granite stones, the brooding black hole which had once been the great cellar where the defenders had finally held out; becoming familiar with the remains of a flight of stone steps, the crumbling walls and ditches which had marked the defensive perimeter of the fortress. The fortress of the Cow Goddess. *Baoí.*

The time arrived when Aunt Rhoda took me back to Cork and put me on the ferryboat to return home. We had made the journey first to her old house on the Sunday's Well Road to stay a day or two. Before she took me down to Penrose Quay to go aboard the *Innisfallen*, she placed a small brown parcel in my hands. I knew by the size and feel that it was a book.

'I think you will like it, *a mhic*,' she smiled. 'I enjoyed it when I was young. It's a good adventure story and something to remind you of this holiday.'

I hesitated.

'I am still not sure about the Way of the White Cow.'

She relented and smiled.

'Bless you, *a mhic*. It's your path from now on until you die and, perhaps, beyond. It will be full of obstacles. Isn't it the same for everyone? But the old ones say that every obstacle yields to resolution.'

My last memory is of my Aunt Rhoda standing on the quay, in her black coat and hat, her features solemn but with a smile threatening at the corners of her mouth. I leant over the rail of the ferry and waved and waved until the *Innisfallen* had backed its way down the River Lee, out of the city towards the choppy seas. It was the last time I saw Aunt Rhoda and I did not know the details of what happened until long after I had returned. I only knew that some days later a telegram arrived to say Aunt Rhoda was dead and that my father had to go to Cork to sort things out. In fact, when she had left me on the ferry and was walking back to her home, she had a heart attack on the steps of Shandon Church on Mulgrave Road and three days later she died.

I still have the book she gave me on my shelf. It is by J. A. Froude, published by Longman, Green & Co of London, in 1891. Its title is *The Two Chiefs of Dunboy*, the story of the conflict between Morty Óg, the last O'Sullivan claimant to the Dunboy estate, and John Puxley. They found themselves on opposing sides at the battle of Culloden with Morty Óg supporting Bonnie Prince Charlie. John Puxley pursued the 'rebel' O'Sullivans with a vengeance, but on 10 March, 1754, not far from the gates of Puxley Mansion, Morty Óg shot Puxley dead. As Aunt Rhoda had promised, it was a stirring adventure novel.

She had put a note inside: 'Remember, *a mhic*, you cannot reach your journey's end by another man's cow-path.'

I did not return to Dunboy until I was in my late twenties. Since then I have returned many times. It continues to be a mystical place for me. The images of that boyhood encounter by Puxley Mansion are still clear and sharp. I can recall my childish boast of one day buying the ruins of Puxley Mansion and its land and restoring it. A youthful dream. It even became a joke between my wife and myself after I had first taken her there and told the story. It would, of course, cost many millions and there are rumours, even as I write, that a consortium plans to buy it and rebuild it as a hotel with adjacent golf course covering the old castle. It will be a grief-haunted place if they do.

Today, the farmer who owns the land at Dunboy will charge you money to go through the gatehouse, beyond the still rusty gate, where there is a little shop for tourists, no more than a wooden shed, selling postcards and souvenirs. The inlet is no longer isolated for you will see in it yachts and powerboats of every description, flying not only the Irish flag, but more numerously the flags of Germany and Holland. New houses and holiday homes have been raised amidst the oaks and conifers around the shores. The area has become 'European' and while in Castletown you may still find MacCarthy's bar and general store, you will also find shops in which you could think yourself in any part of Europe.

But now and then, as I wander around, I sometimes think I glimpse a young girl with golden tresses and a bright emerald green dress with white cuffs. The figure is gone before I can be sure, running, laughing, into the gloom of the surrounding woods.

And sometimes, I have gone to sit at Dunboy in the late summer evenings and gazed up at the cloudless blue night sky and picked out the maze of the Milky Way—*Bealach na Bó Finne.* The Way of the White Cow. The Galaxy. The brilliant path which leads to heaven: our individual heavens. Sometimes I can still hear her passionate voice describing events beyond her time and, surely, beyond her knowledge.

Then I shudder and feel cold and hear the cries, screams and sobs rising all around me. Yet I do not fear them, for that summer, that summer when I was only fifteen, I realised that there had been born in me the idea of what it was I wanted to do in life; *had to do* in life. I had to tell the story of those forgotten victims, and others like them, and by doing so, to exorcise their suffering and sacrifice.

Perhaps that was meant to be? I chose my own cow-path, as Aunt Rhoda said. Now I am an historian; an historian and storyteller. Perhaps that summer when I was fifteen was the first step along the Way of the White Cow?

BELACQUA'S HOMECOMING

Samuel Beckett

The indolent, sexually-curious Irish student Belacqua Shulah, who appeared in the first short stories written by Samuel Beckett (1906–1989), undoubtedly embodied many of the author's own feelings as a young man growing up in Ireland. Yet Beckett, who was born in Foxrock, near Dublin, and came from an upper-middle-class Protestant family, revealed little of this during his traditional education at Portora Royal School, County Fermanagh—where he proved himself a brilliant scholar as well as an outstanding athlete—nor even when he went to Trinity College, Dublin, and obtained a BA in French and Italian. For a time he was a teacher at Campbell College in Belfast, before becoming a lecturer in French at his former college. Suddenly growing tired of teaching at Trinity, he turned to writing and began to develop the unique style which has made him one of the most important literary figures of the twentieth century. His plays such as Waiting for Godot *(1956),* End Game *(1958) and* Krapp's Last Tape *(1959), and his novels including* Molloy *(1959),* Malone Dies *(1958) and* The Unnameable *(1959), are now rightly accepted as classics and are the subject of intense scrutiny and study.*

Beckett has written of youth as a period of great frustration for the young, when they know what they want to say but have not yet got the vocabulary to be able to do so. Indeed, that was one of the preoccupations of his first play, Le Kid, *which he wrote with Georges Pelorson and was first produced in Dublin in 1931. The following year, after he had quit Trinity College, he started work on what was to be his first novel,* Dream of Fair to Middling Women, *in which he introduced Belacqua. The novel, with its early memories of a child at prayer being tempted by a blue devil, and a mother buying turf from two boys who had stolen it from a bog, contained scenes of sexual fantasies which Beckett realised would make it impossible to publish in Ireland. When the manuscript was also rejected by several publishers in England he put it to one side and refused to have the work published until after his death. In 1992 it finally appeared, edited by Eoin O'Brien who declared it 'ranks as one of his [Beckett's] most Irish writings.' The following extract captures, in a way only Beckett can, a young man's homecoming and the emotions from the past which well up in him.*

*   *   *

They took the dull coast road home, three days and three nights they dawdled up homeward along it, by Youghal, Tramore, Wicklow Town, living on the fat of the land. Chas payed, Belacqua having spent his last shillings in Cork on scent for a lady, a neat involucrate flasket of Cologne water, very fine, for his Mother, she stands listening on the perron, for all the stout in bottle they drank on the way, he shelled out for all the stout that helped to bloat the sadness of the sad evenings, and they went down to all the shores, they paced up and down, up and down, side by side, on the firm sand near the waves, and there Chas, in the chill evening and rain of course threatening, did develop his unheard of musical relations with one Ginette Mac Something, the hem of the hem of the hem of the hem of whose virginity (vidual) toga he would never, jamais au grand jamais, presume and was not worthy to lift the littlest notch let alone hoist aloft thigh-high.

'Je la trouve adorable, quoique peu belle. Elle a surtout beaucoup de GOUT, elle est intelligente et douce, mais douce, mon cher, tu n'peux pas t'imaginer, et des gestes, mon cher, tu sais, très désarmants.'

Belacqua saw at once how lovely she must be, he was quite sure she was very remarkable, and dare he hope that on some not too distant occasion he might be privileged to catch a glimpse of her sailing through the dusk when the dusk was she?

'Elle a une petite gueule' moaned Chas 'qui tremble comme un petit nuage.'

Belacqua found that a striking rapprochement, and in the long gloomy silence that ensued he was at some pains to fix it for ever in his mind:

> le ténébreux visage
> bouge comme un nuage . . .

> j'adore de Ginette le ténébreux visage
> qui tremblote et qui bouge comme un petit nuage

'I have a strong weakness' he assured his dear friend 'for the epic cæsura, don't you know. I like to compare it, don't you know, to the heart of the metre missing a beat.'

Chas thought this was a remarkable comparison, and a long gloomy silence ensued.

'There is much to be done, don't you think' said Belacqua 'with a more nervous treatment of the cæsura,' meaning there was nothing at all to be done don't you think, with the tenebrous Ginette, 'just as the preterites and past subjunctives have never since Racine, it seems to me, been exploited poetically to the extent they merit to be. You know:

"Vous mourûtes aux bords . . ."'

'Où vous fûtes laissée' whistled Chas.

'And the celebrated "quel devint . . ." of the unfortunate Antiochus.'

Chas shivered.

'Shall we go in?' he said.

Thus every night for three nights they left a dark shore, the dark sand, on which a soft rain would ere long be softly falling, falling, because it would bloody well have to.

Belacqua was heartily glad to get back to his parents' comfortable private residence, ineffably detached and situated and so on, and his first act, once spent the passion of greeting after so long and bitter a separation, was to plunge his prodigal head into the bush of verbena that clustered about the old porch (wonderful bush

it was to be sure, even making every due allowance for the kind
southern aspect it enjoyed, it never had been known to miss a
summer since first it was reared from a tiny seedling) and longly
to swim and swoon on the rich bosom of its fragrance, a fragrance
in which the least of his childish joys and sorrows were and
would for ever be embalmed.

His mother he found looking worn. She had not been in the
best of health lately, she said, not at the top of her form, but she
was much better now, now she felt fine.

It was really wonderful to get back to the home comforts.
Belacqua tried all the armchairs in the house, he poltrooned in
all the poltrone. Then he went and tried both privies. The seats
were in rosewood. Douceurs . . . !

The postman flew up with letters, he skidded up the drive on
his bicycle, scattering the loose gravel. He was more pleased
than he could say, but compounded with his aphasia to the extent
anyhow of 'Welcome home' in the attractive accent and the old
familiar smile there under the noble moustache 'master Bel'. Yes,
yes, évidemment. But where was the slender one, where was he,
that was the question, as thin and fine as the greyhound he tended,
the musical one, a most respectable and industrious young fellow
he was, by cheer industry, my dear, plus personal charm, those
were the two sides of the ladder on which this man had mounted,
had he not raised himself above his station, out of the horrible
slum of the cottages, did he not play on the violin, own an evening
suit of his own and dance fleetly with the gentry, and: as he lay
as a child wide awake long after he should have been fast asleep
at the top of the house on a midsummer's night Belacqua would
hear him, the light nervous step on the road as he danced home
after his rounds, the keen loud whistling: *The Roses are Blooming
in Picardy* . . . No man had ever whistled like that, and of course
women can't. That was the original, the only, the unforgettable
banquet of music. There was no music after—only, if one were
lucky, the signet of rubies and the pleasant wine. He whistled
the Roses are Blooming and danced home down the road under
the moon, in the light of the moon, with perhaps a greyhound or
two to set him off, and the dew descending.

KOREA

John McGahern

*John McGahern (1935–) has been described as 'a writer akin
to Beckett' and has certainly defied convention and censorship
with equal determination. Indeed, his work reveals a lot of personal anguish, right from his childhood as the son of a senior
Garda officer in Dublin to the publication of his novel* The Dark
*in 1965, which was banned for its 'sexual realism' and lost him
his contract as a teacher.*

*McGahern spent much of his youth in County Roscommon and
was educated at the Presentation Brothers' School at Carrick-on-
Shannon. He subsequently trained to be a teacher and after taking
up an appointment at Clontarf began to write short stories in
his spare time. These presented vivid pictures of village and
schoolroom life.* Barracks *(1963), his first novel, was a dour and
moving portrayal of adolescence which was critically acclaimed
and won several awards. McGahern was now acknowledged as
a major new writer, but following his dismissal over* The Dark
*he decided to leave the country and settled in London for a time.
However, news of this action made him something of a* cause
célèbre *in America and probably played some part in the
subsequent considerable easing of the censor's standards. Ironi-
cally,* The Pornographer *(1979) confirmed his stature as one of
Ireland's leading fiction writers.*

*Short stories have been a constant feature of John McGahern's
output and several of the best deal with childhood and adolescence. Notable are 'Coming into his Kingdom' which focuses on
a young boy's first discovery of sex when he accidentally falls
on a young girl; 'Lavin' about a boy in danger from a degenerate*

old man's attentions; and 'Korea' which is reprinted here. It is a tense little story about the wary relationship between a father and son—the old man, bitter about his life in Ireland, urging the young man to go to America. But there is a motive behind his suggestion and the story has been seen by critics as a grim variation on the perennial theme of Irish emigration to the USA.

*   *   *

'You saw an execution then too, didn't you?' I asked my father, and he started to tell as he rowed. He'd been captured in an ambush in late 1919, and they were shooting prisoners in Mountjoy as reprisals at that time. He thought it was he who'd be next, for after a few days they moved him to the cell next to the prison yard. He could see out through the bars. No rap to prepare himself came to the door that night, and at daybreak he saw the two prisoners they'd decided to shoot being marched out: a man in his early thirties, and what was little more than a boy, sixteen or seventeen, and he was weeping. They blindfolded the boy, but the man refused the blindfold. When the officer shouted, the boy clicked to attention, but the man stayed as he was, chewing very slowly. He had his hands in his pockets.

'Take your hands out of your pockets,' the officer shouted again, irritation in the voice.

The man slowly shook his head.

'It's a bit too late now in the day for that,' he said.

The officer then ordered them to fire, and as the volley rang, the boy tore at his tunic over the heart, as if to pluck out the bullets, and the buttons of the tunic began to fly into the air before he pitched forward on his face.

The other heeled quietly over on his back: it must have been because of the hands in the pockets.

The officer dispatched the boy with one shot from the revolver as he lay face downward, but he pumped five bullets in rapid succession into the man, as if to pay him back for not coming to attention.

'When I was on my honeymoon years after, it was May, and

we took the tram up the hill of Howth from Sutton Cross,' my father said as he rested on the oars. 'We sat on top in the open on the wooden seats with the rail around that made it like a small ship. The sea was below, and smell of the sea and furze-bloom all about, and then I looked down and saw the furze pods bursting, and the way they burst in all directions seemed shocking like the buttons when he started to tear at his tunic. I couldn't get it out of my mind all day. It destroyed the day.'

'It's a wonder their hands weren't tied?' I asked him as he rowed between the black navigation pan and the red where the river flowed into Oakport.

'I suppose it was because they were considered soldiers.'

'Do you think the boy stood to attention because he felt that he might still get off if he obeyed the rules?'

'Sounds a bit highfalutin' to me. Comes from going to school too long,' he said aggressively, and I was silent. It was new to me to hear him talk about his own life at all. Before, if I asked him about the war, he'd draw fingers across his eyes as if to tear a spider web away, but it was my last summer with him on the river, and it seemed to make him want to talk, to give of himself before it ended.

Hand over hand I drew in the line that throbbed with fish; there were two miles of line, a hook on a lead line every three yards. The licence allowed us a thousand hooks, but we used more. We were the last to fish this freshwater for a living.

As the eels came in over the side I cut them loose with a knife into a wire cage, where they slid over each other in their own oil, the twisted eel hook in their mouths. The other fish—pike choked on hooked perch they'd tried to swallow, bream, roach— I slid up the floorboards towards the bow of the boat. We'd sell them in the village or give them away. The hooks that hadn't been taken I cleaned and stuck in rows round the side of the wooden box. I let the line fall in its centre. After a mile he took my place in the stern and I rowed. People hadn't woken yet, and the early morning cold and mist were on the river. Outside of the slow ripple of the oars and the threshing of the fish on the line beaded with running drops of water as it came in, the river was dead silent, except for the occasional lowing of cattle on the banks.

'Have you any idea what you'll do after this summer?' he asked.

'No. I'll wait and see what comes up,' I answered.

'How do you mean *what comes up*?'

'Whatever result I get in the exam. If the result is good, I'll have choices. If it's not, there won't be choices. I'll have to take what I can get.'

'How good do you think they'll be?'

'I think they'll be all right, but there's no use counting chickens, is there?'

'No,' he said, but there was something calculating in the face; it made me watchful of him as I rowed the last stretch of the line. The day had come, the distant noises of the farms and the first flies on the river, by the time we'd lifted the large wire cage out of the bulrushes, emptied in the morning's catch of eels, and sunk it again.

'We'll have enough for a consignment tomorrow,' he said.

Each week we sent the live eels to Billingsgate in London.

'But say, say even if you do well, you wouldn't think of throwing this country up altogether and going to America?' he said, the words fumbled for as I pushed the boat out of the bulrushes after sinking the cage of eels, using the oar as a pole, the mud rising a dirty yellow between the stems.

'Why America?'

'Well, it's the land of opportunity, isn't it, a big, expanding country? There's no room for ambition in this poky place. All there's room for is to make holes in pints of porter.'

I was wary of the big words. They were not in his own voice.

'Who'd pay the fare?'

'We'd manage that. We'd scrape it together somehow.'

'Why should you scrape for me to go to America if I can get a job here?'

'I feel I'd be giving you a chance I never got. I fought for this country. And now they want to take away even the licence to fish. Will you think about it anyhow?'

'I'll think about it,' I answered.

Through the day he trimmed the brows of ridges in the potato field while I replaced hooks on the line and dug worms, pain of doing things for the last time as well as the boredom the knowledge brings that soon there'll be no need to do them, that they could be discarded almost now. The guilt of leaving came: I was discarding his life to assume my own, a man to row the boat would eat into the decreasing profits of the fishing, and it was even not certain he'd get renewal of his licence. The tourist board had opposed the last application. They said we impoverished the coarse fishing for tourists—the tourists who came every summer from Liverpool and Birmingham in increasing numbers to sit in aluminium deck-chairs on the riverbank and fish with rods. The fields we had would be a bare living without the fishing.

I saw him stretch across the wall in conversation with the cattle-dealer Farrell as I came round to put the worms where we stored them in clay in the darkness of the lavatory. Farrell leaned on the bar of his bicycle on the road. I passed into the lavatory thinking they were talking about the price of cattle, but as I emptied the worms into the box, the word *Moran* came, and I carefully opened the door to listen. It was my father's voice. He was excited.

'I know. I heard the exact sum. They got ten thousand dollars when Luke was killed. Every American soldier's life is insured to the tune of ten thousand dollars.'

'I heard they get two hundred and fifty dollars a month each for Michael and Sam while they're serving,' he went on.

'They're buying cattle left and right,' Farrell's voice came as I closed the door and stood in the darkness, in the smell of shit and piss and the warm fleshy smell of worms crawling in too little clay.

The shock I felt was the shock I was to feel later when I made some social blunder, the splintering of a self-esteem and the need to crawl into a lavatory to think.

Luke Moran's body had come from Korea in a leaden casket, had crossed the stone bridge to the slow funeral bell with the big cars from the embassy behind, the coffin draped in the Stars and

Stripes. Shots had been fired above the grave before they threw in the clay. There were photos of his decorations being presented to his family by a military attaché.

He'd scrape the fare, I'd be conscripted there, each month he'd get so many dollars while I served, and he'd get ten thousand if I was killed.

In the darkness of the lavatory between the boxes of crawling worms before we set the night line for the eels I knew my youth had ended.

I rowed as he let out the night line, his fingers baiting each twisted hook so beautifully that it seemed a single movement. The dark was closing from the shadow of Oakport to Nutley's boathouse, bats made ugly whirls overhead, the wings of ducks shirred as they curved down into the bay.

'Have you thought about what I said about going to America?' he asked, without lifting his eyes from the hooks and the box of worms.

'I have.'

The oars dipped in the water without splash, the hole whorling wider in the calm as it slipped on the stern seat.

'Have you decided to take the chance, then?'

'No. I'm not going.'

'You won't be able to say I didn't give you the chance when you come to nothing in this fool of a country. It'll be your own funeral.'

'It'll be my own funeral,' I answered, and asked after a long silence, 'As you grow older, do you find your own days in the war and jails coming much back to you?'

'I do. And I don't want to talk about them. Talking about the execution disturbed me no end, those cursed buttons bursting into the air. And the most I think is that if I'd conducted my own wars, and let the fool of a country fend for itself, I'd be much better off today. I don't want to talk about it.'

I knew this silence was fixed for ever as I rowed in silence till he asked, 'Do you think, will it be much good tonight?'

'It's too calm,' I answered.

'Unless the night wind gets up,' he said anxiously.

'Unless a night wind,' I repeated.

As the boat moved through the calm water and the line slipped through his fingers over the side I'd never felt so close to him before, not even when he'd carried me on his shoulders above the laughing crowd to the Final. Each move he made I watched as closely as if I too had to prepare myself to murder.

DECISION IN BELFIELD

Maeve Binchy

*Columnist and bestselling author Maeve Binchy (1940–) is the
perfect writer to close this anthology, with a story about
the transition from adolescence to adulthood. She has admitted
the process was difficult enough for herself, growing up in the
small holiday resort of Dalkey in County Dublin: 'I remember
as a child asking my mother in wonderment why anyone who
had the money to travel would come to holiday in Dalkey. I once
thought it was the most boring spot on earth, but now I'm a
mature person I realise that it is a great place.'*

*Maeve Binchy's childhood was, however, deeply influenced in
another way by her teacher, Mother St Dominic—'at six I wanted
to be a saint,' she says—and it was the nun who inspired her to
take a history degree and go into teaching. While teaching in
several girls' schools, she began to write in her spare time and
in 1969 abandoned education in favour of journalism. Her column in the* Irish Times *brought her to the attention of Irish
readers and then her first novel,* Light a Penny Candle *(1982),
about the lives of ordinary people in Ireland and London in the
1940s and '50s, was on the bestseller lists for 53 weeks, setting
her on her career as one of the most popular novelists of the
day. Ireland and Irish people appear in all her books and she
makes regular visits to Dalkey where she now has a holiday
home overlooking the picturesque coast.*

*Maeve Binchy has written about life in both the villages and
cities of Ireland, and in this story, 'Decision in Belfield', turns
her attention to Southside, the fashionable district of Dublin
which lies about ten miles from Dalkey and seemed a world away*

to her as a child. It is the tale of an unmarried girl facing the dilemma of pregnancy, and reveals all the skill that is her trademark in its description of a family's emotions and heartsearching.

*   *   *

She had been reading the Problem Pages for years. One or two of them always said things about having done grievous wrong in the eyes of God and now the only thing to do was to Make Restitution. Most of them said that your parents would be very understanding—you must go straight away and tell them. You will be surprised, the Problem Pages said, at how much tolerance and understanding there will be, and how much support there is to be found at home.

Not in Pat's home. There would be no support there, no understanding. Pat's mother wasn't going to smile like people did in movies and say maybe it was all for the best and it would be nice to have another baby around the place, that she had missed the patter of tiny bootees. And Pat's father wasn't going to put his arm around her shoulder and take her for a long supportive walk on Dun Laoghaire pier. Pat knew all this very well, even though the Problem Pages told her she was wrong. But she knew it from personal experience. She knew that Mum and Dad would not be a bundle of support and two big rocks of strength. Because they hadn't been any of that five years ago when her elder sister Cathy had been pregnant. There was no reason why their attitude should have changed as time went by.

Cathy had actually finished college when her little drama broke on the family. She had been twenty-two years old, earning her own living and in most ways living her own life. Cathy had believed the Problem Pages, she thought that Mum wouldn't go through the roof. Cathy had thought that there were ways you could talk to Mum and Dad like ordinary people. She had been wrong. Pat remembered as if it were yesterday the weekend of the announcement. It seemed to have gone on all weekend, Cathy saying she didn't want to marry Ian and Dad saying Ian must be brought around to the house this minute; Mum saying this was the result of trusting people to behave like adults and like responsible people; Cathy looking frightened and bewildered. She had said over and over that she thought people would be pleased.

Pat had been sixteen, and she had been shocked to the core. She had never heard words used like the words that were used that weekend. Dad had even apologised for some of the things he had called Cathy, and Mum had never stopped crying. Cathy came and sat on her bed on the Sunday evening. 'It's not the end of the world,' she had said.

'Oh, but it is,' Pat had said, almost afraid to look at Cathy in case she saw under her waist the whole dreadful shame that was going to cause such trouble.

'It's just that I can't see myself spending the rest of my life with Ian,' Cathy said. 'We'd be ridiculous together, we wouldn't last a year. It's such a terrible way to start a marriage with anyone.'

'But don't you love him?' Pat had asked. The only possible reason you could do the things that Cathy must have done with Ian to get herself to this stage must have been love.

'Oh yes, in a way, I love him, but I'll love other people and so will he.'

Pat had not understood, she had been no help. She had said useless things like maybe it wasn't really positive, the test, and maybe Ian might like to get married if Cathy explained it properly. Cathy had taken the whole thing very badly; she had refused to accept that Mum and Dad might have any right on their side. 'They're so liberal, they *say* they're so liberal,' she had scoffed. 'They keep saying they're in favour of getting divorce introduced and they want contraceptives, and they want censorship abolished, but they refuse to face facts. They want me to marry a man knowing it will ruin my life and ruin his life, and probably wreck the baby's life as well. What kind of liberal view is that?'

'I think they believe that it would be the best start for the . . . er . . . the child,' said Pat uncertainly.

'Great start . . . forcing two people who should love the child most into a marriage they're not prepared for in a country which doesn't see fit to set up any system to help when the marriage breaks down.'

'But you can't have people going into marriages knowing they can get out of them.' Pat was very familiar with the argument from fourth-year debating clubs at school.

'Well, you certainly can't go into a marriage, a doubtful marriage, knowing you can't get out of it,' Cathy had said.

She had gone to London five days later. Everyone else had been told that she was doing this wonderful new post-graduate course. It was a special qualification in EEC law; it was obviously the absolutely necessary qualification of the future. Mum had said that with all the changes that were going to come about from Brussels and Strasbourg and everything, Cathy was doing the right thing. Pat knew that Cathy would not come back. She knew that the family had broken up, and broken much more permanently than when Ethna had gone to be a nun. Ethna hadn't really left at all, even though she was in Australia: Cathy was only an hour away but she had gone for ever.

Ethna had never been told why Cathy had gone to England. At Christmas the long letter with the small slanted writing had wanted to know all about the course that Cathy was doing and what her address was and what holidays she would get for the Christmas festivities. Nobody wrote and told Ethna that Cathy hadn't come home for Christmas. Perhaps Cathy had written, but it was certainly never mentioned in the weekly letters which came and went; every week a green Irish air letter on the hall table begun by Mum, where Dad and Pat added bits; and every week, but slightly out of synch, a blue air letter from Australia with details of Sister this who had done that and Sister that who had done this. And all of the time nothing from Cathy.

At about the time that Cathy's baby should be born Pat had asked Mum for the address. 'I wanted to write and see if there was anything we could do.'

'Oh, there's nothing any of *us* could do,' Mum had said bitterly. 'If there had been anything then we would have been glad to do it, but no, we knew nothing, your sister knew everything. So she knew best and went off on her own. No, I don't think there's anything *we* could do. I don't think it would be welcomed.'

'But, Mum, it's your grandchild. Your own grandchild.' Pat had been almost seventeen and full of outrage.

'Yes, and Ian's mother, Mrs Kennedy, it's her first grandchild too. But are either of us being allowed the privilege of having a grandchild, and a baby we all want, and a christening, and a fuss, and the birthright of any child? No, no, a lot of claptrap about not wanting to settle down and not wanting to be tied down. I wonder does Miss Cathy ever ask herself where she would be if I had felt that way?' Mum had got very pink in the face about it.

'I'm sure she's very grateful to you, Mum.'

'Oh I'm sure she is, very sure. Yes, she must be. Fine life *she'd* have had if she had been given away to an adoption society the moment she saw the light of day because I couldn't be tied down.'

'But you were married already, Mum, and you did have Ethna.'

'That's not the *point*,' Mum had roared.

And suddenly Pat had realised what had been said.

'Is Cathy giving the baby away, she can't be giving the baby away, can she?'

'I'm not permitted to know what she's doing. We're not in her confidence, your father and I, but I *assume* that's what she's doing. If she can't be ''tied down'' to a perfectly reasonable nice boy like Ian Kennedy, then it's very unlikely that she can be tied down to an illegitimate baby which she would have to rear on her own.'

Pat had gone to the firm of solicitors where Ian Kennedy worked with his father. He was a nice, red-haired boy, about the friendliest of all Cathy's boy friends; it was a pity she hadn't married him.

'I came to talk to you about Cathy,' she had said.

'Yeah, great, how is she?' he had asked.

'I think she's fine . . .' Pat had been nonplussed.

'Good, give her my love when you write, will you?'

'I don't have her address, and Mum is being difficult. You know, not being able to lay her hands on it . . .'

'Oh, I don't know where she is now,' said Ian.

'Doesn't she keep in touch?' Pat was shocked again.

'No, she said she didn't want to. Said she wanted to be free.'

'But . . . ?'

'But what?'

'Doesn't she keep you informed . . . let you know . . . ?'

'Know what?'

Pat paused. Now, it had been definitely said, definitely, about six months ago, that Ian had been told of her decision to go to England on account of the pregnancy. Yes, Ian had even been in the house. He had said to Dad that he was very happy indeed to acknowledge that he was responsible for the child, and to marry Cathy if she would have him. Pat knew that he had said he wanted to support the child, and to see it when it was born; he couldn't have forgotten about all that, could he?

'I'm sorry for being silly,' Pat had said. 'I'm the baby of the family and nobody tells me anything.'

'Yes?' Ian smiled kindly.

'But I thought she'd be having the, er, baby, now and I wanted to know how she was . . . that's why I'm here.'

'But didn't she tell you? She must have told you?' Ian's face was lined with concern.

'What? Told me what?'

'It was a false alarm—she wasn't pregnant at all.'

'I don't believe you.'

'Of course! Hey, you must know this. She wrote and told everyone just after she went to London.'

'It's not true . . .'

'Of course it's true. She wrote and told us all. It was a very early test she had here, not a proper one.'

'So why didn't she come back?'

'What?'

'If it was a false alarm why didn't she come back to her job and home and to you and everything?'

'Oh, Pat, you *know* all this . . . she was a bit peeved with your Mum and Dad. She thought there'd be more solidarity, I think. And she was very pissed off with me.'

'Why was she pissed off with you? You said you'd marry her.'

'But that's not what she wanted, she wanted . . . oh, I don't know . . . anyway, it wasn't necessary.'

'So why isn't she back?'

'As I said, we all let her down. She was annoyed. She wrote, when she told me about the false alarm bit, and said she didn't feel like coming back. She must have written to your family too. Of course she did.'

'She didn't,' Pat said definitely.

'But whyever not? Why didn't she put them out of their agony?'

'*Their* agony?'

'You know what I mean. It's an expression.'

'She never wrote.'

'Oh Pat, nonsense, of course she did. Maybe they didn't tell you. You said yourself they kept things from you.'

'They don't know it was a false alarm, I know that much.'

She said goodbye to Ian, and she promised she wouldn't make a lot of trouble for everyone, she'd be a good little girl.

'You're a real *enfant terrible*, you know. You're much too grown-up and pretty to be playing that Saint Trinian's kind of thing.'

She put out her tongue at him, and they both laughed.

Mum said she didn't want to discuss Cathy. Cathy had found nothing to discuss with her, why should she spend time talking about Cathy?

'But Ian says he heard from her as soon as she went. It was all a false alarm, she never had a baby, she was never pregnant at all. Aren't you pleased now, isn't that good news, Mum?' Pat pleaded with her.

'That's as may be,' Mum had said.

Just as she was dropping off to sleep that night, Pat thought of something that made her sit up again, wide-awake.

Now she knew why Mum hadn't been pleased. Cathy must have had an abortion. That's why there was no baby, that's why

Cathy had not come back. But why hadn't she told Ian? Or Mum? And mainly why hadn't she come back?

'Do you think the other nuns read Ethna's letters?' Pat had asked a few days later when the green aerogramme was being sealed up and sent off.

'Very unlikely,' Dad had said.

'It's not the dark ages. They don't censor their correspondence,' Mum had said.

'Anyway she can be fairly critical of some of the other nuns; she gives that Sister Kevin a hard time,' Dad said. 'I don't expect she'd do that if they read her outgoing letters anyway.'

Pat thought that it was nice that Dad read Ethna's letters so carefully that he knew which sister was which.

Pat had written to Ethna; first of all a probing letter. 'I'm getting older and a bit, though not much, wiser. One of the things that upsets me is the cloak of silence that hangs over Cathy, and where she is in England and what she's doing and what the situation is. Could you tell me what the situation is as far as you know it and then I'll take it from there . . .'

She had a letter from Ethna, not on an aerogramme but in an envelope. On the outside of the envelope it said, 'The Stamps You Wanted'. That satisfied any curiosity Mum and Dad might have had. Inside it was very short.

'I really think you are making a mystery about nothing. Poor Cathy has been punished quite enough, she thought that she was indeed going to have a child. And since she was not at all willing or ready to marry the father then it is merciful that this was not so. She is happy in London, where she is doing social work. She has hardened her heart to mother and father, which is a great pity, but in time I am sure she will feel ready to open up doors of friendship again. She doesn't write to me, apart from that one letter which told me all these things; since nobody has ever mentioned anything to me about it in letters from home, I have never mentioned anything either. I pray for her, and I pray for all of you. Life is so short, it seems sad that any of it should be spent in feeling a grievance and a hurt when a hand held out would brush all the unhappiness away.'

Great help, Pat had thought at the time; punished enough, hardened her heart, brush all the unhappiness away; nun's phrases, and not a word of blame about Mum and Dad who were always writing letters to the paper protesting about letting South African rugby teams into the country. They were always talking about itinerants, and they had raised money for refugees. Why were they so hard-hearted about Cathy?

Pat had decided that she was not going to allow Cathy to disappear without trace as if some terrible crime or shame had settled on the family and people hoped that by ignoring it things would return to normal. She had tackled them at supper the night she had got Ethna's letter.

'This family is becoming a bit like nine green bottles,' she said.

'What on earth do you mean?' Dad was smiling.

'First Ethna goes off to the other side of the world, and then we are four. Then six months ago Cathy disappears without trace and now we are three. Will I go off somewhere too?'

Dad was still smiling but he looked puzzled. He stood up to fetch the coffee percolator. He looked tired and a bit beaten. Not the cheerful doctor, always in a smart suit, always optimistic, always seeing the best for patients and neighbours alike. He wore his cardigan at home, and Mum wore an old jumper that was torn under the arms. They looked shabby and a bit dishevelled as they sat in the big dining-room with its good furniture and its expensive cut glass decanters. Pat felt that somehow they didn't make any effort when it was only just her. She was sure they had been far more elegant and lively when Ethna was at home and when Cathy was there.

'Are you just waiting for me to go off and that will be the hat trick?'

'What is this, Pat, what silly game are you playing?' Mum was not very amused.

'No, I mean it, Mum. It's not much of a family, is it?'

'Don't speak to your mother like that.' Dad was surprised and hurt. He had thought that talking about green bottles was going to be a joke; now it had turned into a row.

'It's not normal. People marry and have children, they don't have them just to export them off as fast as possible.'

Mum was very annoyed indeed. 'Ethna was twenty-one when she left. She had wanted to join this order for two years. Do you think we wanted Ethna to go to that outlandish place? Or to be a nun at all? Don't be so ridiculous, and have some thought for other people before you start your hurtful accusations.'

'No, I know that's Ethna, but then Cathy's gone. This house used to be full of people, now it's just us. And soon I suppose you'll want me to go. Would you prefer if I tried to get into UCC or Galway or maybe England rather than Belfield, then you wouldn't have to have me around the place and you could be all on your own?' She stood up, tears in her eyes.

'Apologise this minute to your mother, this minute, do you hear me!'

'Why to Mum? I'm saying it to both of you.'

She was about to leave the room when Mum had said wearily, 'Come back, Pat. Come back and I'll talk to you about Cathy.'

'You owe her no explanation, Peggy, none, not after the way she's spoken to you.' Dad's face was red with disappointment.

'Sit down, Pat. Please.' Grudgingly and shrugging, Pat sat down.

'I'm not going to fight with you. I'm going to agree with you. It's not much of a family, it certainly isn't. When your father and I got married this is not what we had in mind at all.'

'Now Peg, now Peg,' Dad said warningly.

'No, the girl is right to question what's happened. We question it ourselves, for God's sake. Not at all what we had in mind. I suppose we had in mind the practice getting bigger and going well. It has. That's all fine, that side of it. And we had in mind our friends and all the people we like being around, and that's gone well. And our health has been fine. But mainly what we had in mind was the three of you. That's what people do have in mind actually, Pat, that's what they have in mind most of the day and night when they have children. From the time that

Ethna was here we've had you three in mind more than anything else.'

Pat gave a very slight shrug. It was a disclaimer. It was meant to say, you don't have to tell me all this. I know you tried. As a shrug it worked. Mum had known what she meant.

'I know you think I'm just saying this to be nice to you, or maybe perhaps that we started out with good intentions and lost them on the way. But it wasn't like that. I think some of my best times, and yours, Hugh, were when Ethna was about six or seven, and Cathy was five, and you were a baby. Three little girls totally dependent on us, all lighting up with enthusiasm . . .'

'Sure Mum. Yes. Sure.'

'No, give me a very short minute for the sentimental sugary bit because it didn't last long. Then you were all so bright. This was another joy, some of our friends had problems. Well, we didn't call them problems but so and so's child couldn't read until he was seven, or someone couldn't settle at school, or another wouldn't manage to get on with the teachers, or failed the third Honours in her leaving. Not you three, from Ethna on we knew, top of the class, exams no real problem. Do you remember Ethna's conferring?'

'Yes . . . I got the day off school.'

'And she looked so bright . . . that's a funny word, but she did, you know, clear eyes and alert face, compared to a lot of the others. I thought, ours is very bright, there's so much before her when she gets this ridiculous nunnish thing out of her system . . .'

'But I thought you approved?'

'We had to approve in the end.' Dad spoke for the first time. 'Of course we didn't approve. Use your head, Pat, suppose you had brought up a lovely girl like Ethna, as bright as a button as Mum says, who has just got a First class honours degree in history and who wants to go with a crowd of half-educated women to a school in the outback of somewhere because she read a book about the damn place and she met a recruiting team!'

'But you never said. I don't remember . . .'

'You don't remember. How old were you—twelve, thirteen?

What discussions could we have had with you about it that would have helped anything except add to the argument?'

Mum had interrupted. 'We didn't even discuss it with Cathy because we didn't want gangs forming and pressure being put on Ethna. We just talked to her.'

'And what did you want her to do?' Pat wanted to know.

'I'd have liked her to do an MA and then a doctorate. She was very, very good. I spoke to some of the people in there, they said she had the makings of a scholar, and I'd have liked her to have had a good lively life here, instead of putting up with Sister Kevin's tantrums in a jungle.' Dad had sounded very defeated when he said that, as if remembering the whole battle and how it was lost.

'Yes, that's what I'd have liked too. I'd have liked her to go on living here, it was so near and handy, and got a small car and had friends and gone off to the West for weekends. And then married someone in her own field, some professor, and got a house near by and I could have seen the whole thing over again with her children, growing up and learning to walk . . .'

'It's a fairly normal, reasonable wish, isn't it?' Dad had asked defensively. 'Rather than see a whole life, a whole education, and talent, thrown away.'

'She's happy though, she says she is,' Mum had said.

'I suppose her letters to us are about as near the truth as ours are to her,' Dad had said. And there was a silence as they thought about the implications of that.

'So Cathy . . . ?' Pat spoke softly, hoping that the mood hadn't been broken, that she could still get her mother to talk.

'Cathy,' Mum had said.

'Cathy was no trouble either. Everyone else told us of all their sleepless nights over their terrible teenage children. We never had any,' Dad smiled at Pat as if he was thanking her. She felt a twinge of guilt.

'And Cathy did have her friends around much more than Ethna, and they used to laugh, and they were full of life. Do you remember the summer they did the whole garden, Hugh?'

Dad had laughed. 'All I had to do was provide one of those

big cans of beer at the end of the day. They dug and they weeded and they cut hedges and grass.'

'It never looked back since,' Mum had said. 'It used to be a wilderness and they tamed it.'

'All for a few cans of beer,' Dad had said. They stopped talking for a moment. Pat said nothing.

'So Cathy was going to be the one who might be with us, when Ethna went. It wasn't a transfer of love. I suppose it was changing the plans or hopes. And she was so enthusiastic, about everything.'

'We felt we were qualifying with her, she was so entertaining about it all—the lectures, the course, the solicitors' exams down in the Four Courts, the apprenticeship . . . it was all so alive,' Dad had said.

'And she seemed to get on so well with Ian. I kept thinking, she's only twenty-two, she's far too young to settle down but then of course I told myself I was only twenty-two when I married. Then on the other hand, I didn't have a career to decide about. Then I went back to the first hand and said since Ian and Cathy were both solicitors and Ian's father had a firm, well then, surely if they did have a couple of children and she wanted to work part-time it couldn't be too hard to arrange.'

Dad had interrupted. 'This is what your mother meant about you children always being in our minds. We had Cathy married to Ian in our minds long before they even kissed each other.'

'But why couldn't you accept Cathy's decision like you did for Ethna? You didn't want Ethna to go off and be a nun but when she did you sort of acknowledged it.'

'Yes,' Mum had said, 'Yes, it made her so happy and it was her life. Much as I wanted to I couldn't control it any more . . . she had to do what she wanted.'

'So why couldn't Cathy do what she wanted?'

'That was different.'

'But why, Mum, why? It's not as if you and Dad were prudes or anything, it's not as if your friends would cut you off, or as if you'd be ashamed to lift your heads. Why can't Cathy bring her baby home?'

'It's different,' Dad had said.

'I can't think why, I really can't. Nobody minds. Ian doesn't mind. I talked to him. He's very casual about Cathy—''send her my love'' he said. Ethna won't mind. I wrote to her about it, but, but . . .'

'You wrote to Ethna?' Mum had said, surprised.

'Yes, to try and clear things up.'

'And did it?'

'No, not at all.'

'What did you want cleared up?' Dad had asked.

'Whether Cathy is having a baby or not. Something very basic and simple like that, which most normal families would know.'

Dad had looked at Mum, and she had said, 'Tell her.'

'The answer is . . . that we don't know.'

'You don't *know*?'

'No. That's the truth.' Mum had continued, 'We were very shocked by Cathy's attitude. She was very harshly critical of us, and the way we lived, and thought that our attitudes were hypocritical, you know, to preach some kind of broadmindedness and then not to follow it.'

'But we didn't see it like that. You see, it was nothing to do with acceptance or reputations, we thought Cathy was being silly and making extravagant gestures, turning herself into a Protest just for the sake of it. ''Look at me, I'm too modern to do like anyone else, give my child a name and a home and a background, no, I'm far too sophisticated for that!'' We didn't like it, Pat, it was too studenty . . .'

'There's no need to go over all that was said, you probably heard most of it, but to cut a long story short we have only heard from Cathy once since she went to London. I always imply— well, let's be honest, I always tell people lies and say that we've heard from her, but she wrote only once two weeks after she left.'

'Did she say . . . ?'

'She said that it had been a false alarm, that her dates had been wrong, that she was only a shorter time overdue than she thought and that everything was fine.'

There was a silence.

'And did you believe her, Mum?'

'No.'

'Did you, Dad?'

'No. I didn't.'

'It was too far for there to be a mistake?'

'Well, she said she had left a specimen into Holles Street and they had said it was positive. They don't make mistakes.'

'But she says they did.'

'No, she's forgotten she told us that bit, I think.'

'Oh.'

'So we know no more than you do,' Mum had said, spreading out her hands helplessly.

'But why do you say everything's all right . . . ?'

'Because it will be one way or another, sometime, and we don't want Cathy to have to walk back into a whole lot of complications. Keep it simple, is our motto.'

'So what do you believe if you don't believe what Cathy said?'

'Well, what do you think?'

'No, what do you think?'

'Pat, either she had a termination or she is in fact having the child, and as you so rightly pointed out to me, if she is having the baby it's due this month.'

'And we don't know?'

'We don't know.'

'We don't even know where she is?'

'No.'

Then Mum had started to cry, and she cried with her arms down on the table and her head on top of them. Right into the dishes and the food. And Dad had stood up and come over and patted her awkwardly on one side and Pat had patted her awkwardly on the other.

'It's all right, Peg,' Dad had said, over and over.

'It's all right, Mum,' Pat had said, over and over.

It had been a hard thing to sit your Leaving Certificate not knowing where your sister was, whether she was alive or dead, and not knowing if you were an aunt or not. But Pat had gone on and done it: she had got all her Honours and plenty of points. Peggy and Hugh's third daughter was on her way to University College, Dublin, registering as a student in Belfield.

Cathy wrote home that year just before Christmas. She said she had seen enough of other people's miseries in her case-load in London to make her realise that most of life's troubles were caused by families. She would like to say very sincerely that she had been entirely to blame for any little fracas they had had. She asked forgiveness and if they liked she would love to come home for Christmas, but since she had been so difficult and stayed out of touch for so long, over a year, she could well understand if they said no. She gave her address for them to reply. It was in Hackney. Mum and Dad had sent a telegram five minutes after the letter arrived. The telegram had read, 'Welcome home, darling Cathy, to the silliest parents and the happiest Christmas ever.'

Cathy had also written to Pat.

'You may well wonder what the Prodigal thinks she's up to, and I don't want to put your nose out of joint. I'll tell you everything you want to know, if you want to know anything, when I see you, and if you have no time for me I'll understand that too. It was utterly selfish of me to go away and leave you as a teenager, in your last year at school, to cope with all the trauma and drama. But when there's a crisis people only think of themselves, or I did anyway. I hope the reunion won't be a damp squib. I haven't kept in touch with most of my friends, so can I ask you to fill the house a bit with people so that we don't become too hot-house and raise our family expectations too high? I'll stop asking and taking soon and start giving, I promise.'

Pat had thought this was very sensible. She asked her College friends in on the evening that Cathy came back. Mum had gone to the airport to meet her and by the time Pat had come home conversation was quite normal. In fact, so normal it was almost frightening. It was as if Cathy had never gone away, as if no mystery hung over the events of the past year. Cathy had said that Pat looked smashing, and that students must be dressing better than in her day, and there wasn't time for much more conversation because they had to get the mulled wine ready, which involved a lot of conversation about what you did to mull it, and how to ensure you didn't boil the alcohol out of it. Pat had been startled to see that they were all laughing quite naturally in the kitchen when Dad had said he should test each batch they made, just in case the flavouring needed adjusting. 'You haven't changed, Dad,' Cathy had laughed, and nobody made any flicker of an eyelid as the moment passed and Cathy's long absence had now sunk into the collective memory. It could be mentioned without being questioned.

It had been like that all that Christmas, and nothing seemed more natural at the end of the holiday than for Cathy to say that she would be coming back for good as soon as she had found a replacement for herself. She was going to work in Ian's office; they had a vacancy in a couple of months. Pat had been puzzled when she saw Cathy and Ian Kennedy strolling around the wintry wilderness of garden, plucking at bushes and pointing out what should be done with hard, frozen-looking flowerbeds. What was going on inside that red head of Ian Kennedy's? Did he not wonder whether Cathy had given birth to his child in London all by herself in a hospital with no friends to come and visit her? Did he not worry about his child, their child, being given to an adoption society and never knowing what it should have known?

Did Ian Kennedy wonder whether Cathy had gone long, long ago to a doctor in England in order to organise a termination of pregnancy and then overnight in one of those nursing homes everyone knew about, where simple minor surgery under anaesthetic would ensure that Cathy and Ian's child didn't ever come into being? Surely he wasn't so foolish as to think that a girl could be pregnant, disappear for over a year and have some vague belief that the pregnancy was all a false alarm.

People were really behaving more and more peculiarly, Pat decided. The older they got the vaguer they became. Ethna's letters now had nice bland welcoming bits about Cathy in them. Had she forgotten all that earlier stuff about punishment, and hardening her heart, and praying for her? Once people got any way settled they seemed to lose touch with reality and built themselves a comfortable little world like a Wendy House entirely of their own creation.

She had told this to Rory a few times, and he had tried to understand it. But Rory thought that her whole life was a fraud, and that anyone who owned any kind of private house was already out of touch with society. Rory was in her Economics tutorial, by far the most brilliant student of his year, a great thorn in a lot of University flesh. Rory had economic arguments for revolution which could not be faulted. Rory agreed with Pat that the whole Cathy business was very unreal. Rory said he loved Pat, and Pat was very sure that she loved Rory.

'It's a mistake to get too involved with anyone your first year in College,' Cathy had said. 'It ties you down, you should have the freedom to roam round and see who you like and who you don't. You should get to know a lot of people, not just sticking together two by two as if you were the animals going into the ark.' Pat didn't like this remark. It was too reminiscent of Cathy saying she couldn't be tied down to marry Ian. It also implied a criticism of Rory. And that was not allowed.

There was nothing that Mum and Dad could find fault with in Rory; they wanted to, but they couldn't actually put a finger on anything. He certainly didn't distract her from her work; in fact he insisted that she work harder than she was prepared to. He said her essays weren't sufficiently researched; he lent her books, he came with her to the library and sat opposite her. It was easier to do the damn stuff than to find excuses. He didn't keep her out at all-night parties. He had explained to Mum and Dad that he didn't drink much so there wouldn't be any danger of drunken driving late at night in his little beat-up car. When they went away to conferences or student festivals in Cork or Galway, Rory always managed to drop the one phrase which would reassure Mum and Dad about the set-up. 'I'll leave Pat at the girls' house first and then she can settle in and I'll go off and find where they're putting the lads up . . .' Some trivial little remark which would prevent Mum and Dad from wondering what exactly the score was.

The score was exactly as Rory described it for a long time.

'I suppose you think it's silly not to,' Pat had said.

'Silly, no. Wasteful, yes,' Rory had said. 'It's up to you entirely what you would like to do. I don't ever believe in putting on the pressure. Too much of what's wrong is wrong because people felt forced to do things for approval. But I think you're wrong. It would give us both so much pleasure and it would hurt exactly nobody. We aren't betraying anyone, we can be sure that we aren't irresponsibly conceiving a child we don't want. So wasteful is all I think I'd say it was.'

She adored Rory, his intensity and his boyish enthusiasms. She went to the Family Planning Clinic. She knew the doctor who was on duty that day. It was a friend of her father's. 'Glad to see you, that's a good sensible girl,' the friend of Dad's had said. No explanations asked for, no curiosity, no condemnation. It was all so simple. Why hadn't Cathy done this? They had clinics, even in her time.

Cathy was still a mystery. There she was, living at home so calmly. If anyone ever asked about the Common Market Legal course she was meant to have done, she would shake her head and say that she hadn't done it after all, she had worked for the Council in East London. Mum had been right in her way to have kept things simple, to have rocked no boats. Cathy came back and stepped in more or less where she had got out. It was just that time, all those months that remained as inexplicable. What had she been doing, what had she been thinking? She was so placid now, sometimes going out to the theatre with Ian, sometimes with other people. Holidaying with two girls in the Greek islands, sitting with Mum and Dad sometimes in the evenings looking at television.

Pat had insisted on Rory discussing it. 'Is it natural for them not to mention it? Is it normal? I mean, there she is at home, and nobody ever once refers to the fact that she left home pregnant and stayed away from home for fourteen months and came back and everything is as you were.'

'Um.' Rory was reading.

'But why, why do they say nothing? It's like not noticing someone is naked or not referring to someone being in a car crash or in gaol. It's not real.'

'Um. I know,' he said.

'But they don't seem to want to know, it's only me, it's only me that wants to know.'

'Well, why don't you ask her then?' Rory said.

'Cathy, did you have any problems with the Pill, you know, have you had to change brand or anything?'

Cathy looked up from the papers she was studying. She was sitting at the big desk in her bedroom, which she had converted into a kind of study.

'No, I was never on the Pill, so it didn't occur.'

'Never on the Pill, at all?'

'No.'

'How amazing.'

'Pat, you are twenty, going on twenty-one. You aren't actually a wise old sociologist commenting on the funny things society does.' Cathy laughed goodnaturedly as she spoke.

'Yes, but . . . not ever?'

'Not ever. If I *had* been, that little incident which you may remember would never have happened . . .'

'Yes, well, after the little incident . . . ?'

Pat felt she was treading on a minefield. She had to remain light-hearted and casual.

'Oh, after the little incident, I didn't . . . how shall I put it . . . well, I didn't actually need the services of a contraceptive.'

'Not ever?'

'No, not ever.' Cathy smiled, relaxed and calm as if they had been talking about the replanting of the herbaceous border.

'Oh.'

'So I'm not much help. But you could go to the Family Planning Clinic, tell them if it doesn't suit you. They'll change it.'

'Yes, good idea. Cathy?'

'Yes?'

'Remember that time . . . the little incident . . . what happened?'

'How do you mean, what happened?'

'I mean, did you go through with it? Did you have the baby?'

'Did I what?'

'Did you have the baby? In London?'

'Hey, what is this? A joke?'

'No, seriously. I wish you'd tell me. I hate us all pretending, it's so artificial.'

'Tell you what?'

'When you went off to London, did you actually have the baby?'

'No, of course I didn't, are you feeling all right? What an extraordinary question to ask. Have a baby? Where is it, then, if I had it, was I meant to have left it in a telephone box?'

'Well, what did you do? Did you have an abortion?'

'Seriously, is this some kind of game? Of course I didn't. What on earth are you saying . . . ?'

'But you *were* pregnant.'

'No, I thought I was. I wasn't.'

'You were, Dad knows, he said so when you were gone.'

'Oh no, he can't have, I wrote telling them it was a false alarm.'

'He didn't believe you.'

'Listen, don't start stirring up a lot of trouble over nothing. It was nothing. Why all this interrogation?'

'Is that what put you off the whole thing, fellows and making love?' Pat asked. 'They say people can get very depressed.'

'I *didn't* have an abortion, and I wasn't very heavily into fellows and making love, and I haven't gone off fellows.'

'That's all you'll say.'

'Jesus Lord, what is this, Pat, one of Rory's revolutionary tribunals? You've asked me about ten questions. I've answered all of them honestly—which is rather good of me since *none* of them are any of your business.'

'I'm sorry.'

'No, you're not, you want some awful group where everyone sits and tells the most god-awful, self-centred, boring details of

what they did and what they thought and what they felt and what
they did then, and what they thought then and what they felt then
. . . honestly, I can't stand that kind of thing. Even Woody Allen
laughs at it, for heaven's sake. It's not going to solve the world's
problems.'

'What is?'

'I don't know, but a lot of people's are solved by playing down
dramas rather than creating them.'

'And is that what you're doing?'

'I'm refusing to invent them, refusing to make myself into a
tragedy queen.'

'I'm sorry I spoke.'

'I'm not, but I'm glad you've stopped.' Cathy grinned.

Pat gave a watery grin back.

'So you see, she's *got* to be lying. Somewhere along the line she
told a lie.' Pat frowned as she ticked the items off on her fingers.

'There are times you can be very boring, Pat,' said Rory.

She was hurt and upset. 'You're often analysing what people
say and why society forces us to tell lies and role-play. Why is
it boring when I do it?'

'Because it's repetitive and it's slapdash.'

'How do you mean?'

'Well, you haven't even included all the possibilities, have
you?'

'I *have*. Either she was not pregnant, or she was and she had
either a baby or an abortion.'

'She could have had a miscarriage, you clown.'

All that had been a year ago. Pat remembered the conversation
word for word. They had been all at the turning points of things
somehow. The very next day, the day following the interrogation,
Cathy said that she and Ian were going to get married. The news
coincided with a letter from Ethna. She was leaving the order.
And everyone might remember that she had spoken quite a lot
of Father Fergus. Well, Fergus was in Rome at the moment and
the laicisation process was well under way. She and Fergus would

be married in Rome during the summer. Then they would come home, possibly try to get a teaching job. It shouldn't be hard. Both of them had a lot of qualifications and a lot of experience.

'It's all working out as you want, isn't it, Mum?' Pat had said.

'It's what all you girls want that's important, you know that,' Mum had said; she was laughing at herself a little, and she tried to take the triumphant look off her face.

That time had been a turning point for Pat too. Rory had told her about the South American woman, Cellina. Pat had liked Cellina; she had helped her to organise a solidarity campaign for fellow students back home, and she had introduced her to Rory. She had been pleased when Rory had liked Cellina. She had never seen exactly how much he had liked Cellina until he told her.

She had stopped taking the Pill. To use Cathy's marvellous, old-fashioned phrase, she felt she didn't need the services of a contraceptive. She did a lot of work on her thesis, and she did a great deal of work at home too. A family wedding for Cathy, with the Kennedys screaming their delight as loudly as Mum and Dad. Then there was the trip to Rome. Why not? If Ethna was doing something as huge as this they must all be there, and they were. Mother had Ethna back, and she had Cathy back.

But she was about to lose Pat. Temporarily perhaps, who could tell? Rory had come back from Bonn where he and Cellina had been living. He had come home alone. They had met a lot during the two weeks he was back. It seemed silly and wasteful not to go to bed with him. They were giving each other a lot of pleasure and they weren't hurting anyone, since Cellina would never know. And were they betraying anyone? The word betrayal is such a subjective one.

But now Rory had gone back to Bonn, and Holles Street, which is never wrong over such things, had said Positive. And Pat had learned enough over the years not to believe the Problem Pages. It would be best if she went to London, on her own. Connected with work. And the possibility of getting into the London School of Economics—yes, that would be a good one. She had often spoken of the LSE. Mum and Dad would be interested in that as a project.

And as long as she wrote regularly and seemed happy, that was the main thing.

ACKNOWLEDGEMENTS

The editor would like to record his thanks to Brian Cleeve, William Trevor, Edna O'Brien and Peter Berresford Ellis for their help in assembling this collection. He and the publishers are also grateful to the following authors, publishers and agents for permission to reprint copyright stories: Faber & Faber Ltd for 'Mankeepers and Mosscheepers' by Seamus Heaney, 'We Might See Sights!' by Julia O'Faolain and 'Korea' by John McGahern; Penguin Publishing Group for 'The Death of Peggy Meehan' by William Trevor; Victor Gollancz Ltd for 'The First of My Sins' by Brian Friel and 'The Parting' by Liam O'Flaherty; Random House Publishing Group for 'Red Jam Roll, the Dancer' by Brendan Behan, 'Weep for Our Pride' by James Plunkett and 'Decision in Belfield' by Maeve Binchy; Constable Ltd for 'The Trout' by Sean O'Faolain; A. P. Watt Literary Agency for 'The Ring' by Bryan MacMahon; HarperCollins Publishers for 'Not Liking to Pass the Road Again' by Patrick O'Brian and 'Mr Collopy' by Flann O'Brien; Transworld Publishers for 'Lady-in-Waiting' by Anne McCaffrey; Hamish Hamilton Ltd for 'The Face of Evil' by Frank O'Connor; The Mercier Press for 'The Roads' by Padraic Pearse; Poolbeg Press Ltd for 'The Poteen Maker' by Michael McLaverty; C. J. Fallon Ltd for 'The Mystery Play' by Sinéad de Valera; Orion Publishing Group and Weidenfeld & Nicolson for 'Sister Imelda' by Edna O'Brien; Martin Secker & Warburg Ltd for 'The Living Dead' by Roddy Doyle; Writers and Readers Publishing Cooperative Society Ltd for 'Seduction' by Neil Jordan; Gill & Macmillan for 'Red Jelly' by Eithne Strong; A. M. Heath Literary Agency for 'The Way of the White Cow' by Peter Tremayne; Calder Publications for 'Belacqua's Homecoming' by Samuel Beckett.

While every care has been taken to clear permission for the use of stories in this book, in the case of any accidental infringement, copyright holders are asked to write to the editor care of the publishers.